A MISSION FOR DEVELOPMENT

A MISSION FOR DEVELOPMENT

Utah Universities and the Point Four Program in Iran

RICHARD GARLITZ

UTAH STATE UNIVERSITY PRESS

Logan

© 2018 by University Press of Colorado

Published by Utah State University Press
An imprint of University Press of Colorado
245 Century Circle, Suite 202
Louisville, Colorado 80027

 The University Press of Colorado is a proud member of
the Association of University Presses.

The University Press of Colorado is a cooperative publishing enterprise supported, in part,
by Adams State University, Colorado State University, Fort Lewis College, Metropolitan State
University of Denver, Regis University, University of Colorado, University of Northern Colorado,
Utah State University, and Western State Colorado University.

∞ This paper meets the requirements of the ANSI/NISO Z39.48–1992 (Permanence of Paper).

ISBN: 978-1-60732-753-0 (paperback)
ISBN: 978-1-60732-754-7 (ebook)
https://doi.org/10.7330/9781607327547

Library of Congress Cataloging-in-Publication Data

Names: Garlitz, Richard P., author.
Title: A mission for development: Utah universities and the Point Four Program in Iran / Richard
  Garlitz.
Description: Logan: Utah State University Press, 2018. | Includes bibliographical references and
  index.
Identifiers: LCCN 2017033437 | ISBN 9781607327530 (pbk.) | ISBN 9781607327547 (ebook)
Subjects: LCSH: Technical assistance, American—Iran. | Point Four Program (U.S.) | Universities
  and colleges—International cooperation. | United States—Relations—Iran. | Iran—Relations—
  United States.
Classification: LCC HC475 .G37 2018 | DDC 338.955009/045—dc23
LC record available at https://lccn.loc.gov/2017033437

The University Press of Colorado gratefully acknowledges the generous support of the
Department of History and Philosophy at University of Tennessee at Martin toward the publication of this book.

CONTENTS

ACKNOWLEDGMENTS

It is a pleasure to thank the many people who helped me research, write, and think about this book. I especially want to thank Jessie Embry of the Charles Redd Center at Brigham Young University for sharing her vast knowledge about the Utah families that went to Iran. As the daughter of Utah State University (USU) adviser Bertis Embry, she spent two years of her childhood in that country. Much of this book could not have been written without the interviews she conducted with former advisers and their spouses in 1998 and 1999 as part of the Utah Universities in Iran Oral History Project. I sincerely appreciate the transcripts of those interviews she gave me on my first research trip to Utah in 2006. I also want to thank Bob Parson, longtime university archivist at Utah State University, who provided expert guidance throughout my research. I still owe you a Logan's Hero. Richard Saunders encouraged me to pursue this project, and Michael Spooner at Utah State University Press supported it from an early stage. Kylie Haggen at Utah State University Press and Laura Furney at the University Press of Colorado helped bring the project to the finish line. Cheryl Carnahan did a superior job copyediting the manuscript. Keith Erekson, director of the Church History Library in Salt Lake City, made the Franklin Harris diaries available to me for research. Dan Davis, photo archivist at USU, helped me find appropriate photos. I want to thank the many friends and colleagues who read initial drafts or provided helpful suggestions, especially Ervand Abrahamian, Lois Beck, Robert Davis, John Ghazvinian, Jim Goode, Lon Hamby, Renee LaFleur, Amanda McVety, Richard Saunders, and Matthew Shannon. I have benefited from a great many dedicated teachers in my life. Two who had an important impact on this book are Chester Pach, my dissertation adviser, and Sholeh Quinn, who tutored me in Middle East history, both at Ohio University.

The University of Tennessee at Martin funded part of my research and awarded me a semester's leave to write the book. The Department of History and Philosophy also contributed research funding and continues to be a supportive intellectual environment. The friendly and professional staff at the Paul Meek Library provided quiet office space where I wrote most of the manuscript. Director Sam Richardson graciously allowed me to use the building when it was closed to the public, and Dana Breland helped me track down materials through Interlibrary Loan. The Charles Redd Center, the John F. Kennedy Library Foundation, and Phi Kappa Phi all provided generous research funding.

Finally, I want to thank my family for their steadfast encouragement. I inherited a love of international travel and learning about the world from my grandparents, Richard and Loretta Breunlin. My mother, Kathy Garlitz, a dedicated schoolteacher and principal, taught me the importance of committing to a task and paying attention to detail. My father, Leo Garlitz, who passed away unexpectedly in early 2015, encouraged me to study abroad as an undergraduate and to pursue a career in history. I dedicate this book to the two most important people in my life, Renee and Eleanor. You are a blessing every day, even when life's little inconveniences make me grumpy and irritable.

NOTE ON USAGE

"Point Four Program" was a popular name for American technical assistance to developing countries threatened by international communism during the 1950s, but it holds an ambiguous place in both the US government's foreign policy nomenclature and historical writing about international development. The program began under the Technical Cooperation Administration (TCA) in the spring of 1950 but underwent three major administrative reorganizations during the decade. The Truman administration folded economic and development aid, including the TCA, into the Mutual Security Administration (MSA) in October 1951. The Eisenhower administration deemphasized the Point Four name, which the public associated with President Harry S. Truman, in favor of the more neutral "technical assistance" and reorganized all foreign aid into the Foreign Operations Administration (FOA) in June 1953. For that reason, some historians use Point Four only in relation to the Truman years. The International Cooperation Administration (ICA) replaced the FOA in the spring of 1955. The Kennedy administration consolidated technical assistance into the US

Agency for International Development in the fall of 1961 and dissolved the ICA. The acronym USAID or simply AID thereafter replaced Point Four in common usage. Public records from the 1950s sometimes refer to the Point Four Program, but most bear the name of the administrative agency at the time of their creation. To avoid potentially confusing jargon, I use Point Four Program throughout this book except when discussing how specific administrative changes affected its projects. In such cases, I have tried to include appropriate clarification.

Utah State University was called Utah State Agricultural College (USAC) until 1957. For simplicity's sake, I refer to the institution as Utah State University or USU throughout the book, except in a few cases of quoting primary documents that precede the name change.

Iran was known as Persia in the West before the mid-1930s, and many Americans continued to use that name well into the 1960s. Again, for consistency, I use Iran throughout this book. Spelling Persian words and names can be daunting for anyone not familiar with that language, especially given the variations that exist in Western sources. Readers will, for example, encounter the famous nationalist prime minister as Musaddiq, Mossadeq, Mosaddeq, and Mossadegh, among other variations. For the most part, I have followed the *International Journal of Middle East Studies* word list, except insofar as I have substituted the "o" for "u" to reflect common spelling in Iranian names: Mohammad rather than Muhammad, Hossein rather than Hussein. I hope readers will overlook my errors in the understanding that I have aimed for clear and consistent spelling.

A MISSION FOR DEVELOPMENT

INTRODUCTION

The United States must devise a means to develop Iran for the benefit of all its people.

T. Cuyler Young, 1950

Bruce Anderson was just trying to finish a master's degree in agricultural engineering at Utah State University (USU) in mid-1951 when he encountered an opportunity that changed his life. His research on an irrigation canal in Vernal had stalled when his adviser, Cleve Milligan, suggested that Bruce accompany him on a new venture USU was organizing halfway around the world in Iran. The university had agreed to send specialists to help the Iranian Ministry of Agriculture improve farm production, and Milligan had been chosen to head the project's engineering operation. He could use another irrigation specialist, and Anderson would no doubt find plenty of suitable research projects in that mostly arid country. As exciting as the prospect sounded, it also inspired "fear and trembling" in this married father of four who had difficulty finding the country on a map. Nevertheless, the families

DOI: 10.7330/9781607327547.c000

of Bruce Anderson, Cleve Milligan, and three of their USU colleagues set off for Tehran that September.[1]

The Anderson family spent most of the next decade living in Iran, first in and around the historic southern city of Shiraz and later in the sprawling capital of Tehran. Bruce and his wife, Lula's, youngest son, Mark, was born in Iran; the children attended an American school there. They witnessed an intense political crisis unfold between 1951 and 1953 that culminated in a fateful military coup that cast a long shadow on the country and shaped US-Iranian relations for a quarter century. They observed the country's grinding poverty, but they also experienced the warm hospitality of the Iranian people. Bruce's work took him to rural villages and to remote highland pastures of tribal nomads. He helped improve irrigation methods and assisted the government in organizing an agricultural extension service.[2] It was an "enriching and enlightening" experience, recalled Lula nearly four decades later, adding that in her estimation, "we did a lot of good."[3]

The work Anderson and dozens of his Utah colleagues did in Iran was part of the US government's Point Four initiative to provide technical assistance to poor countries that seemed susceptible to communist influence. Driving this new approach to foreign policy was a firm belief that American influence, including technical know-how, would naturally promote economic prosperity while also incubating democracy around the world.[4] Its original architects in the Truman administration conceived Point Four as a low-cost program of on-the-ground teaching and demonstration in which American advisers would work directly with the people of host countries to improve the quality of life in rural communities. The goal was to demonstrate the superiority of the American way and thereby blunt the appeal of international communism. Its first director, Henry Bennett, called Point Four "a 'down-to-earth' method of working which brings modern methods to the villagers in a form readily understood by them and easily adapted to their problems."[5] Sociologists and historians have sometimes used terms such as "low modernization" and "development through citizen participation" that highlight the emphasis on small-scale, locally directed projects.[6]

This book tells the story of how three Utah universities—Brigham Young University (BYU), the University of Utah, and USU—contributed to Point Four technical assistance in Iran between 1951 and 1964. The Utah projects generally fit within Point Four's original low-modernization framework, though some stretched the limits of that approach. They contrast with the more familiar stories of foreign aid that often stress large-scale modernization and generous military grants the US government doled out to help stabilize friendly governments. The grandiose visions of modernization theorists in particular, with their compressive plans and faith that superhighways and hydroelectric dams would propel non-Western societies toward an age of mass consumption, came to dominate American development thinking by the second half of the 1950s and remained prominent throughout most of the 1960s.[7] This "high modernization" has therefore commanded the bulk of attention historians have directed toward understanding economic development as a component of American foreign policy during the Cold War.[8] One objective of this book, then, is to direct attention back to the smaller localized projects that preceded the ascendency of modernization theory and ambitious seven-year development plans.[9]

A second major aim of this book is to examine an important link between American higher education and international development. American colleges and universities emerged as prominent partners in the dissemination of technical aid during the 1950s. They employed top scientists who conducted vital research in fields that were at the heart of socioeconomic development. Influential academic leaders promoted the Point Four Program, either out of a sense of patriotism or with an eye toward enhancing their institutions' global reach. Many individuals who participated, including Bruce Anderson and his USU colleagues, wanted to do something beneficial for the people of less developed countries. In all, more than seventy American universities supported technical assistance projects through Point Four and its successor, the US Agency for International Development (USAID, or AID), during the 1950s and 1960s. This book focuses on three of them. Utah State University held four Point Four agricultural contracts in Iran and maintained a continuous presence in that country between 1951 and 1964. BYU sent two teams of advisers to assist in the modernization of Iranian education, one from 1951 through 1955 that emphasized teacher training and another between 1957 and 1961 that helped modernize Iran's National Teacher's College, Daneshsaraye Ali, in Tehran. The University of Utah also sent a small team of public health advisers to Iran between 1951 and 1956. Taken together, the Utah projects represent a cross-section of university contributions to US technical assistance, an aspect of early Cold War foreign policy historians have so far left unexplored.

Point Four technical advisers represented the US government and became ambassadors for the American way of life. The Utahans wholeheartedly believed their work would uplift Iranians while striking a blow against the dangerous march of international communism. They approached that work with sincerity and enthusiasm. The missionary spirit of the Latter-day Saints community, to which most of the Utah families belonged, encouraged and sustained them. But theirs was not a religious mission; rather, it was a mission for socioeconomic development. Larry Grubbs has called the academics and technical experts who carried out American development schemes in Africa at the same time "secular missionaries," and most of the characteristics he identifies with those individuals—a high level of personal commitment, faith that Western science and technology could solve a wide range of poverty problems, and a strong belief in American exceptionalism—were also present in the Utah advisers.[10] Dedication to the job, honesty, and clean living helped the Utahns connect with their Iranian partners and made them stand apart from the many American diplomats who became notorious for carousing and careerism. They displayed a humanitarian spirit that led them to leave the comforts of middle-class American life and serve impoverished people in a remote, strange, and often intimidating land, confident that their own experience in transforming the American West qualified them for the task.

A third purpose of this book is to explain why Point Four achieved only limited success in Iran. Americans believed their abundance of technical knowledge would help underdeveloped nations achieve efficient and peaceful economic development, but that did not happen in Iran and many other countries. The program was modest in scope and could do little more than provide a primer for Iranian development in a few select fields. While American advisers possessed an abundance of technical knowledge, they lacked a deep understanding of Iranian culture and society. Despite their good intentions, then, technical advisers faced a steep learning curve. From negotiating with cabinet ministers and village leaders to living and working in a country where clean water and paved roads were still rare, they encountered a bewildering array of challenges. Like all technical experts, the Utahns had to show patience and flexibility. Projects that displayed too much American influence or that pushed too strongly to Americanize Iranian practices often met resistance, especially in education. Even when they enjoyed Iranian support, Point Four advisers operated amid myriad bureaucratic obstacles that limited their effectiveness, including instability and inefficiency within the Iranian government and a frustrating lack of continuity in US foreign aid policies. The onset of a process known as integration further undermined technical assistance in 1956. Integration sought to reduce American costs and commitments by having Iranians take over more of the planning and execution of the projects, that is, integrate them more fully into Iranian development schemes, while American advisers continued to provide technical support. Unfortunately, many Point Four projects floundered under Iranian control during the second half of the 1950s.

Point Four was never a very high priority for the US government. While it was much smaller than most other Cold War foreign aid programs, many conservatives nevertheless dismissed it as wishful thinking and a wasteful misallocation of tax dollars. To provide some fiscal perspective, Congress allocated just under $150 million to the program in 1952 while spending $6 billion on military assistance that year and more than $13 billion on the reconstruction of Western Europe, the Marshall Plan, between 1948 and 1952.[11] The US government's total commitment to technical aid in Iran amounted to about $120 million between 1951 and 1967, or approximately half of 1 percent of all US foreign aid to that country during those years.[12] The US government put much more emphasis on using foreign aid to preserve friendly regimes around the world than it put on Point Four's belief that democratic socioeconomic development would lead to a more peaceful world. To put it plainly, Point Four's goal was to achieve stability *through* democratic development, but American foreign policy makers prioritized stability *over* democratic development.[13] That is not to say that US leaders ignored Point Four's goals altogether; they clearly recognized that rampant poverty and political repression left many countries, including Iran, unstable and susceptible to communist influence. But the first priority was to protect friendly anti-communist regimes. Point Four's low-modernization approach to development became less significant in Iran by the mid-1950s as the overriding American goals shifted to bolstering the regime of Mohammad Reza Shah Pahlavi and assisting large-scale infrastructure and industrial projects.

A final goal of this book is to explore how the Utahns both understood and misunderstood the relationship that developed between the United States and Iran from the mid-1950s through the late 1970s. The first Utahns arrived in Iran during pivotal years when the country became more significant to US foreign policy. Washington's interest stemmed from the growing importance of Persian Gulf oil, from the country's strategic location along the southern border of the Soviet Union, and from a fear that communist activity was increasing.[14] The early 1950s marked a watershed moment when Prime Minister Mohammad Mossadegh rallied Iranian nationalists in a campaign to wrest control of the country's greatest natural resource from the British-owned Anglo-Iranian Oil Company. The resulting oil nationalization controversy plunged Iran into a crisis that British and American leaders feared would embolden Iranian communists and perhaps the Soviet Union itself. In August 1953 they supported a military coup that removed Mossadegh from power. Like many American leaders, the Utahns welcomed the ouster of a leader they came to see as too chaotic and too tolerant of communism. The 1953 coup marked a major turning point in US-Iranian relations. US policy makers threw their lot in with the regime of Mohammad Reza Shah Pahlavi, the shah who ruled Iran from 1941 until 1979.

Though the Utahns felt great sympathy for the Iranian people, their reading of Iran's development under the shah proved flawed. While the Utahns celebrated the overthrow of Mossadegh as a necessary step in restoring stability and democracy, Iranians came to see it as a case of foreign powers thwarting their national sovereignty. The Utah advisers applauded as the shah led Iran through a period of tremendous economic growth during the 1960s, but many Iranians resented his increasingly authoritarian leadership and the chaotic nature of Iran's economic development. Moreover, American intelligence agents helped train his notorious secret police, SAVAK, and supplied the regime with lavish military aid that the shah often used to suppress dissent. This book draws on the experience of the Utah advisers to explain how Americans misread the era of the shah's modernizing dictatorship between 1953 and 1979.

IRAN AND THE WEST BEFORE 1950

Iran is one of the world's oldest civilizations, though few Americans paid much attention to it before the Cold War. Some could probably recall school lessons about its great ancient history: the massive Persian Empire that Cyrus and Darius built five centuries before the birth of Christ followed by the epic wars with Greece and subsequent conquest by Alexander the Great. More worldly

Americans might be acquainted with the country's distinguished medieval poets or its beautiful carpets and architecture. But Iran was far removed from American commercial and diplomatic concerns. The United States did not establish formal diplomatic relations with the Iranian government until 1883, and the US Department of State did not appoint a desk officer for the country until World War II. American diplomacy largely restricted itself to protecting scattered missionaries and overseeing the little business transacted between the two countries.[15]

The once-great nation fell on hard times during the nineteenth and early twentieth centuries. Russian expansion toward the Persian Gulf absorbed much of the Caucasus region between the Black and Caspian Seas by 1830; the czar's armies extended Russian power over the vast Asian steppe on Iran's northern border by the end of the 1870s. The Iranian government had to accept humiliating treaties in 1813 and 1828 that made Russia master of the Caspian Sea and gave Russian citizens immunity from Iranian prosecution. This history of Russian aggrandizement at Iran's expense loomed large in American thinking about the Middle East during the Cold War. Britain like-wise expanded its presence in Afghanistan and along the Persian Gulf during the nineteenth century to strengthen its control of the approaches to India and deny Russia access to the Indian Ocean. Fearing the growth of German influence in Iran immediately before World War I, the Russians and British put their "Great Game" rivalry on hold in 1907 to divide Iran into spheres of influence. Russia entrenched itself as the dominant power in the north, while Britain became practically sovereign in the southeast around the strategic strait at Hormuz where the Persian Gulf empties into the Gulf of Oman and the Indian Ocean.[16]

Meanwhile, the extravagant but feeble Iranian government squandered the nation's wealth on lavish royal trips abroad and by selling to British and Russian investors the rights to exploit key sectors of the economy. The grand prize of these foreign concessions went to William Knox D'Arcy, a British businessman who made his fortune in mining and land speculation. In 1901 D'Arcy acquired the sole right to explore for oil in most of Iran for sixty years. In return, he paid less than $100,000 in cash—a modest sum even in 1901— granted the shah another $100,000 worth of stock, and promised the Iranian government 16 percent of future petroleum profits. The Anglo-Persian Oil Company (renamed the Anglo-Iranian Oil Company [AIOC] in 1935 and now

British Petroleum [BP]) bought the concession in 1908 and retained control over all aspects of the Iranian oil industry for the next half century. The British government acquired a controlling share of the AIOC in 1914, and the company soon emerged as the United Kingdom's most valuable foreign asset.[17] Other agreements gave British or Russian interests almost complete control over banking, mining, communications, and public finance.[18] As a consequence of these foreign concessions, few Iranians learned the technical skills necessary to build a modern country. Moreover, European exploitation of the nation's economy inspired Iranian antipathy toward the West.

British and Russian operatives blocked several attempts at meaningful reforms in Iran during the first half of the twentieth century. Popular dissolution with the country's plunge toward colonial servitude culminated in a constitutional revolution that produced Iran's first elected parliament (Majlis) the fall of 1906. But Mohammad Ali Shah (r. 1907–9) sought Russian help in squashing the revolution. He ordered the Russian-led Cossack Brigade to bombard the Majlis building in the summer of 1908, and Russian forces occupied Tabriz, a city in northern Iran to which the constitutionalists fled, the following spring.[19] When Reza Shah (r. 1925–41) attempted to cancel the British oil concession in 1932, Anglo-Persian executives agreed to increase the Iranian government's share of profits and royalties, but they retained complete ownership and control of the company.[20]

The Bolshevik Revolution raised Western fears that Russian communists would export their ideology to Iran. Iranian socialists formed a Justice Party at Baku across the Russian border in 1917 and renamed it the Communist Party of Iran in 1920. The party sent delegates to the Sixth Bolshevik Congress, organized workers, recruited for the Red Army, smuggled socialist newspapers into Iran, and supported a socialist republic in the province of Gilan on the southern coast of the Caspian Sea. Leftist ideas continued to circulate, especially in Tehran and Tabriz, during the interwar years despite Reza Shah's concerted attempts to stamp them out. A socialist party began organizing the lower classes in 1921. One of its leaders, Sulayman Iskandari, became the first chairman of the pro-Soviet Tudeh (Masses) Party, which was formed in 1941 and became the focal point of Anglo-American fears about communism in Iran during the 1950s.[21]

Though Iran was remote from US government interests before World War II, a handful of American missionaries had been active since the 1830s ministering to the Armenian and Assyrian Christian communities and building hospitals and schools. The Church Missionary Society established a hospital outside Isfahan in 1875.[22] Dr. Adelaide Kibbe Frame Hoffman, a Presbyterian missionary, worked as a physician in Iran from 1929 until 1957, primarily in Mashhad and Rasht.[23] Presbyterian missionaries founded a boys' school in Tehran, later Alborz College, in 1871. American missionary schools, according to historian Robert Daniel, "provided an indispensable institution for modern society" and began to attract the sons of leading Iranians by the turn of the twentieth century.[24] Dr. Samuel Jordan, who along with his wife, Mary, taught at the school for more than forty years, could boast by the 1930s that "probably no other school in the world has ever enrolled so many of the children of the leading men of any country."[25] American missionaries also helped pioneer practical education for girls, especially in home economics, in an era that offered few other educational opportunities for them.[26] Historian Monica Ringer writes that missionary girls' schools were "significant for the impetus they provided to women's education" because they "viewed women's education as a means of improving general living standards."[27] Jane Doolittle, a missionary who "dedicated her life to furthering the education and health of the Iranian people," served as principal of the Presbyterian girls' school in Tehran for more than four decades, between 1925 and 1968.[28]

Americans also contributed to other aspects of Iranian development that anticipated Point Four technical assistance. In 1911, for example, the Iranian government hired W. Morgan Shuster to reorganize the country's finances. Anglo-Russian pressure truncated that effort, which led Shuster to write a scathing criticism of British and Russian imperialism titled *The Strangling of Persia*.[29] Arthur Millspaugh, a former college professor and trade adviser to the Department of State, spent five years in Iran during the 1920s reorganizing tax collections at the request of Reza Shah. A second Millspaugh mission during World War II tried to create order from the endemic corruption within the Iranian government. He was a sincere and principled civil servant, but his rigid manner made him many enemies among the Iranian elite. Millspaugh, according to historian James Bill, "drove an American-made bulldozer into the Iranian labyrinth." His efforts bore little fruit.[30] Finally, the Near East Foundation (NEF) emerged as a major philanthropic organization in Iran by the 1940s. It grew out of American missionary relief to victims of the Armenian Genocide during World War I.[31] In 1946 the NEF pioneered a rural improvement program in northwest Iran that embraced the same low-modernization techniques in agriculture, education, and public health that would characterize Point Four work in the next decade.[32]

IRAN AND US FOREIGN POLICY

World War II and the onset of the Cold War made Iran much more important to American foreign policy. The Allies wanted to keep German forces out of Middle East oilfields, and Iran's position along the Persian Gulf made it an important supply conduit to the Soviet Union.[33] In January 1943 the Department of State endorsed a memorandum written by its Iran desk officer, John Jernegan, urging that the United States provide Iran with "American specialists and application of American methods in various fields." He believed that preserving Iranian independence after the war would be important to American strategic interests and that the United States should therefore assist the country's economic development.[34] The substance of the memorandum reached President Franklin D. Roosevelt, who gave it an informal endorsement. The US government subsequently promised Iran "such economic assistance as may be available" as part of an Allied Tripartite Declaration on Iran.[35] Jernegan's memorandum proved prophetic, as Iran was at the center of an early Cold War showdown in early 1946. The Allied powers had all agreed to withdraw their troops from Iran within six months of the end of the war. The United States and United Kingdom complied; the Soviet Union did not. Instead, Joseph Stalin hoped to use the Soviet presence to leverage an oil concession out of the Iranian government. Meanwhile, Soviet troops encouraged separatist republics in Kurdistan and Azerbaijan. The Truman administration denounced the Soviet behavior as imperialism, and Iranian prime minister Ahmad Qavam negotiated an oil agreement that he knew the Majlis would not ratify. The Soviet Union withdrew its troops from northern Iran in May 1946, but the episode left US and Iranian leaders deeply suspicious of Soviet intentions.[36]

In January 1950 historian T. Cuyler Young offered an analysis of the situation in Iran that was designed to show Americans how important Truman's Point Four proposal could be for that country. World War II brought crippling inflation and extensive economic dislocation as the Allied occupation forces commandeered much of the country's agricultural output. The government of the young Mohammad Reza Shah Pahlavi was struggling to implement basic measures to improve quality of life, such as expanding public education and controlling malaria, but it lacked resources and dedicated civil servants. Powerful politicians, landlords, and clergymen opposed meaningful democratic reforms. Meanwhile, Young warned, the Soviet Union still viewed the country as a target of influence and possibly of expansion.[37] George McGhee of the Department of State was even more direct: "We can be sure that the Kremlin is losing no opportunity to fish in the troubled water of Iran."[38] For Young, the challenge required a robust American response. "The United States must devise a means," he concluded, "to develop Iran for the benefit of all its people."[39] Once remote from American interests, Iran had suddenly become a focal point of US strategic thinking.

1

FORGING A PARTNERSHIP FOR DEVELOPMENT

Point Four and American Universities

We cannot hope to be rid of human tyrants, until we wipe out the impersonal tyranny of hunger, misery and despair on which human tyrannies thrive.

Henry Bennett, Point Four Program director, 1951

The principal currency of Point 4 is not the American dollar, but American know-how.

Benjamin Hardy, "Point IV: Dynamic Democracy"

President Harry S. Truman wanted his January 20, 1949, inaugural address to reinvigorate American foreign policy in a time of increasing Cold War tensions. The president celebrated American diplomatic and economic leadership in the wake of the cataclysmic world war. "Our efforts," he declared, "have brought new hope to all mankind." Having "beaten back despair and defeatism," the United States now stood ready to "build an even stronger structure of international order and justice" and "to improve the standards of living of all people." To accomplish this lofty goal, Truman

DOI: 10.7330/9781607327547.c001

outlined four main priorities. The first two, support for the United Nations and European recovery, reaffirmed existing US policies. The third, participation in the collective security of the "free world," was about to become reality in the form of the North Atlantic Treaty Organization. But the fourth point, which the president talked about as much as the other three combined, was new to most Americans. "We must embark on a bold new program," he said, "for making the benefits of our scientific advances and industrial progress available for the improvement and growth of underdeveloped areas."[1]

Truman presented international economic development as a significant component of the country's Cold War strategy. He reminded his listeners that most of the world's population lived in or near poverty. Inadequate food, lack of clean water, insufficient access to education, poor healthcare, and little upward mobility—these were the conditions that sparked violent revolution and made the "false philosophy" of communism deceptively attractive to millions of people. But the middle of the twentieth century offered new hope because, the president declared, "humanity possesses the knowledge and skill to relieve the suffering of these people." Furthermore, Truman boasted that "the United States is pre-eminent among nations in the development of industrial and scientific techniques." Americans should, in conjunction with suitable international partners, provide technical assistance and promote investment in poor countries to help them produce more and better food, improve education and housing, and expand industrial activity. The result would be "the achievement of peace, plenty, and freedom."[2]

The resulting program, popularly called Point Four in reference to Truman's speech, became a modest but consistent part of US foreign policy during the 1950s. American universities soon emerged as attractive partners in this venture for international development. The 1950s and 1960s marked great expansion and internationalization of American higher education. Enrollments soared, research programs proliferated, and more professors and students went abroad than ever before. Thousands of foreign students also flocked to the United States to study, especially in fields such as engineering, agriculture, education, and medicine that were at the heart of national development. Early forays into overseas technical aid raised hopes that members of the academic community would "make both competent and selfless ambassadors—better, on average, than protocol-minded diplomats and bureaucratic civil servants."[3]

This chapter traces the origins of the Point Four Program and discusses how and why universities became involved. The Point Four Program was a contested piece of US foreign policy that encountered turbulence as it went through major reorganizations and corresponding policy changes during the 1950s. The partnership for international development that emerged between the US government and universities also produced difficulties that are illustrated in the Utah universities' work in Iran, especially between 1951 and 1955.

TRUMAN'S BOLD NEW PROGRAM

Harry Truman felt he needed something big to capture the public's imagination following his unexpected victory in the 1948 presidential election. The three-and-a-half years since he had inherited the presidency upon the death of Franklin Roosevelt had been filled with ominous international crises. While the Allies emerged victorious from World War II during his first year in office, the Grand Alliance fell apart over the next three years. The Soviet Union tightened its grip on Eastern Europe, attempted to starve its erstwhile allies out of Berlin, and sought strategic advantages in the straits of Istanbul and in northern Iran. Farther east, Chinese communists under Mao Zedong pushed toward victory in a long and bloody civil war. All along the Eurasian periphery of these two behemoths, from Turkey to Korea, poor and weak nations appeared susceptible to communist expansion. Meanwhile, the United States and its partners struggled to contain that expansion and to rebuild Western European economies shattered by fifteen years of depression and war. Truman attacked these grave challenges with steadfast resolve despite having assumed the presidency with little foreign policy experience.

The American public, however, showed only lukewarm confidence in his presidential leadership. Plainspoken and occasionally given to frank self-deprecation, Truman lacked his predecessor's charisma and towering prestige. Roy Roberts, a longtime acquaintance and managing editor of the Kansas City *Star*, once described him as "the average man"; *Time* more bluntly called him "a man of distinct limitations, especially . . . in high level politics." His political prospects appeared to dwindle during three tumultuous years in office. Roosevelt loyalists blamed him for the Republican sweep of the US

Congress in the 1946 midterm elections; former interior secretary and New Deal stalwart Harold Ickes even suggested that he should resign. Public opinion polls in the spring of 1948 predicted that Truman would lose to any of the leading Republican challengers in the upcoming election. Liberal publications such as *The Nation* and *New Republic* called on him to step aside; Roosevelt's sons lobbied Dwight Eisenhower to run for the Democratic Party nomination. Throughout the fall campaign, the press seemed more enamored with the crisp and confident Republican candidate, Governor Thomas Dewey of New York. The conservative *Chicago Daily Tribune* declared "Dewey Defeats Truman" in the early morning hours after the election. The actual results, however, showed Truman to be the winner in one of the most dramatic presidential elections in modern American history.[4]

Emboldened by the victory and adamant that the United States must lead the "free world" through a time of crisis, Truman set out to build public support for the nation's much-expanded foreign policy. When presidential aide Clark Clifford solicited the Department of State for recommendations on how to make Truman's inaugural address "a democratic manifesto" to the whole world, a public affairs officer named Benjamin Hardy responded with a proposal for a program of technical assistance for economic development in poor nations threatened by international communism. Hardy had formerly been a reporter for the *Atlanta Journal* and a press officer for the US government's embryonic technical assistance program in Brazil during World War II. Both positions gave him a firsthand appreciation for how the targeted spread of new technologies could improve underdeveloped rural areas. Hardy hoped his idea would "capture the imagination of the peoples of other countries" and create a "democratic campaign to repulse Communism."[5] Undersecretary of State Robert Lovett balked at the idea, but Hardy had the gumption to pitch it directly to George Elsey, Clifford's assistant. Clifford sent the proposal back to the Department of State, but he presented it as Truman's idea to protect Hardy, who had risked his career by going outside channels. Again, Department of State officials brushed the idea of technical assistance aside, claiming they could not study it sufficiently. Clifford nevertheless began working Hardy's idea into drafts of the president's upcoming inaugural address.[6] Truman embraced the proposal. His reading of American history and his previous experience as a rural county judge had acquainted him with problems of rural development. His top priority more than two decades earlier had been to extend well-paved roads to all farms and businesses in Jackson County, Missouri.[7]

Truman's "Point Four" proposal, as the idea soon became known, received enthusiastic applause and an almost immediate groundswell of public support. The *Washington Post* said it would "electrify the world," while the *Christian Science Monitor* called it "a tremendous idea, not only humanitarian but practical."[8] Economist John Kenneth Galbraith observed that "few actions by an American Chief Executive ever produced a more whole-souled response."[9] David Lilienthal, then chairman of the Tennessee Valley Authority (TVA), described it as "the most potent weapon ever devised, a weapon that makes the atomic bomb seem a firecracker by comparison."[10] Clifford added that the proposal "tapped a deep wellspring of altruism and idealism within the American people."[11] Secretary of the Interior Julius Krug called the president's speech "one of the most constructive and far reaching statements of foreign policy of our time." He wrote incoming secretary of state Dean Acheson imploring that the technical assistance proposal be "implemented as soon as possible."[12]

For Truman, Point Four was neither inaugural bluster nor a dose of sugar aimed at enticing poor countries to choke down American foreign policy objectives. Rather, it was a serious call for Americans to do something bold to help with the development of poor countries while simultaneously beating back the advance of international communism. "It was an adventurous idea," the president recalled in his memoirs, adding with some exaggeration, "such as had never before been proposed by any country in the history of the world."[13] Though it was the smallest of four major foreign aid initiatives the Truman administration created, Point Four was the program "for which Truman personally felt a great deal of enthusiasm."[14] He sincerely believed that an expanded technical assistance program would be a foreign policy asset. Diplomat Capus Waynick called it "the long-range answer to communism."[15] Historian Amanda McVety observed that Point Four "promised to help the United States by helping others. It offered a Cold War weapon that was not a weapon and promised peace through peaceful means."[16] Truman himself called it "a practical expression of . . . our policies of preventing the expansion of Communism" that would help "insure the proper development" of recipient nations. Point Four would bring to the downtrodden peoples of the world "not the idealism of democracy alone, but the tangible benefits of better living through intelligent co-operation."[17]

MAKING THE POINT FOUR PROGRAM A REALITY

Turning Truman's proposal into a working component of US foreign policy proved difficult throughout 1949 and 1950. The first task was to sell the concept to a reluctant Department of State, which, according to Clifford, "looked down on activities that were not purely diplomatic."[18] Acheson, who himself had little enthusiasm for Point Four, recalled that Lovett and Paul Nitze of State's policy planning staff "were neither enthusiastic nor impressed with its utility."[19] They would have preferred that the president not mention it. No one at State had a very clear idea of what Truman had in mind. "I think the first problem that the State Department had to figure out," recalled legal adviser Ben Hill Brown, "was what in the hell the man was talking about."[20]

Administration officials indeed struggled to define the president's idea. A week after his address, Truman responded to a reporter's question about Point Four with "I can't tell you just what is going to take place, where it is going to take place, or how it is going to take place. I know what I want to do."[21] Acheson tried to put aside his misgivings but likewise found he could speak only in generalities. Technical assistance would "help in the ancient struggle of man to earn his living and get his bread from the soil," and that would in turn help people obtain "freedom and dignity, the fullness of life." The new secretary attempted to head off potential criticism, especially concerning the plan's potential to expand American financial commitments to nations far removed from the historical scope of US foreign policy. Point Four, he asserted, would not burden American taxpayers with the cost of international development. Instead, it would emphasize the dissemination of know-how and encourage private investment. Acheson also reiterated that the United States was prepared to cooperate with the United Nations and other countries that could provide sound assistance.[22] Beyond that, he could provide few specifics.

Point Four presented the Department of State with a host of logistical questions. How much good would technical know-how do in countries that lacked modern infrastructure? Would technical assistance require a new government agency, or would responsibility be spread among the roughly two dozen federal agencies already engaged in some kind of relief, reconstruction, or development work in Latin America and Western Europe? What countries would be eligible to receive technical aid, and would they have to be aligned with the United States in some way? Should the US government or recipient

nations determine which projects to fund?[23] Truman's stress on cooperation
with the United Nations was appealing on the surface, but that would also
mean funneling taxpayer dollars to multilateral projects over which the US
government could not exercise unilateral control. What portion of the cost
should the United States bear? The Department of State noted that the UN
budget for technical assistance was modest and that the United States was
already covering almost 40 percent of the UN World Health Organization's
budget. Legislative ceilings would likely preclude any substantial increase
in US government support for multilateral technical assistance.[24] The president's emphasis on encouraging private investment likewise raised thorny
questions, especially in the wake of a destructive world war.[25] It remained to
be seen how willing Americans—or anyone else—would be to invest in countries that lacked a stable economy and government. From Latin America to
Asia, American diplomats scrambled to dampen expectations that Point Four
could become a Marshall Plan for the world.[26]

The Department of State developed a broad, though still not precise,
vision for the Point Four Program throughout 1949. It would enhance world
peace by promoting democratic government and sound and stable economic growth, and it would encourage the expansion of global trade. A
State pamphlet published in December 1949 anticipated a first-year budget
of around $85.6 million—nearly three times what the program eventually
received—with just over half the money going to agriculture and forestry,
health, and education. Promoting industrial development would be the
next-highest priority. Other areas such as transportation, social services,
and public administration would receive more modest support.[27] Recipient
nations would have to bear a significant portion of the cost, and US investment would have to come primarily from the private sector. The US government would not carry out development projects; rather, it would provide
technical support for countries to do more for themselves. Already in 1949,
US policy planners acknowledged that American technical experts could not
risk the appearance of coming into countries as neo-imperialists in the garb
of altruistic advisers.[28]

The next hurdle, getting appropriate legislation through Congress, took
nearly a year to clear. The congressional agenda was already crowded, and
divergent visions for the program both inside and outside the government
made arriving at a consensus difficult. Fiscal conservatives were reluctant to

embrace another program that would ship millions of US tax dollars overseas in the wake of the capacious Marshall Plan and $400 million in "Truman
Doctrine" economic and military aid to Greece and Turkey. Representative
Otto Passman (D-LA) of the House Appropriations Committee doubted that
Point Four would win the United States many long-term friends. Rather, he
argued that recipient nations would resent the appearance of being dependent
on American resources and know-how.[29] Senator Kenneth Wherry (R-NE)
similarly decried spending "billions" on the "fatuous idea that friendship of
nations can be won with bribery." Representative Christian Herter (R-MA),
who later helped implement Point Four late in the Eisenhower administration, expressed support for the plan but wanted to ground its humanitarian idealism in economic reality. He therefore tried to steer legislation away
from a large-scale commitment to foreign aid and toward the promotion and
protection of private American investment in other countries.[30] For his part,
Secretary of State Acheson was preoccupied with Germany and finalizing
the North Atlantic Treaty; he did little to encourage Point Four legislation.[31]

The chair of the House Foreign Affairs Committee, John Kee (D-WV),
introduced a bill in July 1949 that reflected the administration's emphasis on
technical assistance.[32] Herter warned that Point Four legislation must offer
"no illusions whatever" of "a large-scale, give-away program." Recipient governments had to create conditions that would attract private investment and
improve productivity.[33] He therefore offered an alternative bill that emphasized the protection of American investment from foreign currency restric-
tions, uncompensated nationalization, and double taxation.[34] Kee acknowledged that both bills aimed to use economic development as a weapon
against communist expansion, but he felt that Herter's version would put
that weapon in the hands of business leaders who would be less interested
in the community-oriented projects Kee felt would be most effective in promoting democratic growth in poor countries.[35] Hearings revealed strong support for the Point Four idea but significant differences on how the program
should work. Representatives of business and international trade showed
more enthusiasm for Herter's approach, while administration supporters
argued for more vigorous emphasis on technical assistance. The 1949 legislative session ended without the House taking action on either bill. Kee and
Herter jointly introduced a compromise bill early the next year that passed
the House as part of the Foreign Economic Assistance Act of 1950. Herter

attached an amendment that reduced the initial allocation from $35 million to $15 million, both to make the bill more palatable to fiscal conservatives and because he recognized that Point Four work would require multi-year commitments.[36]

Point Four legislation faced a tougher fight in the US Senate where Eugene Millikin (R-CO) and Robert Taft of Ohio, "Mr. Republican," led a spirited opposition.[37] Taft had long favored minimizing US commitments abroad and was uneasy about the expansion of US foreign policy during the second half of the 1940s. He saw foreign aid as a wasteful scattering of US taxpayer dollars around the world that would force the government to raise taxes and thereby stifle economic growth at home. He further worried that the Soviet Union would use an increased American presence in Asia as justification for a more ambitious Soviet policy in Latin America. More philosophically, Taft feared that the multifaceted expansion of Cold War foreign policy would erode the hallowed American tradition of limited government. Like many of his conservative colleagues, Taft reluctantly accepted the Marshall Plan and the Truman Doctrine because they showed that the administration was serious about stopping the communist advance, though he sought to limit both. He even embraced US aid to Taiwan in light of the communist victory in the Chinese civil war. But the Point Four concept smacked of a worldwide New Deal—Taft himself called it a "global WPA" in reference to the 1930s Works Progress Administration—and that was something this arch-opponent of the actual New Deal could not stomach.[38] When Point Four legislation came before the Foreign Relations Committee in the spring of 1950, several senators including Walter George (D-GA), Henry Cabot Lodge Jr. (R-MA), and Howard Smith (R-NJ) sought to impose limitations similar to those Herter had attached to the House bill.[39]

As Congress debated Point Four legislation, a growing chorus of skepticism appeared in public discussion. The *Chicago Daily Tribune* denounced it as a "spendthrift policy," while the *Wall Street Journal* surmised that its full cost would be ten times the administration's estimates and worried that it would legitimize open-ended commitments to economic development in non-communist countries.[40] Respected journalist Henry Hazlitt's influential criticism, *Illusions of Point Four*, opened with the sensational charge that the entire scheme originated from a more ambitious proposal by American communist leader Earl Browder. Hazlitt also suggested, without a hint of irony in Jim Crow America, that "instead of adopting a caste system or ancestor worship," poor countries should have embraced "free competition, free initiative, [and] equality of opportunity." Hyperbole aside, Hazlitt articulated important concerns about the Point Four concept. There was simply no guarantee, he observed, that potential recipient governments possessed either the will or the means to make effective use of American aid. Rather, Hazlitt presumed that development aid would primarily strengthen corrupt regimes and hasten "the present fashionable trend away from free enterprise and toward statism and socialism." The administration's talk of promoting private investment also struck Hazlitt as a chimera. Poor countries were poor precisely because they lacked a business climate conducive to attracting investment. Their entrenched social hierarchies stifled individual initiative and offered few opportunities for upward mobility. Publicly funded development loans made at discounted rates would actually make the problem worse by effectively undercutting private investment.[41]

Liberal economist John Kenneth Galbraith echoed many of Hazlitt's concerns. He wondered, for example, if American development aid would actually reach the people who needed it most. After all, the widespread misuse of military aid to Chiang Kai-shek's nationalist regime in China during World War II illustrated how rulers could instead channel US aid toward their own petty and corrupt purposes. Galbraith also joined Hazlitt in pointing out the folly of counting on private investment to develop politically unstable areas of the world where there was little history of American business activity. Finally, he noted the very real possibility that peasant farmers in far-flung lands would largely reject American technical innovations.[42]

After considerable debate in both the US Capitol and the press, the Senate passed by one vote Point Four legislation that resembled the House bill in its technical assistance aspect.[43] The Foreign Economic Assistance Act that Truman signed into law on June 5, 1950, put several conditions on participation. Recipient nations had to shoulder a fair share of the cost, demonstrate that they were making effective use of US aid, and cooperate with other nations in the mutual exchange of technical skills. Congress also retained the right to terminate any project it judged to be inconsistent with broader US foreign policy goals.[44] Conference negotiations between the two houses authorized $35 million for fiscal year 1951, but the actual appropriation was just under $27 million—less than a tenth of what the US government spent on the occupation of Germany that year and slightly more than 1 percent of the $2.25 billion it sent to Western Europe for the Marshall Plan.[45]

The modest scope of the Point Four Program belied the rather grandiose vision on which it rested. Point Four was firmly grounded in the belief that spreading American values—the American way of life—would naturally lead to a more stable, peaceful, and democratic world. It drew on the near-messianic American sense of being a "city upon a hill," a shining beacon for humanity. Truman, writes historian Amanda McVety, cherished Point Four's place in the "long tradition of American humanitarianism—an urge to share the [American] experiment with others."[46] Indeed, Point Four drew from the same well that inspired nineteenth-century missionaries to build hospitals and schools in the Middle East and China. It incorporated and expanded the US government's early technical assistance programs in Latin American during the 1940s and those the Near East Foundation pioneered in Iran.[47] Americans had long believed that their way of life could improve the human condition; the hardening of the Cold War helped convince more of them to take that light into distant corners of the world. Department of State leaders might balk at this newfangled approach to "public diplomacy," and congressional conservatives might try to limit the government's role, but few Americans doubted that their benevolent influence could make the world wealthier and more peaceful.

If the Point Four Program grew out of America's loftiest principles, its architects were not blind to the self-serving motives that often accompanied those principles. Americans like to think that their influence promotes prosperity and democracy abroad, but history paints a more complex picture. The "civilizing missions" military men and philanthropists imposed on the Philippines and a host of Caribbean nations in the first half of the twentieth century, for example, reflected an often violent adherence to racial hierarchy. Economic and infrastructure improvements tended to favor American investors rather than the indigenous populations, and none of these interventions produced genuine democracy.[48] Senator Tom Connally (D-TX), chair of the Foreign Relations Committee, was adamant that Point Four should avoid any hint of exploitation; it could not allow Americans to "go abroad and invest abroad and get money out of those poor devils that we are supposed to help."[49] Stanley Andrews, who led the Point Four Program during the final years of the Truman presidency, emphasized that American pride coupled with insensitivity to local conditions could negate the goodwill technical projects were supposed to create.[50] Milton Eisenhower, president of Pennsylvania State University, enthusiastic supporter of the Point Four effort, and brother of the future US president, emphasized that Americans had "to understand people of other nations and cultures as people" to "develop a genuine comprehension of those specific economic, social, and psychological situations" that often determined "the ever-present issue of war and peace."[51] Point Four work, then, would have to avoid the appearance of exploitation lest it incubate anti-American resentment in those countries the US government was trying to court.

ENTER THE UNIVERSITIES

American colleges and universities were involved in the Point Four Program almost from the beginning. In early 1951 Truman asked Nelson Rockefeller, a moderate Republican who had spent most of the previous decade working on the US government's nascent technical assistance program in Latin America, to establish an advisory board that would coordinate planning for Point Four among business, philanthropic, and education leaders. The academic community was well represented, as seven of the nineteen members had ties to higher education. Rockefeller established a good working relationship with Henry Bennett, president of Oklahoma Agricultural and Mechanical College (Oklahoma State University [OSU]), who became the first director of the Point Four Program.[52] Interest was especially high among leaders of the nation's land-grant colleges. These institutions represented a pragmatic American innovation in higher education in that they emphasized teaching and research in fields of applied knowledge such as agriculture, engineering, public health, and home economics.[53] Land-grant colleges played an important role in American agricultural and economic development during the late nineteenth and early twentieth centuries. They pioneered, for example, modern extension services, the arm of higher education responsible for disseminating practical scientific knowledge about farming and health to rural families. Both academic and government officials believed their collective expertise would prove valuable to international development work.[54] John Hannah, president of Michigan State College of Agriculture and Applied Sciences (Michigan State University [MSU]) and also of the National Association of Land Grant

Colleges and Universities (NALGCU), wrote to Truman just weeks after the inaugural address offering the services of land-grant institutions to the Point Four effort.[55] Land-grant college officials reaffirmed their "definite responsibility and desire" to assist with agricultural training in foreign countries when they met with their government counterparts in the spring of 1952.[56]

More traditional institutions of higher education also showed interest. Many were coming into their own as comprehensive research centers during the early postwar period, and overseas technical assistance held promise for broadening their intellectual horizons, extending the scope of their expertise, and enhancing institutional prestige. The American Council on Education recognized the duty of colleges and universities to "contribute ideas, resources, and techniques" to programs that "strengthen bonds of international understanding." Its Committee on Institutional Projects Abroad declared university participation to be "natural and fitting" because universities are "fundamentally concerned" with "the raising of intellectual and living standards upon which, in the last analysis, the welfare of mankind depends."[57]

Truman's choice of Bennett to head the Technical Cooperation Administration (TCA), a new agency within the Department of State created to oversee the Point Four Program, further cemented its relationship with the nation's universities.[58] Described as a "loveable man with a genius for inspiring people," Bennett had served as president of OSU since 1928 and developed an interest in international agricultural development.[59] In 1931, for example, he told alumni that the college would eventually develop an institute to help poor countries increase food production. He helped the US Army plan land reforms and other agricultural improvements in occupied Germany in 1949.[60] Administration officials were impressed with his guidance of OSU through a period of tremendous growth that saw enrollment more than triple and the curriculum expand to embrace more emphasis on international subjects, including the teaching of "Oriental languages."[61] Bennett traveled to Addis Ababa, Ethiopia, in the spring of 1950 to initiate an agreement through which OSU would assist the Ethiopian government in setting up an agricultural school that would function like a US land-grant college. That collaboration became an early model for similar Point Four projects.[62]

Bennett devoted considerable attention in 1951 to promoting Point Four among college faculty and administrators. To the National Conference of

Supervisors of Home Economics Education, he stressed the low status of women as a persistent barrier to economic and social development in many parts of the world. Point Four would encourage professional opportunities for women in less developed countries by providing training in fields such as dietetics and rural health. It also needed female advisers to organize food preservation and sanitation demonstrations in gender-segregated societies.[63] He emphasized to the American Society for Engineering Education that infrastructure improvements would facilitate economic development. Planning new transportation systems would require civil engineers; sanitary engineers could help develop water purification and distribution systems. Geologists and hydroelectric engineers would be crucial in controlling flooding and finding new sources of power.[64] Bennett emphasized the importance of racial justice in promoting democracy to leaders of historically black colleges and universities and touted that scientists from those institutions were already working to solve technical problems in Liberia, Iran, and Mexico.[65] The nation faced a grave threat from international communism, he told academic leaders in November, but military power alone could not stop its advance. Winning the postwar peace would require eliminating the conditions on which "stomach communism" thrives. "We cannot hope to be rid of human tyrants," Bennett reasoned, "until we wipe out the impersonal tyranny of hunger, misery, and despair on which human tyrannies thrive."[66] Point Four advisers could not be just technical experts, though; they had to possess a social conscience and a flexible diplomatic personality. "We should not try to transplant our own institutions on foreign soil," he warned, "but rather to help other people develop the kind of institutions that suit their own particular needs."[67]

Henry Bennett died in a plane crash outside Tehran while on Point Four business in December 1951. Also killed in that tragedy was Benjamin Hardy, the Department of State public affairs officer who two years earlier had risked his career to send his technical assistance idea to the White House. Both men devoted the final years of their lives to laying the foundation for a new approach to foreign policy that they believed would bring a peaceful, humanitarian, and non-communist revolution to the world's less developed nations. Given the resistance Point Four faced in the Department of State and Congress, it is doubtful that the program would have existed at the end of 1951 without their vision and dedication.

The first Point Four university contracts began in 1951; among them were the first agreements for the Utah schools to begin work in Iran.[68] Harold Stassen, a former university president who led Point Four from the fall of 1953 to the spring of 1955, greatly expanded university participation. "It has been my observation," he told reporters soon after taking over the project, "that many of the best developments overseas have occurred in those instances in which colleges and universities of our countries have been brought into a direct relationship."[69] Citing the successful OSU project in Ethiopia and similarly successful efforts by MSU advisers in Colombia and India, Stassen proclaimed that the participation of more colleges and universities "would be one of the most desirable methods of carrying forward our technical cooperation program."[70] He also told Senator J. William Fulbright (D-AR), another strong proponent of international cooperation, that universities brought a "depth of the people-to-people warmth" to projects that often achieved "greater results than the hiring of governmental technicians."[71] Stassen was particular eager for universities to establish partnerships with counterpart institutions in developing nations that would continue long after their Point Four contracts ended.[72]

Most university projects took place in Asia and Latin America, which reflected Point Four's broader strategic priorities. Five American universities undertook technical assistance work in India, the world's largest democracy and an impoverished country of nearly 370 million, in 1950. The number of Point Four university projects in that country reached thirteen by the early 1960s. Many of these early partnerships were university-to-university arrangements, a pattern that became standard by the end of the 1950s. Those projects varied a great deal in scope and in the level of university involvement. Some lasted just two years and sent fewer than five advisers; others, such as USU's agricultural work in Iran, continued for more than a decade and involved more than fifty individuals. The faculty and administrations of some participating universities showed little interest in Point Four projects, while others, especially Oklahoma State, Michigan State, the University of Nebraska, and Utah State, made technical assistance a centerpiece of their emerging international programs.[73]

The work also varied a great deal. The University of Tennessee provided home economists to help eight colleges and universities in India develop curricula and applied research in nutrition, while the University of Illinois helped Allahabad Agricultural Institute, a former missionary school, modernize its educational programs. Perhaps not surprisingly, many of the university-to-university projects involved expanding and modernizing teacher training programs. BYU, for example, provided advisers to help improve the University of Tehran's teacher training college between 1957 and 1961. Only 2 percent of adults in Nepal could read and write when the University of Oregon began assisting the Nepal Teacher Training Center in September 1954. Prairie View Agricultural and Mechanical College, a historically black university in Texas, assisted the Booker Washington Agricultural and Industrial Institute in Kakata, Liberia, in expanding vocational training courses in carpentry and other skilled trades. Land-grant institutions such as the University of Arkansas, the University of California, Cornell University, Michigan State University, the University of Nebraska, North Carolina State University, Oregon State University, Purdue University, the University of Wyoming, and Washington State University helped establish or improve agricultural and engineering colleges in countries as diverse as Afghanistan, Brazil, Chile, Colombia, Pakistan, Panama, Peru, Philippines, South Korea, Thailand, and Turkey. Those projects usually involved adapting elements of the American land-grant method of higher education to fit the needs of host countries.[74]

Other early contracts partnered American universities with relevant government agencies in the host countries, particularly ministries of agriculture, education, and health. All of the initial Utah university advisers worked directly with agencies of the Iranian government. The University of Florida, the University of Idaho, Kansas State University, the University of Missouri, Ohio State University, the University of Pennsylvania, and the University of Wisconsin all engaged similar efforts between 1952 and 1956 that sought to eradicate diseases, build better schools, develop heartier crops, purify water supplies, and improve childhood nutrition. These projects generally included both planning and consultation with ministry officials in the capital and fieldwork in training extension agents and demonstrating improved techniques in rural villages.[75]

Improving public administration was one additional area of university concentration in the Point Four Program. Advisers from the University of Michigan, for example, helped establish an Institute of Public Administration at the University of Philippines between 1952 and 1956. A 1954 University of Southern California project allowed Iranians to study public administration at the university's Institute for Public and Business Administration. The framers of that project hoped the participating Iranians would return home to initiate a "re-examination of all educational attitudes and institutions in their home country."[76] MSU supported an extended mission in South Vietnam that worked to improve both public administration and police training between 1955 and 1962. Its close association with the unpopular regime of Ngo Dinh Diem and its emphasis on enhancing internal security made that project a lightning rod for criticism at MSU as the United States became more involved in the Vietnam War; it caused John Hannah to resign as president of the university in 1969.[77]

University contracts accounted for around 20 percent of the US government's technical assistance personnel working abroad by mid-1953.[78] A total of fifty-six American colleges and universities had entered eighty Point Four contracts in thirty-three countries by the fall of 1958.[79] By that point, most were working directly with universities or postsecondary vocational schools in host countries. The number of American universities participating grew to seventy by the early 1960s, and the annual budget for such contracts had grown to $136 million, a nearly tenfold increase over that of 1955.[80]

CHALLENGES TO THE PARTNERSHIP FOR DEVELOPMENT

The partnership between the Point Four Program and universities was not problem-free, however, and tensions grew by the mid-1950s as university involvement increased. The bureaucratic practices and strategic priorities of universities often differed substantially from those of the federal government. Academic officials usually emphasized the research and technical dimensions of overseas development work, but government officials had to give primacy to larger foreign policy objectives and to domestic political considerations. The two communities often took divergent views of project funding as well. Some university administrators saw Point Four contracts as just another source of research money, and they all wanted assurances that funding would be available for the entire duration of projects. Yet federal expenditures are always subject to annual congressional appropriations, for which Point Four was never a very high priority. Moreover, participating universities had to play by the frequently shifting rules of federal contracts, something that rarely came naturally to academic leaders who treasured their autonomy from government oversight. Many project coordinators soon found themselves bogged down by the federal bureaucracy and by a host of procedural matters such as acquiring security clearances for new advisers and filing the necessary periodic reports.[81] Finally, some universities showed a greater commitment to supporting their overseas technical assistance contracts than did others. Fortunately, all three Utah institutions provided adequate support for their field teams, with BYU and USU earning praise from Point Four officials for their exemplary commitment to development projects.[82]

Finding qualified people to commit to two-year assignments overseas, usually in remote parts of poor countries, also presented difficulties. It was not easy to pry top scientists and engineers away from their competitive salaries, comfortable homes, and modern labs. Untenured faculty members risked losing two years of career growth and job security. Some universities showed reluctance to release their more experienced specialists for so long a leave of absence, and many senior faculty members had too many other commitments to consider an overseas assignment.[83] Consequently, universities sometimes recruited less qualified individuals including, apparently, some "misfits and drifting adventurers."[84] John Hannah lamented in 1955 that "one of our faults is that sometimes we haven't sent people particularly well fitted to do the job."[85]

The Point Four Program's continued evolution during the 1950s became yet another source of conflict between government and universities. It endured major reorganizations during the decade, which meant that policies concerning university projects rarely remained static for long. The new Eisenhower administration, for example, junked the Technical Cooperation Administration in favor of a Foreign Operations Administration (FOA) in June 1953.[86] Administration officials even tried to discourage the use of the common "Point Four" name because the public so thoroughly identified it with Truman. Harold Stassen, FOA's energetic new director, proved an enthusiastic supporter of university involvement. A moderate Republican who won fame for being elected governor of Minnesota at age thirty-one, Stassen had also served as president of the University of Pennsylvania for five years before accepting the leadership of the Point Four Program. He oversaw more than twenty new university contracts during his eighteen months in charge.[87]

The rapid proliferation of university participation did not lead to harmonious relations between government and higher education leaders. One reason was that Point Four had a chaotic feel under Stassen, and coordination with participating universities was often uncertain. USU, for example, still had not received a renewal of its Iran project in mid-September 1953, six months after the original contract had expired. Dean of Agriculture Rudger Walker acknowledged an obligation "to carry the program through to completion" but wondered how the college could meet project expenses.[88] Delays again hit the USU field team in early 1954 when changes to the process for acquiring necessary clearances held up the appointment of twenty new advisers in plant science and agricultural engineering.[89]

More fundamental, however, Stassen was an outlier within an Eisenhower administration that was less impressed with foreign development aid than was its predecessor. Administration officials believed promoting international trade held much greater long-term potential for developing poor countries than did foreign aid, including technical assistance. Secretary of the Treasury George Humphrey observed that "foreign aid obstructed the release of market forces around the world." The administration therefore sought to restrict economic aid to only those countries directly threatened by communism.[90] It again reorganized technical assistance into the International Cooperation Administration (ICA) in the summer of 1955, and Eisenhower appointed former congressman John Hollister (R-OH) to succeed Stassen. Hollister was a fiscal conservative who did not share Stassen's enthusiasm for university contracts. Like many in the Eisenhower administration, he thought about foreign aid primarily in terms of promoting national security rather than economic development. Hollister also observed that many university projects yielded disappointing results, which he blamed on haphazard organization and the failure of participating institutions to provide adequate support.[91] The administration's reappraisal of foreign aid priorities therefore led to a reduction of university involvement in technical assistance in 1955 and 1956.[92] Both the University of Utah's public health project and BYU's teacher training initiatives were terminated during this consolidation. Academic leaders at BYU and around the country found Hollister's new policies troubling, and some threatened to quit the technical assistance program. They felt that Point Four contracts had become too rigid and no longer enjoyed support at the highest levels of the federal administration.[93]

CONCLUSION

From the bold new proposal President Truman first articulated in his 1949 inaugural address, Point Four technical assistance had become a regular component of US relations with thirty-five countries by the mid-1950s. While it was always a contested piece of foreign policy, viewed with skepticism by traditionalists within the Department of State and congressional conservatives, Point Four nevertheless tapped the American sense of mission to remake the world and embodied its popular spirit of exceptionalism. Men such as Truman, Benjamin Hardy, and Henry Bennett touted Point Four as the humanitarian, even altruistic, face of US foreign policy. Its primary purpose, however, was strategic. The program aimed to align recipient nations closer to the United States, reduce their need for Soviet foreign aid, and lessen the appeal of international communism. Cold War concerns therefore placed the nexus of Point Four technical assistance along the Middle Eastern and Asian periphery of the Soviet Union and China, but Point Four missions also existed in Latin America and a handful of African nations.

The participation of American universities grew steadily, from the first contracts in 1951 to more than fifty by the middle of the decade. The partnership for development that evolved between the federal government and the academic community experienced plenty of turbulence, but sufficient support remained to continue it within both the diplomatic and academic communities. It was in this hopeful but often chaotic context that the three Utah institutions began their work on Iranian rural improvement in the fall of 1951.

2

UTAHNS IN IRAN

Utah and the college are known very favorably in this country . . . I know of
no other institution that can carry on the work in Iran as well as I think Utah
State [University] can do it.

Franklin Harris, 1951

This was indeed a strange land into which we had flown. Strange in custom,
strange in human action, and degenerate in appearance.

A. Reed Morrill, BYU adviser in Iran, 1953

Government officials began recruiting Utah's major research universities to
participate in the Point Four Program even before Truman signed the Act for
International Development in May 1950. That March, Glen Taggart of the
US Department of Agriculture contacted Franklin Harris to see if he would
consider an appointment in Iran with the Department of State's new technical assistance program. Taggart, a Utahn who later served as president of
Utah State University (USU), emphasized that Harris was the government's
top choice.[1] Harris was widely respected in Utah as an agronomist, a leader in

DOI: 10.7330/9781607327547.c002

the Church of Jesus Christ of Latter-day Saints (LDS), and an accomplished university administrator. He had served as president of Brigham Young University (BYU) from 1921 until 1945 and held the same post at USU for the next five years until he joined the Point Four staff in the spring of 1950. His career gave him influence among higher education leaders across the state and familiarity with a broad pool of technical experts. Soon after joining Point Four, Harris suggested that the state's main universities would make good partners for the work to be done.[2]

The Department of State looked to Utah for a variety of reasons. Soil and climate conditions in the state resembled those in Iran, and Utahns had a well-earned reputation for embracing the hard work that brought forth agricultural abundance from that semiarid state. The *Deseret News* [Salt Lake City] proclaimed that Utah's sons of Mormon pioneers could make Iran "bloom as a rose." Moreover, the Utah scientists enjoyed the confidence of Henry Bennett, the first director of the Point Four Program. "I like these Utah fellows," Bennett wrote to Rudger Walker, dean of agriculture at USU, in March 1951, "they usually get things done."[3] Finally, the history of cooperation between USU agronomists and the Iranian Ministry of Agriculture made that institution an attractive choice. BYU, USU, and the University of Utah were all receptive to the call and accepted contracts to support Iranian rural improvement the following summer.[4]

The Utahns' experience in Iran proved daunting, but it was not altogether unpleasant. The first families to arrive were mostly from around Logan and Provo, home to USU and BYU, respectively, and most had ties to those college communities. Many knew each other prior to departure, and those stationed in Tehran lived near each other north of the city—two factors that helped the Utah families cultivate an unusually strong expatriate community. Their close personal relationships and shared dedication to their work helped these Utahns navigate a country that often seemed incomprehensible to middle-class American families. In addition to learning how to operate within what to them seemed a very strange society, the Utah advisers and their families had to work within a still-evolving US government program for foreign development aid. Most of the problems were ultimately worked out to at least basic satisfaction, but a major rift between the Utahns and the US government emerged in the summer of 1955 when Point Four officials abruptly terminated the BYU project for teacher training.

UTAHNS IN IRAN BEFORE POINT FOUR

The agricultural connection between Utah and Iran began in 1912 when President John Widstoe of USU met Mirza Ali Gholi Khan, consul general for the Iranian government, at an agricultural conference in Alberta, Canada. The two developed a friendship, and Widstoe invited Ali Gholi to speak at the college's 1915 baccalaureate.[5] That initial exchange resulted in the first Iranian students enrolling at the Logan campus. The Iranian presence at USU remained limited during the interwar years but increased significantly after World War II and reached 20 percent of the college's international enrollment by the early 1950s.[6] Many Iranian graduates returned to their home country to take up positions within the Ministry of Agriculture; six served on Harris's initial Point Four staff in early 1951. The most famous, Ardeshir Zahedi, served as principal assistant and interpreter to the first director of Point Four operations in Iran, William Warne.[7] Zahedi was the son of General Fazlollah Zahedi, who served as prime minister from August 1953 until the spring of 1955. Ardeshir first met the shah in Utah in 1949 when the young monarch visited the United States, and the two quickly became friends.[8] Between 1960, when the shah appointed him ambassador to the United States, and the fall of his regime in 1979, Ardeshir Zahedi remained one his closest and most trusted political allies.

Franklin Harris also advanced the Utah connections within Iran. A specialist in soil science, Harris had directed agricultural experiment stations in Utah prior to entering higher education. He also lived a life of international service.[9] Harris helped organize a branch of the LDS in Japan in 1926, assisted in the resettlement of Jewish refugees in the Soviet Union in 1929, and studied agricultural problems in Syria and Lebanon in 1946.[10] When the Iranian government requested an American adviser to help reorganize the country's Ministry of Agriculture in 1939, the Department of State recommended Harris, who was then president of BYU. He and his wife, Estelle, spent eleven months touring the country's agricultural facilities between the summers of 1939 and 1940.[11] Jafar Madani, a young Iranian graduate of USU, served as his primary assistant and interpreter.

A year in Iran familiarized Harris with the country's range of agricultural industries and challenges. He studied cotton and citrus fruit production in the humid subtropical Gilan, just south of the Caspian Sea, and experimental wheat farms in the temperate province of Azerbaijan, near the Soviet border.

He learned that irrigation depended heavily on a network of underground canals known as *qanats*, many of which were centuries or even millennia old and required constant maintenance to function properly, to distribute water from mountain sources to the arid interior. He gained insight into the special problems nomadic tribal groups faced herding flocks of sheep and goats from summer to winter pastures. He observed the processing industries for sugar beets and tea. Harris also gained some understanding of Iran's stratified social structure. He met with the prime minister and conferred with cabinet ministers in Tehran, but he also rubbed shoulders with ordinary farmers and soldiers while visiting farms and rural villages.[12] He toured oil installations in southern Khuzestan on the Persian Gulf, though his glowing description of the British-owned refinery at Abadan does not mention the abysmal conditions of most of the company's Iranian workers and instead suggests that he saw only what the company's British executives wanted him to see.[13] Harris spent much of September 1939 in Karaj outside Tehran consulting with Ministry of Agriculture officials about the agricultural college that was about to open there.[14] USU advisers later spent nearly fourteen years working at the college as part of their Point Four contracts. Finally, Harris showed an interest in Iranian culture and history. He read Persian poetry in his spare time and visited many of the country's historic and religious sites with Estelle.[15] By the time he left in July 1940, Franklin Harris had developed a grasp of Iran's development problems.

After leaving Iran, Harris recommended two USU faculty members, agronomist Don Pittman and irrigation engineer Luther Winsor, to continue his work. Pittman traveled to Iran with his wife in September 1940 but left the country in September 1943 amid the turmoil of World War II. Winsor arrived with his family just a week before the Japanese attack on Pearl Harbor in December 1941 and remained through 1946.[16] He held the position of director general of irrigation during his five years in Iran, a post that gave him access to key Iranian leaders. Winsor even took a three-day horseback tour of irrigation facilities with the young shah, who had shown interest in agricultural improvements.[17] His detailed reports painted a picture of a country with vast agrarian potential but one that was in immediate economic and political crisis. The agricultural sector was woefully underdeveloped and dominated by a small class of landlords who monopolized the harvest and showed little interest in peasant welfare or agricultural improvements. Most of the population was illiterate, sick, and never far from starvation. The central government was ineffective in most rural areas, and foreign experts had failed to improve the country's financial and administrative structures.[18] Winsor was convinced that the young shah could be a productive conduit for Iranian development, but the Allied wartime occupation greatly curtailed his power. "Iran keeps coming back to America," he wrote, because "America is her last hope." American missionaries had helped improve Iranian education, and a team of American agricultural experts that arrived in 1949 seemed to be making some headway.[19] Still, Winsor believed Iran showed all the hallmarks of a society susceptible to communist insurgency. Moreover, the Soviet Union demonstrated its appetite for expansion in 1946 by its refusal to remove its troops from the country and its encouragement of leftist breakaway republics in Azerbaijan and Kurdistan. Winsor implored his Utah colleagues to contribute to the burgeoning American effort to help the country.

USU agronomist George Stewart was among the agricultural experts who went to Iran in 1949. His team recommended "practical plans" for rural development the following spring. Writing in *The Improvement Era*, an LDS magazine for young men, Stewart argued that the "struggle for ideals" being played out in Iran should appeal to Mormon humanitarianism. "Those holding the democratic ideology must be more active," he wrote, because communist propaganda from across the Soviet border was a constant presence in this desperate nation. What Iran needed most, he concluded, was "plain industry and practical know-how such as the Utah pioneers had used so effectively."[20]

UTAH UNIVERSITIES JOIN POINT FOUR

Franklin Harris pressed his Utah colleagues to participate in the Point Four Program from his new post as technical director for Iranian rural improvement. "I am thoroughly convinced," he wrote to Rudger Walker in February 1951, that Utah State "is better suited to sponsoring Iran than any other institution."[21] He prompted the college's president, Louis Madsen, with "Utah and the college are known very favorably in this country . . . I know of no other institution that can carry on the work in Iran as well as I think Utah State Agricultural College [USU] can do it."[22] Later that spring he reminded Madsen that the college "stands very high in Iran" because its Iranian graduates have "returned to serve in the country."[23] Henry Bennett likewise contacted Walker to explain that Point Four needed "exceedingly good scientists" to work on a project to which the Department of State "attached great importance." Madsen discussed the idea with the college's board of trustees before going to Washington, DC, to get more information.[24] Meanwhile, E. Reeseman Fryer of State reached a mutual understanding with Brigham Young University on May 1 for the latter to recruit all the initial personnel for rural development in Iran.[25] Five days later, however, Harris wrote that he still expected Point Four to make use of three Utah institutions: BYU, USU, and the University of Utah. Point Four officials also clarified that they wanted all three to participate, though they noted that since BYU had already reached a tentative agreement to send technicians in all fields, "Washington would not open [the program] to the other two Utah institutions unless it was agreed to by President [Ernest] Wilkinson" of BYU.[26] Bennett asked the leadership of each university to work with Harris to establish a satisfactory scheme under which all would contribute commensurate with their capabilities.[27] Harris then traveled back to Utah and met with Presidents Madsen, Wilkinson, and Ray Olpin of the University of Utah in an effort to work out an arrangement acceptable to each university.[28]

Wilkinson and BYU agreed to cooperate with the other two universities under an agreement that would allow each institution to specialize in the field for which it was best suited. BYU would concentrate on education, the University of Utah on public health, and USU on agriculture. A pleased Bennett said the Utah universities would amplify the "effective work" being done in Iran.[29] But the arrangement was not problem-free. Agriculture and agricultural extension commanded the largest share of the budget and required the most advisers, so USU stood to have a greater presence than the other two schools.[30] That bothered BYU officials, who felt they had been generous in agreeing to share responsibility with the other schools and who believed they should be able to play some role in agricultural projects.[31]

Franklin Harris spent the summer of 1951 working to assemble the field teams. He wanted to launch the program "as quickly as possible," but recruiting university faculty to work as Point Four advisers was no simple matter.[32] Potential recruits had to commit to a two-year term of service and possess a flexible and diplomatic disposition. The job would be physically taxing, so candidates had to be in good health and under sixty years old.[33] Graduate students and young professionals often made attractive prospects because they possessed current knowledge but were not yet ensconced in secure high-paying positions.[34] Accommodating the families of potential advisers presented additional complications. The Department of State agreed to pay for a spouse and up to two children to accompany each adviser, but it discouraged those with larger families because of cost and the difficulty of traveling to and living in Iran. In reality, many of the top candidates had more than two children, so suitable arrangements had to be negotiated.[35] Cleve and Helen Milligan did not know with certainty that they would be allowed to join the initial USU agricultural team until just a few weeks before their scheduled departure in September because they had four children.[36] Congress had not yet made the final appropriations, so Harris did not know exactly how many people he could use; nor could he always tell potential advisers what they would be doing or where they would be posted.[37] Complicating matters even more, Iran experienced significant civil unrest and mounting political violence from 1951 through the summer of 1953. Harris therefore had to convince both university administrators and potential advisers that Iran was safe for American families to live and work.[38]

The Utah families brought a wide range of experiences and expectations with them. Some had prior experience abroad and were comfortable operating in foreign cultures, but none had much familiarity with Iran. Bruce Anderson and his wife, Lula, were excited but a little taken aback at the challenge. Imogene Wood recalled being "a little fearful" at the prospect of moving to an unfamiliar country halfway around the world, but she ultimately decided it was her duty to join her husband, Jim, a machinery adviser on the USU agricultural team.[39] The opportunity to visit a land awash in ancient and biblical history intrigued some of the Utahns.[40] Many thought the experience would be a good way to see the world, to learn from another culture, or to do something to help less fortunate people.[41] "The cry of the peasant everywhere is[,] ask America to help get doctors and schools," proclaimed USU sociologist Richard Welling Roskelley in an effort to inspire the LDS community. "She will teach us how to farm, so that we can help ourselves."[42] A. Reed Morrill of BYU expressed appreciation for Point Four's "high type of service" and thought his university could still become "the leader in this type of humanitarian work."[43] Some Utah families acknowledged that they hoped to spread the gospel, though they understood that as representatives of the US government in Iran, they could not preach their religion.[44]

The Utah advisers only occasionally mentioned the financial ramifications of going to Iran, but they were substantial. Point Four work brought a considerable increase in salary for some participants. Fulltime USU faculty members working in Iran in 1953, for example, received higher salaries than most of the college's senior administrators, and the income from overseas assignments was exempt from federal income tax.[45] Those stationed in remote areas received additional hardship allowances. Other advisers, however, such as L.H.O. Stobbe, a physician on the University of Utah team, earned "far less" than he had in private practice.[46] The Department of State covered travel expenses to and from Iran and agreed to pay for the shipping of household goods, but hidden ancillary costs invariably appeared. Many Utah families took time for sightseeing on the way to Tehran, and most had to purchase at least some furniture or appliances once they got settled. Some hired Iranian servants to help manage life in an unfamiliar culture, especially in the traditional markets.

Preparing to move entire families to Iran for two years also required extensive and careful planning. George Stewart, who returned to Iran in the summer of 1951 to assist Harris in getting the program off the ground, tried to prepare his colleagues for what they should expect. Modern apartments with electricity were available in Tehran and other large cities, but furnishings varied widely; many units lacked bathtubs, toilets, and refrigerators. Fresh fruits and vegetables were plentiful in season, but dry staples such as flour and sugar were of a lower quality than those in the United States. Fresh milk was unavailable, though processed substitutes usually were. Both childcare and maintaining a vehicle were more difficult than in Utah. Stewart warned against bringing infants under age one because of the "extreme danger of infant diarrhea."[47] Sanitary conditions would present additional challenges in the rural villages, as most lacked access to clean water and modern sewer systems. Diseases such as malaria, typhoid, dysentery, and tuberculosis were common, especially among the very young and the very old.[48] The Utah families did not always know what kind of schools, if any, would be available for their children. There was an American school in Tehran, but families stationed in the provinces often had to make do on their own. Several families packed books and makeshift school materials so the mothers could conduct lessons at home.

The Utah families also had to wade through the vexing web of federal bureaucracy. The Point Four Program was still taking shape in 1951, so information and sometimes the policies themselves changed often. Salaries and post allowances for remote assignments had to be negotiated, then often clarified and sometimes adjusted.[49] Arrangements to ship household items and automobiles had to be coordinated through the Department of State and cleared by the Iranian government.[50] Expense allotments for travel between Utah and Iran had to be worked out with Point Four officials. Many logistical questions remained unresolved as the first Utah families embarked that fall; some resulted in disputes that continued well into 1952.

The first Utah families received a scant two-week orientation in Washington, DC, prior to their departure. The course included a cursory introduction to Farsi (Persian), the majority language, but it was too short to do much good. Wives and children received immunizations but no real instructions, though they were apparently promised an orientation once they arrived in Iran.[51] Not surprisingly, the Utah people found this training lacking. "I was not thrilled with it[,] very frankly," recalled Vern Kupfer, a psychologist from the College of Southern Utah who joined the BYU education team. "As far as telling us anything about the living conditions in Iran[,] that was almost humorous."[52] Facilitators had been to Iran only for brief visits and had rarely ventured outside the major cities. But Kupfer and his wife, Nola, were stationed in Kerman, a remote city in the sparsely populated southeast more than a two-day drive from Tehran. Cleve Milligan called the training "harassment" and surmised that "one day in a village in Iran is worth a month in Washington as far as orientation is concerned." Experience soon taught him that "endless discussions and meetings . . . give a person the wrong perspective." Instead, "a trip into the country, talks with simple people, [and] observations of their conditions" provided new advisers with much better insight. Milligan found especially amusing the advice one instructor gave that all the new advisers purchase a hat box "because toilet facilities were few and far between in Iran." He concluded, "I suppose she had never heard of a sagebrush."[53]

Five USU families departed from Utah in early September 1951, while the first BYU and University of Utah families left at the beginning of October. Both groups traveled across the country by car caravan to Washington, DC, for training and then up the East Coast, where they embarked on comfortable ocean liners bound for Beirut, Lebanon. Ships carrying the Utah families called at Barcelona, Marseilles, Naples, and Alexandria, which allowed the families to explore those storied Mediterranean ports. Beirut itself was a splendid city in the mid-twentieth century, one of the cultural and tourism gems of the Middle East.[54] After leaving Beirut, however, the journey became much more arduous. The USU families traveled overland to Tehran by way of Damascus and Baghdad. Lula Anderson recalled that driving conditions worsened the deeper they drove into Syria and Iraq. "The roads were almost nonexistent" from Baghdad to Tehran, and "the few gas stations and hotel accommodations were very bad." Second thoughts set in quickly.[55]

Meanwhile, a shipping strike in New York City prevented the BYU families' automobiles from being loaded onto their ship. They therefore had to fly from Beirut to Tehran, and the men returned to Beirut to reclaim the cars when they arrived in December. Their drive back to Tehran turned harrowing when several inches of snow fell unexpectedly on Lebanon and Syria. Max Berryessa, Reed Bradford, and Glen Gagon found themselves marooned in the storm and forced to sleep in their cars one night and in "an opium den" on another. The experience was hardly any easier for their families, though, as the men's telegrams failed to reach Tehran. US ambassador Henry Grady considered the party lost until it showed up two days before Christmas.[56] The overland trip from Beirut to Tehran proved a grueling introduction to the Middle East for many of the Utah families. "We were very, very weary from a strenuous ride with no overnight stops to rest," wrote A. Reed Morrill soon after arriving in the autumn of 1953, "lonesome for our own families; and distraught over the appearance of these ancient lands."[57]

The difficulties of travel through the heart of the Middle East notwithstanding, a fledgling community of expatriate Utah families emerged in Tehran by the end of 1951. In addition to Harris and Stewart, who had been in Iran since the summer of 1950, Dean Peterson of BYU arrived at the end of October 1951 to serve as economic administrator and liaison officer for the Utah contracts.[58] Peterson also headed Point Four's education and training division as a member of Warne's staff.[59] High school teacher and livestock specialist Jay Hall arrived at about the same time, along with veterinarian Hendrik Versluis; Hall supervised agricultural work in Fars.[60] The first five USU families—those of rural sociologist Richard Welling Roskelley, agricultural engineer Cleve Milligan, horticulturalist J. Clark Ballard, irrigation engineer Bruce Anderson, and construction specialist Joe Coulam—arrived in

Tehran on November 6. Five BYU families arrived twelve days later—those of Berryessa, Bradford, and Gagon, along with the families of Troy Walker and Douglas Brown—as did the families of the first two University of Utah advisers: L.H.O. Stobbe and Orrin Miller, a sanitary engineer.[61] The families spent their first weeks in a comfortable westernized Tehran hotel while Fereidun "Fred" Saleh, an Iranian student who had studied at BYU, helped acquaint them with the city.[62] Four more people from the University of Utah, nurses Ruth Brown and Cecile DeMoisy, along with sanitary engineer Scott Brandon and his wife, arrived at the end of November.[63] Some of the new arrivals enjoyed Thanksgiving dinner at the home of Ardeshir Zahedi, who had become a personal friend of both Harris and Warne.[64]

LIFE IN IRAN

All of the Utah families had to work through some degree of culture shock. "This is indeed a strange land into which we have flown," wrote Morrill to Wilkinson in October 1953, "strange in custom, strange in human action, and degenerate in appearance."[65] It was a "shock" for agricultural economist Deon Hubbard and his wife, Louise, "to see the beggars, the camels, and the donkeys in the street" when they arrived in 1954. Prior to leaving Utah, Iran had been a "fairy tale fantasy," but the reality of seeing "the poverty and the peculiarities of the Middle East was a shock."[66] Maxine Shirts, who arrived with her husband, Morris, and the second BYU team in the spring of 1957, was struck by the glaring disparity in wealth. The first home her family rented was modern and spacious, with a balcony overlooking the street below. Across the street, however, stood a ramshackle mud hut, half the size of a middle-class American living room, which two poor families shared. "They had nothing," she later recalled, "we could see because they didn't even have a door." Americans also soon discovered that Iran was a land of sharply contrasting traditions and modernity. Shirts remembered attending the wedding of an Iranian army officer. "I've never seen fancier clothes than some of those Iranian women had," she thought. "And then we'd see the ones with the chadors on the streets," a reference to the simple dark garments that cover women from head to ankle.[67]

Plunging headfirst into a completely new and foreign environment heightened the sense of adventure. "I think our first impressions were ones of curiosity at the way people lived and the way they dressed," recalled Gordon Van Epps.[68] The Hubbards were a young couple without children; they saw the assignment as an opportunity to "travel and explore." Armed with a National Geographic Bible Lands map, they "took a three thousand mile trip down to Ur and Chaldea." They also visited Baghdad and Babylon and spent an evening in the desert outside Mosul enjoying the hospitality of a tribal sheik. They later visited Afghanistan, Pakistan, and India during the course of their assignment.[69] Once settled, it was not difficult for the Utah families to link their new surroundings with imagery familiar from the Bible. Helen Milligan described why her church group chose to study the Old Testament: "We could look out our windows and see them [Iranian peasants] harvesting the grain with a sickle and tying it up." The sight brought to mind images of the barley harvest in ancient Judah: "It was like being transported back to biblical times to see the way they did things."[70]

Almost all of the Utah families were Mormon, so church activities naturally became the center of their social and spiritual lives.[71] The Tehran LDS branch already had seventy-three members, including children, when it elected Harris president at the end of November 1951.[72] The Utah families created other branches as they spread to different parts of the country. Bruce Anderson headed the Shiraz branch in Fars province that also included the families of Hall, Gagon, and Stobbe. Some groups found it difficult to hold meetings on Sunday, a work day in Iran, so they occasionally had to worship and hold Sunday school on Friday, the Islamic day of worship and a weekly holiday in Iran.[73] Utah families sometimes joined with members of other Christian denominations in remote locations where there were not enough Mormons to make a branch.[74] Church activities became a source of emotional and spiritual renewal for these American expatriates who found themselves struggling to make progress amid unfamiliar and often stressful circumstances. Boyd McAffee of BYU, who arrived in 1953, found that the LDS communities in Tehran and Shiraz "made us appreciate our blessings even more . . . These weekly meetings do much to keep us united and spiritually geared to the huge task at hand: That of helping other people."[75] Roskelley felt similarly: "The many specific teachings of the Mormon church proved to be a great source of strength for me in the work that I was asked to do."[76] "Our church was very close," recalled Lula Anderson decades later. Through devastating automobile accidents and the deaths of two infants born to Utah families, "the Utah people rallied around and helped each other out."[77]

Local officials made no effort to discourage the Utah families from worshiping among themselves, but Iranian law placed strict prohibitions against preaching to Muslims. In at least one case, a policeman initially stood watch outside the home where the Tehran group had gathered to ensure that no Iranians took part.[78] US government policy likewise forbade religious proselytizing. Most Utah families complied, though some individuals expressed internal conflict between the spiritual responsibility they felt to preach the gospel and their professional responsibility to abide by Point Four regulations.[79] Many Utahns chose simply to preach by example. Erza Benson, a prominent LDS official and future secretary of agriculture in the Eisenhower administration, cautioned the families against proselytization, but he did encourage them to demonstrate their faith and to answer any questions about it that Iranians asked. "I promise you this," he told Helen Milligan just weeks before her 1951 departure, "you can live your religion." He added that if the Utahns approached their work with dedication, both the Iranians and Americans would respond favorably: "You'll go there and return home in peace and safety."[80] Joseph Bentley reported to BYU officials in 1954 that the approach was paying dividends. "Many individuals who have participated in the Iran program feel that a great amount of missionary work and untold benefits are derived directly from the work or the people here," he noted. "As a result of the acquaintances with Latter-day Saints people at least one Iranian has been baptized and a great many more are interested."[81]

The Utah families also tended to live close together whenever possible, sometimes sharing enclosed compounds and in some cases even sharing homes.[82] "We were all LDS and pretty much all from the Logan area and BYU," remembered Mildred Bunnell. "We'd known each other before we even went over. If somebody got sick, two or three people went [to help]."[83] Those stationed in Tehran congregated in Shimron, a suburb north of the city located on the slopes of the Alborz Mountains, "where homes were a little better and the temperature was a little more temperate."[84] Most of the homes in this "Utahville" were comfortable enough for the Utah families and often included quarters for live-in servants and gardeners, who assisted many of the families with cooking, cleaning, shopping, and taking care of children. Many of the homes had a swimming pool and tennis courts. They became

FIGURE 2.1. An LDS gathering of Utah families in Tehran, June 13, 1954. A. Reed Morrill is on the far left in the first row. Next to him is Dean Peterson. Joe Coulam is fourth from the right in the first row, Roy Bunnell is third from right, Rudger Walker is second from right, Richard Welling Roskelley is on the far right. Mildred Bunnell is fifth from the right in the second row. Janet Berryessa is third from the left in the third row. *Courtesy*, Richard Welling Roskelley Photograph Collection, Special Collections and Archives, Merrill-Cazier Library, Utah State University, Logan.

the focal points for church meetings and large social gatherings, such as the Fourth of July and Pioneer Day.[85] Living in close proximity to one another undoubtedly made life in a strange country more pleasant for the Utah families in Tehran, especially the wives and children. The community provided a sense of belonging and regular social interaction with other Americans. According to Max Berryessa, "It was a desirable situation."[86]

Contemporary commentators and historians have criticized American diplomats and foreign aid workers for cloistering themselves in affluent "golden ghettos," where they lived comfortably insulated from the ordinary people of host countries, whose customs and language they rarely understood.[87] That criticism perhaps fits the Utah families stationed in Tehran, few of whom ever learned more than the basics of Persian. But it is also important to acknowledge that the American families banded together for security. Max Berryessa remembered that "because the Iranian[s] were poor, there were a lot of robberies; constant robberies." Dean Peterson lost all his suits in one burglary; others lost expensive Persian rugs and silverware.[88] On one particularly harrowing occasion, Mildred Bunnell saw her daughter grab a butcher knife to confront a would-be thief who had entered their house through a door left open to provide ventilation. After that her husband, Roy, created a homemade alarm that, when tripped, rang a bell and released a large lightbulb to crash down onto the back porch.[89] Richard Griffin returned home one evening to find a burglary in progress; on two other occasions the ferocious barking of a family dog saved his household from thieves who had gained access to their roof.[90] Moreover, the political crisis Iran experienced between 1951 and 1953 sparked a sharp rise in anti-Americanism, especially in Tehran and Shiraz. The Utah families experienced increasing intimidation, and they witnessed rioting and the destruction of Point Four offices throughout 1952 and 1953. Safety, then, as much as social interaction dictated that the Utah families remain close to one another.

Critics of the "golden ghetto" mentality cite Americans as living extravagant lifestyles in poor countries, abusing diplomatic privileges, breaking local laws, and behaving boorishly toward the people they were sent to assist.[91] But most Utah families lived modest lives without the drinking and carousing that characterized much the American diplomatic corps in the developing world. The Mormon influence created a wholesome living environment that helped the Utah families thrive under strange and often difficult circumstances. Dean Farnsworth, a librarian who joined the BYU team in 1959, later recalled that "most of our social contact was with the LDS people." He found socializing with many non-Mormon Americans "a disappointment." Recreational and social facilities were "heavy with smoke and with alcohol. Drinking was the principal scene."[92] The Utahns' religious devotion and social gatherings might have bored the American "cocktail circuit," but the LDS lifestyle seems to have won the respect of Iranians, especially those pious Muslims who were taken aback by the extravagance and drinking of some Americans.[93]

At the same time, however, some American officials found the close-knit Utah communities off-putting. Clark Gregory, who succeeded William

FIGURE 2.2. Utah advisers at Shimron, north of Tehran, spring of 1952. *From left*: Hendrik Versluis, Cleve Milligan, J. Clark Ballard, Richard Welling Roskelley, and Dean Peterson. *Courtesy*, Richard Welling Roskelley Photograph Collection, Special Collections and Archives, Merrill-Cazier Library, Utah State University, Logan.

Warne as director of the Point Four Program, complained that the Utahns "were rather clannish."[94] Maxine Shirts indicated that there was something to this claim when she acknowledged that some Utah families "didn't have much of a relationship" with other Americans in Iran. "It was friendly," she explained, "but we had our church groups on Sunday and just didn't have reason to get that close to them."[95] Bruce and Lula Anderson, in contrast, struck up friendships with American families from outside the Utah contracts that continued four decades later.[96] If the Utahns could appear standoffish to other Americans working in Iran, the feeling seems to have been at least partially reciprocated. Jay Hall recalled getting along well with Point Four's regional director in Shiraz and inviting his family to parties and to LDS services. But Hall later found out that when he was in Tehran, the director "would complain about having to live with those Mormons."[97] William McSwain of the University of Utah public health team observed that Point Four employees were "a bit suspicious of all these Utah people," but he also noted that the

Americans who got to know the Utahns "discovered that we were people just like themselves."[98]

Of course, living in proximity to other Utah families was far easier for those posted in Tehran than for those sent to regional cities or remote rural areas. BYU adviser Richard Brown was stationed at Ahwaz in southwestern Iran near the Persian Gulf, and the Kupfers were sent to Kerman in south-central Iran; each lived more than a day's car journey from Tehran and enjoyed the company of just one other American family.[99] "It was isolation," remembered Mildred Bunnell of those families who worked in such remote settings.[100] The scorching city of Ahwaz proved trying for Jim and Imogene Wood. Language and cultural barriers prevented their children from attending local schools, so Imogene taught her younger children at home. They had to send their oldest child home to the United States to attend high school. There were just two Point Four advisers along with a small American military post in the city. The soldiers invited the Wood children to watch movies in the house they shared. "That's the only thing my children really had to look forward to," she remembered four decades later.[101]

All of the Utah families had to adjust to new ways of living in Iran. Local sources of water, including that which flowed from the mountains into cisterns built under some Tehran homes, invariably became polluted with all manner of debris. The US Embassy in Tehran provided clean water to American families, but the Iranian workmen who delivered it sometimes cooled their feet in it. Nicer homes had rooftop tanks that provided running water, but the tanks had to be filled and chlorinated daily. Other families had to purify drinking water through small, slow charcoal filters in the kitchen or boil a daily ration. A few homes had modern electric water heaters, but most had charcoal-fired models that could explode if soot built up on the exhaust pipes. Electricity was rationed in some of the provincial cities, including Shiraz and Ahwaz where summer daytime temperatures often exceed 100°F. Food preparation was also more complicated than in the United States. Shopping in bazaars could be overwhelming for American housewives and even dangerous in times of political unrest. Mutton and chicken were usually available in the markets, but cuts had to be fresh and carefully selected. Some Utah families simply instructed trusted gardeners or housekeepers to do the shopping. Local flour, even the variety sold at the American commissary, contained smut that had to be carefully sifted out. Most of the homes included indoor kitchens, but others had detached kitchens behind the house or in the courtyard. Modern appliances such as gas ranges and washing machines were not readily available in most of Iran, so the Utah families either had to bring them from home or make do without them. Cooking on a charcoal stove and washing clothes on a washboard in a tub was time-consuming, especially for families who had small children and no hired help.[102] Americans could rarely use telephones unassisted because none of them could understand the Iranian operators. Driving was also difficult, even hazardous, especially in Tehran. The Point Four advisers initially could not use the US Army's post office, so mail took several months to cross from Iran to Utah.[103]

Maintaining personal health also required extra diligence. Maxine Shirts noted that most of the Utah families stayed reasonably healthy despite the limits of public sanitation as long as they took adequate care to purify their water and wash food.[104] Despite the precautions, however, some children did become seriously ill, and when that happened it could be a challenge to find Western doctors. The families in Tehran could use a US Army hospital, but they were the lowest-priority patients, and the wait to see a doctor could take several hours. More often, they asked for one of the doctors on the University of Utah public health team or sought out British or French doctors from missionary hospitals. Those families stationed outside Tehran had to travel to the capital to receive significant medical attention, including giving birth and caring for sick infants. Many of the advisers spent extended time in rural villages and tribal areas. In addition to being physically taxing, those trips increased the chances of becoming ill, especially when locally prepared food and water was all that was available.[105] Mildred Bunnell often accompanied her husband, Roy, on such journeys despite the discomfort of travel in rural Iran and the pervasive gender segregation in Iranian villages. She usually packed army rations because "we were just a little afraid of their food." On one occasion when the couple's nineteen-year-old daughter also came along, however, they found themselves without any food. The family became so hungry that they ate a chicken that had not been fully plucked in a dimly lit caravansary (inn) along the road.[106]

For all the challenges of navigating life in a strange and sometimes perilous environment, most Utah families adapted reasonably well. Maintaining good working relationships with Iranian partners helped facilitate the work the Utah advisers were doing. Mildred Bunnell observed that some Iranian Point

Four drivers and technicians preferred to work for the Utahns, who did not indulge in "tobacco, liquor, and women." Iranian dignitaries were likewise relieved to learn that they did not have to ply the Utah families with alcohol at official functions.[107] The Utah families occasionally attended extravagant Iranian dinner parties that lasted very late into the evening and included feasting on fruit, nuts, roasted lamb, rice pilaf, and a variety of breads and sweets. Many Utah families likewise celebrated Nowruz, the Iranian New Year, on the first day of spring and Eid-e Fetr at the end of Ramadan, the Islamic month of fasting. Celebrations sometimes lasted for days, with Utah families attending lavish feasts and offering gifts to their Iranian neighbors and colleagues.[108] Other religious holidays included Ashura, a Shi'i commemoration of the martyrdom of Husayn in the seventh century during which the pious practice self-mutilation, which perplexed and even frightened the Utahns.[109] Housing and transportation improved at Karaj Agricultural College in the early 1960s, which made life more comfortable for the USU families working there. They helped plan and equip modern single-family and duplex homes that were fully electrified for faculty use on the campus. The USU families were able to live in some of these homes beginning in late 1961.[110]

TENSIONS WITHIN THE UTAH CONTRACTS

Like most American universities that participated in the Point Four Program, the Utah institutions encountered administrative difficulties, both within the academic community and with the federal government. USU's involvement in the Point Four Program apparently did not enjoy unqualified support among the university's board of trustees. Madsen noted that some members questioned the institution's legal right to participate and expressed concern that overseas technical assistance was "weakening our own programs at the college by sending our good faculty members away on extended leave." Difficulties inherent in contract negotiations and "bickering among the advisers themselves" continued to surface through the early months of 1953.[111] Roskelley's leadership of the agricultural program became an early source of debate among the field team. An accomplished rural sociologist, Roskelley was the most senior of the initial USU advisers. But he lacked administrative experience in 1951 and never felt entirely comfortable in his leadership role.

An early challenge from the government arose in the summer of 1952 when federal officials proposed amending university contracts to make university advisers government employees. Point Four administrator Avery Johnson explained to University of Utah president Ray Olpin that the "sandwiching of government and university employees" into a "single administrative structure" produced "serious disadvantages" and made "difficult the efficient management of the Iran program." But Johnson also reassured Olpin that Point Four officials were pleased with the work the Utah advisers were doing and would therefore encourage their "eventual transfer" to federal employment.[112]

Most of the Utah people balked at the idea. Glen Gagon of BYU objected to the potential financial consequences of losing the exemption from federal income tax that university advisers enjoyed and of the possible reduction in his post allowance if he went to work for the Department of State.[113] Both he and L.H.O. Stobbe of the University of Utah rural health team pointed out that they had accepted a Point Four position out of a desire to help the Iranian people, not because they wanted to become federal employees.[114] Tenured faculty members naturally worried that moving to the government payroll would jeopardize their permanent positions at home. A concerned I. O. Horsfall, who administered the University of Utah contract in Salt Lake City, wrote to Johnson that his team was "getting along very nicely" under the original arrangement and saw no reason to change it. Moreover, "it took a lot of persuasion" to get some of the advisers to go to Iran. They would be "very disappointed" if those satisfactory arrangements suddenly changed, and the quality of their work would likely suffer.[115] William Warne intervened on behalf of the Utah advisers by telling Point Four officials that the Utahns had "worked earnestly" in Iran and that the rural improvement program would be "on the rocks" if it lost the Utah schools.[116] Point Four ultimately decided not to pursue the transfer of Utah advisers to federal employment, but future contracts were extended for only short periods of between twelve and eighteen months.[117]

A much more serious problem arose in the summer of 1955 when Point Four officials abruptly announced the termination of BYU's teacher training project against the university's wishes. The government's decision reflected a reorganization of the Point Four Program that was then under way under the leadership of its new director, John Hollister. Federal officials decided to reduce the number of university contracts and to narrow the scope of their work to partnerships with similar institutions of higher learning in host countries.[118] The BYU project, which involved multiple teacher training efforts carried out through the Ministry of Education, did not fit the new mold. BYU and some USU officials felt, however, that there was more afoot than just a reprioritization of university involvement in the Point Four Program. They pointed out that BYU's work could fit the new model for university involvement under a new contract the university had recently negotiated with the University of Tehran. They charged instead that key members of the Point Four leadership in Iran were trying to discriminate against Mormons.[119] Chapter 5 contains a more thorough discussion of that controversy.

CONCLUSION

Utah's main research universities were well positioned to contribute to Point Four's rural improvement initiatives in Iran. USU had already built a strong relationship with Iranian agricultural officials by 1950, and individuals such as Franklin Harris, Luther Winsor, and George Stewart had distinguished themselves in their service to that country. Harris in particular proved an invaluable asset. He enjoyed a favorable reputation among US government officials and possessed a working knowledge of Iran's agricultural problems. Extensive experience in Utah higher education made him influential at both BYU and USU and gave him connections with potential advisers. Finally, the Utah advisers approached the Iranian rural improvement program with a missionary-like sense of purpose and commitment that earned the respect of most of their American and Iranian partners.

Life in Iran nevertheless presented formidable challenges for middle-class American families. Upon departing in the summer of 1959, BYU education adviser Morris Shirts composed a poem that captures well the difficulties and frustrations but also hints at the rewards:

"NO MORE—ENSHALAH!!!"[120]

No more wetting on the walls.
No more fancy "know it alls."
No more jubes, no more coolies,[121]
No more dirty swimming poolies.
No more chickens; no more goats.

No more summer-winter overcoats.
No more "balies"; no more "kube,"[122]
No more washing in the jube.
No more sleepers on the street.
No more beggars with calloused feet.
No more stealing; no more flies.
No more wild taxi rides.
Kurdahfez[123] all—and to all goodbye,
We leave to you our mahst and chi.[124]
We're off to the land of milk and honey.
Rich in experience, but short on money.
May we see you soon—pas Fardah.[125]
We won't be back—En-Shalah!![126]

The logistical challenges of moving entire families halfway across the globe and then learning how to function in a very different society were daunting; the culture shock was at times overwhelming. But the Utah families adapted well. They formed a tight community that provided its members with support, encouragement, and spiritual sustenance. Amazingly, despite periodic tragedies that included the deaths of two infant children and one nurse in a plane crash,[127] only two of the Utah advisers went home before the completion of their assignments, for personal reasons. The reality of Point Four working within contracts added another layer of headaches. This required both the universities and the individual advisers to wade through a complex and still-evolving government foreign aid bureaucracy that often made little sense to either the advisers or university administrators.

3

POINT FOUR AND THE IRANIAN
POLITICAL CRISIS OF 1951–1953

We realized that we were actually participating in a struggle for supremacy of
two ideologies, i.e., democracy or another way of life.

> *Richard Welling Roskelley, USU adviser in Iran, 1951–54*

If Americans could have just supported him [Mossadegh] we would really
have had a lot of support in Iran.

> *Jay Hall, USU adviser in Iran, 1951–53, 1954–56*

Iran experienced an intense political crisis that destabilized the country and
ultimately created the foundation for the ill-fated US-Iranian alliance during
the first two years of Point Four work. At the heart of the crisis was Prime
Minister Mohammad Mossadegh's attempt to nationalize the Iranian oil
industry in the spring of 1951. Nationalization, or the transfer of ownership
and control of the British-owned Anglo-Iranian Oil Company (AIOC) to
the Iranian government, was at the heart of a popular nationalist struggle to free the country from foreign domination. It ignited an international

DOI: 10.7330/9781607327547.c003

dispute, however, that led to the prime minister's overthrow in August 1953.[1] Agents of the British and American governments helped organize and finance the coup, but it was primarily carried out by Iranian operatives. Mossadegh's political coalition, commonly known as the National Front, also challenged the shah for control of the Iranian government. This contest was part of a struggle, ongoing since the constitutional revolution of 1906–11, to vest supreme political authority in the Majlis (lower house of the parliament) and to restrain the power of the monarchy. Finally, the Iranian communist movement reemerged as a considerable, though hardly decisive, presence on the political scene. While the struggles over oil nationalization and constitutional authority were the most significant, it was the possibility of a communist insurgency that provoked the greatest concern among Point Four workers, including the Utah families. They did not participate directly in any of these controversies, but they could not escape the far-ranging effects of all three. This proved especially true during the chaotic thirteen months between July 1952 and August 1953 when Iran's cities experienced escalating political violence fueled in part by foreign agitators, in part by pro-shah forces within the military and the clergy, and in part by Iranian communists.

As instability worsened, the Utah advisers lost faith in Mossadegh's leadership. They ultimately welcomed the overthrow of a government they had come to associate with political chaos, economic stagnation, and menacing communist agitation. The Utahns tended to interpret developments through their understanding of the Cold War, a point of view that allowed them to overemphasize the role of communism in what was essentially a nationalist revolution. Their understanding of events led them away from a conclusion that the coup had abridged Iran's national sovereignty and stunted its constitutional development. Rather, they came to see Mossadegh's downfall as good for the country because it replaced a chaotic regime with a more stable foundation for economic growth. The Utahns had some help in reaching those conclusions. The Western press and US propaganda depicted Mossadegh as an irrational and despotic ruler who had become increasingly dependent on communist support to implement his agenda. The Central Intelligence Agency (CIA) cooperated with British agents in carrying out covert operations designed to convince Iranians that their country was on the verge of a communist revolution.

MOSSADEGH, OIL NATIONALIZATION, AND
THE ANGLO-IRANIAN CONFRONTATION

Mohammad Mossadegh rose to political power in 1951 on the shoulders of widespread support for the nationalization of the AIOC and a growing popular demand for more constitutional accountability in the Iranian government. Born in 1882, Mossadegh descended from the Qajar family that had ruled Iran in the nineteenth century. He was also a European-educated lawyer who had acquired a reputation for honesty and respect for the rule of constitutional law while holding a variety of public positions during the 1920s. He held cabinet posts as justice minister in 1920, finance minister in 1921, and foreign minister in 1923 and then represented Tehran in the Majlis from 1924 until 1928. He also briefly served as governor of two important provinces, Fars in 1920 and Azerbaijan in 1923. A strong opponent of Reza Pahlavi's seizure of the Iranian throne in 1925, Mossadegh withdrew from politics and was briefly imprisoned in 1940. Reza Shah's abdication the following year, however, allowed him to return to public life. He was again elected to parliament in 1944 and had emerged as the de facto head of the Iranian nationalist movement by the end of the decade. Mossadegh distrusted all foreign influence in Iran. Whereas previous Iranian leaders had attempted to leverage the Anglo-Russian rivalry to curry aid from both sides, Mossadegh developed a policy of "negative equilibrium" that stressed ending concessions to all foreign powers, Russia and Britain alike. He organized nationalist deputies into a coalition known as the National Front in October 1949.[2] The National Front was not a traditional political party that drew on mass public support. Rather, it was a parliamentary caucus united behind nationalizing the oil industry and asserting the constitutional role of the elected parliament, Majlis, over the monarchy.

The National Front moved toward full oil nationalization early in 1951. It organized a nationwide campaign in January that enjoyed the support of the vocal anti-British cleric and speaker of the Majlis, Ayatollah Abol-Ghasem Kashani. Though the National Front held a small minority of the seats in a Majlis that was still dominated by conservative landowners and royalists, it won support for an oil nationalization bill—first by unanimous vote in the oil committee on March 9, then by unanimous vote of the ninety-five deputies present in the Majlis on March 15, and finally by unanimous vote in the Senate, the newly formed upper house of the Iranian parliament, on March

20.[3] The Majlis unexpectedly nominated Mossadegh as prime minister on April 28, 1951, by a 79 to 12 vote.[4] Mossadegh said he would accept the nomination only after the oil nationalization bill had been passed into law. Both houses unanimously complied. The shah resented the legislature taking such a monumental step without consulting him, but there was little he could do in the face of widespread public support for Mossadegh and oil nationalization. He reluctantly agreed to both. Thus, Mohammad Mossadegh became the constitutional prime minister of Iran, and oil nationalization went into effect on May 1. He stated that his government would have only two goals: implementing oil nationalization and reforming electoral laws. He received a vote of confidence in the Majlis on May 6.[5]

For the British, Iranian oil nationalization was tantamount to theft and represented a threat of the highest order. The AIOC was Britain's most lucrative foreign asset. It had poured hundreds of millions of pounds into the British treasury since the government acquired a controlling share of its stock in 1914. The AIOC also sold much-needed fuel to the British Navy, and British statesmen believed successful Iranian oil nationalization would inspire other countries to nationalize similar assets, such as the Suez Canal in Egypt.[6] The British government rejected Mossadegh's offer of compensation at the full value of the company in 1951. Furthermore, few British officials thought Iranians could run a complex oil industry. The inevitable result of nationalization would be economic disaster for Iran. British ambassador Sir Francis Shepherd dismissed Mossadegh as a "lunatic" and a "demagogue"—imagery that quickly caught on in the United States.[7] The British government responded to Iranian nationalization by blockading the port at Abadan, organizing an international boycott of Iranian oil and other essential exports, and drawing up plans for possible military intervention.[8] Iranian oil production, which had reached 660,000 barrels per day in 1950, dwindled to a mere 20,000 by early 1952.[9] Mossadegh gave British workers a week to decide whether to go to work for the new Iranian National Oil Company or leave the country; all of them were gone by early October 1951.

The US government inevitably found itself pulled into this volatile dispute. American diplomats such as Ambassador Henry Grady and Middle East specialist George McGhee sympathized with the Iranian desire for a better deal and urged the British government to adopt concessions they hoped would resolve the crisis short of full nationalization.[10] Truman was cordial but noncommittal when Mossadegh visited the United States in October to make his case before the United Nations and ask for American economic aid.[11] Both the president and Secretary of State Dean Acheson held firm that the Iranian government had first to reach an agreement with the British. Once that happened, the British government would lift its embargo; oil would once again flow out of Abadan, and Iran would have plenty of money for economic development. Truman acknowledged that such an agreement had to be fair to Iran, though he did not specify what that meant. He did make clear, however, that the United States would not undermine the British.[12] When Mossadegh protested that Iran was a poor desert country with nothing but a few sheep and camels, Acheson replied "and with your oil, rather like Texas!"[13]

The Utah advisers who arrived in Iran in the fall of 1951 soon learned how serious the crisis had become. Dire predictions swirled around Tehran that the country would be in financial ruin before the end of the year. Education professor Max Berryessa of Brigham Young University (BYU) later recalled that Iranians and Americans alike could plainly see that "Britain had already milked Iran of the proceeds of their oil industry."[14]

THE IRANIAN RED SCARE

The specter of a communist insurgency became the dominant prism through which many Americans viewed developments in Iran, even though communism never enjoyed widespread support in the country. British and American officials understood that Mossadegh was no communist; his "negative equilibrium" strategy plainly rejected Soviet interference as strongly as British interference. British diplomats nevertheless exaggerated the strength of communist influence to goad the US government into action.[15] American leaders worried that the unresolved oil dispute would destroy Iran's economy, embolden the communist element, and perhaps invite Soviet intervention.[16] Mossadegh ironically reinforced American fears during his October visit when he invoked the communist threat in an effort to leverage a larger commitment of US aid. Communist subversion, he told Truman, "would gravely endanger" Iranian independence. Poverty and unrest were "prevalent throughout the country." Teachers barely made enough money to rent a room. He warned that "many of them had become sympathetic to communism and were spreading this idea throughout the school system." A cautious Truman acknowledged that "Russia was sitting like a vulture on the fence waiting to pounce."[17]

The American press reinforced a sense of the red menace in Iran. *Time* magazine's January 7, 1952, article naming Mossadegh "Man of the Year" for 1951 was particularly significant. It mixed stereotypes about the exotic Middle East with the fear of communist expansion to paint an unflattering portrait of the man it called a "dizzy old wizard" and "an appalling caricature of a statesman." The prime minister was "not in any sense pro-Russian," the magazine told its readers, "but he intends to stick to his [oil nationalization] policies even though he knows they might lead to control of Iran by the Kremlin." The article concluded that Mossadegh was leading a nationalist charge toward chaos. Without Western intervention, it warned, Iranians would reach a point where they would "welcome communism."[18] Such rhetoric resonated among the generally conservative Utahns. Franklin Harris told the influential *Deseret News* [Salt Lake City] in May 1951 that communism was "boring from within" the country. Communists were gathering strength and "continuously stirring up trouble."[19] A 1952 political cartoon by Dorman H. Smith that ran in the Logan *Herald Journal*, titled "His Favorite Chef," presented Iran's political problems as the product of Soviet mischief. A cook labeled "political unrest" stands proudly beside two boiling cauldrons, one labeled "Iran" and the other "Egypt." Joseph Stalin, the dominant figure in the cartoon, sniffs the stews approvingly.[20] The implication was clear, especially to readers who had a limited understanding of those far-off countries.

Utah State University (USU) professors Luther Winsor and George Stewart, both of whom had worked in Iran during the 1940s, also warned about the growing communist influence in that country. Winsor described Iran as a "tinder box" through which "the evil monster on the north [the Soviet Union]" could "set fire to the entire world." "The threat is real," he warned, "and cannot be passed off with the turn of a wrist."[21] Stewart reinforced that assessment. "Iran is one of the key fronts on which this battle [the Cold War] is being fought and is likely to be fought," he wrote in 1950. Low standards of living, close proximity to the Soviet Union, and a history of leftist influence from Russia all made the country highly susceptible to communist propaganda.[22] The communist threat in Iran was real and immediate, then, for the Utah families who accepted Point Four work.

Iranian communist activity did increase, especially in Tehran and other large cities, during Mossadegh's tenure in office. The most significant communist organization in the country was the openly pro-Soviet Tudeh (Masses) Party. Founded in 1941, the party was officially banned in 1949, but Mossadegh allowed its organizations—including newspapers, youth groups, and women's groups—to operate as part of his liberalization of civil society.[23] The party held a major demonstration in Tehran that coincided with the passage of the oil nationalization bill in April 1951. Sixty thousand rallied in front of the American embassy on May 12, shouting support for Stalin as "the standard bearer of peace" and demanding the expulsion of American military personnel from Iran.[24] Another large anti-American demonstration in July coincided with the arrival of veteran diplomat Averell Harriman to facilitate Anglo-Iranian negotiations. More than thirty people died when authorities fired on the crowds.[25] A large Tudeh demonstration in opposition to Mossadegh's visit to the United States degenerated into a street brawl in December.[26] William Warne, who had arrived just a few days earlier to direct Point Four operations, was "deeply shocked at the intensity of the disorder."[27]

Still, Iran was not as close to a communist revolution as Americans often feared. Since mid-1945 the Iranian communist movement had been divided between the Persian-based Tudeh Party and the Democrat Party of Azerbaijani Turks in the north.[28] Tudeh membership was itself divided over Mossadegh. The leadership denounced him as an imperialist stooge for seeking American aid, but moderates came around to supporting his oil nationalization scheme.[29] The Tudeh Party's atheism and its open ties to the Soviet Union also put it at odds with most of the Iranian public.[30] This was especially true for rural peasants, who accounted for more than 70 percent of the population and among whom the party had little support. Moreover, both Iranian and Western propaganda had conditioned the Iranian public against communism. Reza Shah waged an effective battle against leftist movements in Iran during the interwar years.[31] The CIA began disseminating anti-communist propaganda in that country after World War II.[32] Voice of America initiated Persian-language radio broadcasts in 1949, and by 1951 both the United States Information Service and the American embassy were circulating anti-communist literature and films.[33]

The most important reason why communism did not flourish in Iran during the early 1950s was that Mohammad Mossadegh proved to be a much more attractive alternative. The National Front drew broad support from the non-communist left, especially Khalil Malcki's Third Force, and Mossadegh had positioned himself squarely at the head of the most important issues of the day—oil nationalization and constitutional political reforms.[34] Communists had no comparable issue with which to seize momentum.[35] Even in the summer of 1953, when communist agitation reached its peak, the CIA estimated that Tudeh Party membership totaled no more than 22,000 nationwide and that the party could count on a voting strength of around 25,000 in Tehran, a city of 1.2 million people. CIA director Allen Dulles told the National Security Council in March that there was little danger of a communist takeover as long as the Mossadegh government survived.[36] The Tudeh Party "was not talking about revolution," concludes Ervand Abrahamian. "It was not really preparing for either an uprising or an armed struggle."[37] Maziar Behrooz similarly finds "no evidence that the party had a plan for securing political power for itself in the foreseeable future."[38]

POINT FOUR AND MOSSADEGH'S FIRST GOVERNMENT: APRIL 1951–JULY 1952

The situation in Iran raised concerns among officials at the Utah universities during the early months of 1951. Franklin Harris tried to reassure his colleagues back home that the country was safe for Americans. Life in Iran could be "pure velvet," he wrote USU dean of agriculture Rudger Walker, once folks got the hang of living in a foreign country. People should not be afraid to go "where the world is so upset," Harris opined, with the spurious logic that if war did come, "there is danger living anywhere these days of possible bombings. Even Ogden and Salt Lake might be good targets."[39] He assured President Ray Olpin of the University of Utah that things were alright following the row surrounding Harriman's arrival in July. "Living conditions here are very pleasant," Harris wrote. "We hear about occasional riots in different parts of the country, but they seem to be no worse than Utah Copper and other strikes in the United States."[40]

The first Utah families to arrive in Iran soon noticed signs of the political troubles. Bitterness toward Western foreigners became more pronounced as the Iranian economy, deprived of oil revenue, ground to a halt. Angry Iranians occasionally harassed Americans in public; Max and Janet Berryessa noted that the "Yankee Go Home" slogan appeared with increasing frequency on buildings adjacent to American offices and homes in Tehran.[41] Point Four came under intense criticism when it began importing sturdy donkeys from Cyprus to improve Iranian mule breeding. The communist press griped that "the great United States comes to help Iran and what does Iran get? A few jackasses! The people are hungry, but what do the promises of the wealthy imperialists amount to? Jackasses."[42] Anti-American rhetoric increased throughout 1952 as the British departed and left Americans as the only large group of Western foreigners.[43] Lula Anderson wrote to her parents that the closure of British consulates in January provoked public celebrations in Shiraz. "We feel it prudent to stay at home until the feelings quiet down," she continued, "so we won't be mistaken for the British."[44] Vern Kupfer felt uneasiness upon arriving in Tehran after the Iranian government severed diplomatic relations with the United Kingdom in October: "I felt we were not welcome . . . we were as bad as the British."[45]

Still, the Utah families faced little real danger in those first months, and they do not seem to have been overly concerned about their safety. Cleve Milligan, whose family was among the first to arrive in November 1951, quipped that sporadic unrest was "quite harmless. More people get hurt in a Stanford-California football rivalry." He did, however, note that political turmoil made it "most difficult" to establish a working technical assistance program.[46] His wife, Helen, recalled one instance when unruly demonstrators almost prevented Cleve from collecting their children from school, but she usually received warnings from Iranian friends prior to disturbances: "As a rule, they'd know ahead of time when there was going to be a riot."[47] Bruce Anderson wrote to his family in January 1952 that Shiraz was "very quiet and peaceful with no demonstrations. There is no danger to us and we want you to cease worrying."[48] Likewise, Nola and Vern Kupfer soon discovered that "most of the [Iranian] people were cordial." The Kupfers were stationed in Kerman where there was less political turmoil. "They [communists] were there," the Kupfers recalled, "but we were able to work."[49]

The summer of 1952 marked an important turning point in the ongoing Iranian political crisis. Mossadegh resigned in protest on July 16 when the shah refused to allow him to assume control of the Ministry of War. Twenty-seven of the thirty National Front deputies then boycotted a secret Majlis meeting that nominated Ahmad Qavam, a distinguished statesman, as prime minister.[50] A week of chaotic unrest in Tehran culminated in mass demon-strations in support of Mossadegh on July 21, 1952, that devolved into brutal street fighting in which several hundred people lost their lives. Caving to public pressure and eager to end the violence, that evening the shah asked Mossadegh to form a second government. The episode left an indelible imprint on William Warne, who later wrote: "It was a bloody day. Inflamed mobs fought one another. Some gruesome events transpired. One hospital caring for wounded and dying from an earlier affray was raided. The dead were carried off, hoisted by many hands. Grim leaders headed a marching column bound in furious zeal on further depredations. Rioters burned news-paper plants. Other mobs set other establishments afire in retaliation. Shops were looted."[51]

Historians who are sympathetic to Mossadegh tend to portray the July demonstrations as a genuine show of popular support for the prime minister, a view Minister of Court Hossein Ala, an opponent of Mossadegh, inadver-tently echoed that afternoon when he acknowledged that the prime minister seemed to enjoy "tremendous popular appeal."[52] Warne, however, called it "organized rabble rousing," and Ambassador Loy Henderson reported that thousands of rioters took to the streets shouting "death to the Brit[ish] and Ameri[can] imperialists. Down with the Shah."[53] Their views have some merit. According to journalist and historian Sepehr Zabih, "Communists took control of strike-ridden streets" that afternoon, chanting "down with the Shah" and demanding a people's republic; National Front supporters clashed with Tudeh factions in violent confrontations.[54] The events of that July engendered serious misgivings about Mossadegh's leadership among Point Four officials. "Many of us had become used to fighting in the streets," Warne later recalled, but now "riotous displays disconcerted us because they empathized that no effective government existed."[55]

Warne also became genuinely concerned about the safety of Point Four personnel working in Tehran. "This was a period of great trial," he later confided, noting that anti-foreign propaganda had become more promi-nent.[56] Point Four work experienced fewer disruptions outside the capital. Lula Anderson wrote to her family that Point Four personnel in Shiraz were directed to stay home during the July demonstrations and that a guard was stationed in front of the local office. But otherwise, nothing happened. She seemed almost to lament the fact that "we miss out on all the excitement and demonstrations." The Point Four office in Isfahan was broken into, apparently because it did not close to observe a period of mourning for those killed on July 21. Anderson reported that things had quieted down in Shiraz by the end of July, but she was uncertain about what was going on elsewhere in the country: "There were many stories that came out [about] the trouble, but it's hard to know what to believe."[57]

Iran's political problems complicated the inherently difficult tasks of adjusting to life in a foreign country and initiating a working technical assistance program, but they do not seem to have dominated the Utahns' attention before the summer of 1952. Advisers occasionally commented on the diplomatic and economic ramifications of the oil embargo, but most of their energy was focused on the daily tasks of forming expatriate communities and beginning their work. Lula Anderson wrote to her parents in early September that there were "communist inspired uprisings occasionally," but she assured them, "so far we haven't been bothered."[58] Warne and Harris did their best to protect the safety of the Utah families and to encourage university leaders back in Utah to continue participating in the program. None of the Utah families were so concerned about the political situation that they felt they had to leave the country. "I feel that all of our people are enjoying their work and their experience in Iran," wrote Dean Peterson to University of Utah officials in February.[59] But the crisis soon intensified, and the Utah families increasingly found themselves in the path of the storm.

POINT FOUR AND MOSSADEGH'S SECOND
GOVERNMENT, JULY 1952–AUGUST 1953

The summer of 1952 marked the apex of National Front power and popularity in Iran, but difficulties began to mount in the following months. The Majlis granted Mossadegh extraordinary powers to enact economic and political reforms for up to six months without parliamentary approval. Such measures helped restore order and insulated the prime minister from political gridlock, but they came at a high price. Several key members of the National Front opposed the emergency powers as dictatorial and began to abandon Mossadegh. The most influential of the defectors, Majlis speaker Ayatollah Kashani, soon emerged as one of Mossadegh's sharpest critics.[60] Moderates within the Tudeh Party rallied support for the embattled cabinet in newspapers and on the streets, but their activities also linked the National Front more closely with communism in the public eye.[61] Mossadegh's plan to produce an "oil-less economy" had not worked, and deteriorating economic conditions incubated unrest. The prime minister also clashed with military brass when he forced into retirement more than 100 army officers who had suppressed demonstrations during the July uprising. General Fazlollah Zahedi, chief of police in Tehran and a leading opponent of the prime minister in the Senate, helped organize the officers into an association that plotted against Mossadegh. The Iranian government formally severed diplomatic ties with the United Kingdom in October after discovering that British officials had entertained Zahedi's overtures to initiate a coup against the government.[62] Mossadegh asked Warne to dismiss Zahedi's son Ardeshir, a USU graduate, from the Point Four staff after he became convinced that the younger Zahedi "was engaging in activities hostile to the government of Iran."[63] Both Ardeshir and his father played significant roles in the overthrow of Mossadegh the following summer.

The political crisis became more visible to the Utah families in the fall of 1952. Those stationed in Tehran became used to the tanks, barricades, soldiers, and other trappings of martial law. The Utahns generally considered the unrest to be communist-inspired, a view bolstered by both the Iranian press and the communist activity in the streets. Mildred Bunnell, who arrived with her husband, Leroy, that fall, recalled that a shop owner warned her of a "communist plot" to round up Americans living in the city, though Point Four officials were unable to verify it.[64] In Shiraz, Bruce Anderson thought newspaper reports were causing "undue concern" about communism in early September, but he had grown more despondent by November. A constant chorus of "Yankee Go Home" and talk of ridding the country of American imperialists now made it appear that "commies were ready to take over the country."[65] His wife, Lula, later recalled that there were "a lot of anti-American feelings . . . it was a bit scary."[66] Communist influence was much weaker in rural areas, but it could still be disruptive. Americans had to be withdrawn from the Caspian region in early 1953, and angry students sometimes damaged Point Four vehicles as they traveled through Abadeh, between Shiraz and Tehran.[67]

Mob violence again disrupted Point Four work in Tehran on February 28 as the shah and Queen Soraya were preparing to leave the country for a vacation and to seek medical advice in Switzerland. The royal couple's departure was supposed to be confidential, but leaks tipped off two Mossadegh opponents, former prime minister Ahmad Qavam and General Zahedi. Ardeshir Zahedi apparently then informed Ayatollah Kashani, who had emerged as a vocal and influential opponent of Mossadegh.[68] The shah met with the prime minister and cabinet members for about an hour just prior to his departure, during which time the retired officers and Kashani whipped a crowd of between 1,000 and 3,000 into a frenzy by giving anti-Mossadegh speeches.[69] Kashani exclaimed that the shah's absence would "leave the prime minister in a virtually dictatorial position."[70] Mossadegh heard the crowd when he attempted to leave for the Majlis and had to be escorted out of the palace through a side gate. In his memoirs, Mossadegh recalled that a police squadron blocked the crowd from moving toward his nearby residence until the shah's brother, Prince Hamid Reza, appeared in the street and ordered the police away, "saying that the people were free to go where they liked." The police retreated, and the crowd rushed toward his house. One of the street toughs who was leading the crowd attempted to crash a jeep through the prime minister's front gate, and rioters also broke into the home of his son next door.[71] At the urging of his son and Foreign Minister Hossein Fatemi, Mossadegh climbed over the wall into a neighboring compound, which Point Four leased from the prime minister. It housed the Tehran regional offices, including those of Leroy "Roy" Bunnell, a USU agronomist, and Max Berryessa. Mossadegh flagged down a stunned Bunnell, who had just arrived on the scene. Bunnell had the prime minister get into his car and whisked him "out of the grasp of the rioters."[72]

The rioting and its aftermath caused a considerable disruption of Point Four operations in Tehran. A detachment of machine gunners occupied the Point Four premises for several days to protect Mossadegh's home. The captain invited the Americans to keep working there, but they chose to relocate to other offices. According to Warne, "an uneasy calm returned" to Tehran, but "civil unrest deepened." He reported that mass demonstrations became more frequent and unruly, and "extreme nationalists," that is, the National Front, increasingly welcomed Tudeh support in the streets.[73] Warne later reflected that Mossadegh's fate appeared to be sealed that February afternoon; he might have been more correct than he realized. Recent research indicates that the February 28 attack on the prime minister's home became a model for mob manipulation during the coup that ousted him from power in August.[74]

William Warne put the best possible spin on the situation in his correspondence with President Madsen of USU. While not denying the potential dangers in Iran, he assured Madsen that no Americans had been injured or "seriously threatened." He pleaded for the college to continue to support Point Four's work: "We have had a great influence in the effort to keep Iran free." The people "are looking with hope to us." The United States was "absolutely right in going ahead with its Point 4 Program," he insisted, using blatantly patronizing language. "In this desperately confused and hopeless country," Point 4 represented "hope in the future." Warne closed by urging Madsen to see the program through troubled times. "We shall, on occasion, have to swallow our Yankee pride," he concluded, "like a big brother in his relationship with a child who has been mistreated."[75]

The "comic-opera" of the February fracas in Tehran gave way to "grimmer realities" on April 15 and 16 when nationwide demonstrations for and against the government turned bloody. In Shiraz, a raging mob plundered and destroyed the Point Four regional headquarters on April 15.[76] Witnesses to the April attack reported that the police allowed the rioters free access to Point Four facilities, where they destroyed everything in the building including data Glen Gagon of the BYU team had been compiling in preparation to develop mobile schools for nomadic tribes.[77] When news of the attack reached Tehran, Warne and US ambassador Loy Henderson protested directly to Mossadegh, who assured them he had instituted martial law in the city and sent a new governor and military commander to restore order.[78] The following morning, however, another unruly mob marched toward the homes of the Utah families, "throwing rocks, shouting, and being very ferocious."[79] This time, the police held the crowds back and allowed the Point Four families to make a frantic escape to the Baq-e Eram, the "Garden of Heaven," headquarters of the Qashqai tribe located outside town.[80] Thirty-three Americans, many of them families of the Utah advisers, huddled there for the next three days until local authorities restored order.

The Department of State declared the situation too dangerous to allow the families of the Point Four advisers to remain in Iran. A few that were nearing the end of their two-year assignment went back to the United States. Most of the rest went to Europe because State would not pay for families

FIGURE 3.1. Demonstration outside the Point Four building in Shiraz. *Courtesy,* Richard Welling Roskelley Photograph Collection, Special Collections and Archives, Merrill-Cazier Library, Utah State University, Logan.

to go back to the United States and then subsequently return to Iran. Lula Anderson and her children accompanied four other families to Switzerland.[81] Janet Berryessa and her two sons stayed with relatives in Germany. Newly arriving Point Four personnel were not allowed to bring their families until 1954, a reality that no doubt complicated the task of recruiting qualified advisers.[82]

It was difficult to tell who was responsible for the destruction of Point Four offices, given the murky character of mob demonstrations and the widespread distrust of foreigners in the city. Mossadegh blamed British agitators for inciting the violence and cited local officials for their failure to keep order.[83] Dean Peterson of BYU wrote that "it appears on the surface as if a religious motivation was back of it all" and noted that Americans were not the only targets. The main bazaar as well as Jewish and Armenian neighborhoods were also damaged.[84] Other Point Four officials, however, pointed to communists. Elmer C. Bryant, who had recently become Point Four's regional director in

Shiraz, told Warne that "Tudeh students from the medical school first turned the mobs" on April 16.[85] Gagon likewise held "communist mobs" responsible for the destruction of Point Four property and data.[86] The CIA judged that the violence was "apparently caused by communist exploitation of demonstrations by rival factions."[87] It is far from certain, however, that communists were responsible. There had long been a stifling Western presence in the area, as the British Army had used Shiraz as a base to commandeer food and supplies during World War II while the population was reduced to near starvation.[88] Much of the population no doubt saw Americans as a similar threat. A range of political operatives—royalists, nationalists, leftists, foreign agents—employed street thugs to organize and manipulate crowds throughout the Mossadegh era. These semi-organized mobs often included large numbers of paid rowdies who marched alongside committed demonstrators. Rabble rousers frequently provoked violence in the name of their political opponents as a way of discrediting them. British intelligence and royalist army officers, for example, fomented "communist mobs" to create a "palpable fear of a communist takeover."[89] CIA agents likewise provoked acts of violence that they then blamed on communists.[90] The Utahns' tendency to finger communists therefore probably reflects the common American belief that communists were the ultimate source of political instability in Iran.

Mossadegh still believed he had public opinion on his side, but developments soon called that into question.[91] The entire National Front caucus resigned from the Majlis that summer when conservative delegates balked at a bill aimed at reducing the influence of the royalist Senate. The body therefore lacked a quorum. Rather than follow constitutional procedure of asking the shah to dissolve the parliament and call for new elections, Mossadegh proposed a national referendum on the matter in July and declared that "the people of Iran—and no one else—has the right to judge."[92] But he went a step too far. Ballot boxes for "yes" and "no" votes were placed in different locations, and goons intimidated voters who attempted to cast "no" votes. The government won an overwhelming, but hollow, victory. As historian Ervand Abrahamian points out, "The great admirer of Montesquieu was now echoing Jean-Jacques Rousseau."[93] More moderate constitutionalists abandoned Mossadegh, some out of disgust for the blatant ballot rigging, others because the prime minister refused to curb communist agitation. Furthermore, two years of economic crisis and mounting political chaos had taken a heavy toll. The summer of 1953 became the "most riotous" Warne had experienced in Iran. "The whole stream of activity" in Tehran seemed to be "rushing toward disaster."[94]

POINT FOUR AND THE OVERTHROW OF MOSSADEGH

It was during this crescendo of volatility that British and American agents cooperated with Iranian operatives to overthrow the Mossadegh government. British intelligence officers had first approached their American counterparts about finding a way to overthrow the prime minister in the fall of 1952, but US officials feared that any possible alternative to Mossadegh would increase instability in Iran.[95] American politics were transitioning toward the incoming Eisenhower administration, however, and soon-to-be CIA director Allen Dulles thought his new boss might be brought onboard. Eisenhower initially hesitated before coming around when Mossadegh broke off oil negotiations with the British in early 1953. The president approved $4 million for the CIA to bring down Mossadegh's government.[96]

The CIA prepared the ground by intensifying its misinformation campaign designed to erode the prime minister's domestic support.[97] It planted articles in the Iranian press that linked Mossadegh to communists; others incited the clergy and conservative Muslims by claiming that he was Jewish and anti-Islamic. The CIA also funded "Tudeh-inspired" demonstrations and circulated threatening "communist" handbills, all in an effort to convince Iranians that the country was in the midst of a communist insurgency. It likewise planted articles, including one that ran in *Newsweek* just days before the coup, that played up the communist presence in the Iranian Army and government. The article concluded that Mossadegh "appears to be irresistibly driven toward more reliance on Tudeh" support.[98] Donald Wilbur, an archaeologist who helped the CIA organize the coup, reported "there can be no doubt whatsoever" that the misinformation campaign "directly influenced" Iranian public opinion "in a most positive way."[99] It is hard to imagine that such a concerted propaganda campaign failed to make a strong impression on the Utah families as well.

Meanwhile, Ali Akbar Akhavi, the Iranian minister of national economy, implored Warne and Ambassador Henderson that Point Four should continue to support the Mossadegh government. Akhavi assured the Americans that the prime minister recognized the danger of communist activity, but he could not fight both the British and the Tudeh at the same time. As soon as he had resolved the oil issue, Mossadegh would turn his attention to suppressing the communists. In the meantime, Iran desperately needed American aid.[100] But Warne's close working relationship with the prime minister concerned CIA officials, who feared that Mossadegh was attempting to exploit that relationship to create the impression within the Iranian public that he still enjoyed American support. Kermit Roosevelt, a leading American planner of the coup, cautioned that Warne not be notified about the evolving plans, codenamed AJAX, and that he instead be encouraged to leave Iran for a month-long vacation in August. Warne remained in Iran throughout the summer, though it does not appear that he was ever brought into the planning or execution of the anti-Mossadegh coup.[101]

British and American officials preferred that the overthrow be constitutional, so they first tried to buy a no-confidence vote in the Majlis. That effort failed when Mossadegh adjourned parliament in early August. The planners next tried to persuade the shah to dismiss the prime minister and appoint General Zahedi in his place. The shah hesitated, citing doubts about the army's loyalties, before signing the necessary decrees on August 14. He then left the country to ride out the uncertainty in Baghdad. Mossadegh learned of the plot, however, and had the officer who attempted to serve him the orders arrested.[102] Zahedi went into hiding, protected by the US Embassy staff.[103] Army units loyal to the prime minister still controlled Tehran on Sunday morning, August 16, and it looked as though the coup had fizzled.[104] Resigned to his fate, the shah told the American ambassador in Iraq that he would soon be looking for work, as he had a large family and no means of support outside Iran. The royal family then departed for Rome.[105]

The next two days brought uncertainty, more demonstrations, and considerable destruction of property in Tehran. Warne urged Point Four personnel to stay off the streets except when on official business. He noticed that several statues of the shah and his father had been torn down and destroyed; a communist slogan was painted on one of the pedestals. He received "at least a hundred reports that the communists controlled the streets" and got the impression that "Tudeh mobs ruled the city" while driving around town on August 18.[106] Warne probably overestimated the level of communist control in the streets, but he was not altogether wrong. The Central Council of the

Anti-Colonial Society, a Tudeh Party organization, met that morning and unanimously adopted a resolution calling for the end of the monarchy and a national referendum on establishing a "democratic republic." Tudeh supporters subsequently hoisted banners and staged demonstrations around the city, all of which contributed to a sense of an imminent communist takeover in Tehran.[107] Ambassador Henderson reported that "hooligans bearing red flags and chanting Commie songs began tearing down statues of Shah and father" and breaking into homes to destroy images of the shah.[108] But it is unlikely that communists were exclusively responsible for the looting and destruction of property. Wilbur's account acknowledges that pro-shah gangs were also responsible for vandalism, as were CIA-paid "Tudehites."[109] The real communist presence, however, undoubtedly inspired many Iranians to take up the cause of the shah and added legitimacy to the CIA's portrayal of the previous two days as a genuine communist revolution.[110]

Mossadegh ordered the streets cleared on the evening of August 18 amid fighting between Tudeh supporters and the police.[111] The resultant calm cleared the way for a "great demonstration" in favor of the shah the following day, Wednesday, August 19. The organizers wanted this demonstration to appear to be a spontaneous display of popular support for the monarchy, but it was carefully planned by American agents and Iranian army officers at the US Embassy on the evening of August 17. Both General Fazlollah Zahedi and his son, Ardeshir, were present at the embassy meeting. Ardeshir Zahedi took responsibility for organizing and paying ruffians from south Tehran athletic clubs to demonstrate in favor of the shah and attack Mossadegh supporters. Perhaps most important to the ultimate success of the operation, these mobs were to surround and overwhelm pro-Mossadegh tank units, thus preventing them from defending the prime minister. Meanwhile, army units loyal to the shah were dispersed on orders to suppress communist activities. In reality, they targeted all Mossadegh supporters and any opposition to the shah.[112]

Warne closed the Point Four offices early in the afternoon of August 19 and found it difficult to navigate the streets on his way home, where he intended to continue working. Sporadic brawls and some machine gun fire broke out across Tehran. Supporters of the shah took control of a radio station near Shimron, where many of the Point Four families lived, in the early afternoon with the help of sympathetic soldiers.[113] After returning home,

Warne received a call from Gholam Mossadegh, the prime minister's son, who said that the situation would not allow him to have dinner with the Warnes that night as scheduled. Gholam and his wife, Warne later confided, "were among my favorite people." He then heard frenzied voices on the radio shouting "General Zahedi is Prime Minister" and "long live the Shah!"[114]

The news that Zahedi had emerged from hiding to take control of the government threw Tehran into a bloody convulsion. Dean Peterson wrote that "open warfare" broke out in the streets when soldiers arrived to arrest Mossadegh.[115] Mobs descended on the prime minister's residence as they had at the end of February. This time, a mass of raging humanity broke into the Point Four compound adjacent to Mossadegh's home. From his bathroom window Max Berryessa saw "rioting soldiers within the mob . . . exchanging shots" before he and Peterson fled toward the safety of Shimron along with the rest of the Point Four staff and their families.[116] Mossadegh was again forced to flee through the Point Four compound, in a manner reminiscent of the February 28 incident, and he went into hiding. Rioters ransacked the education office and destroyed several American vehicles. They broke all the windows and mangled a heavy iron gate; bullet holes were peppered around the main building's exterior. They also stole everything they could— including bathroom fixtures, mirrors, cupboards, and a fireplace mantle.[117] Pro-Zahedi army units took control of the city by nightfall but not before 300 people had died.[118]

The reactions of Point Four personnel to the violence of August 19 show how firmly their views of events were rooted in Cold War anti-communism. Warne saw signs of a communist uprising all across Tehran during the previous two days. Berryessa wrote that "a Communist Party revolt was almost successful in overthrowing the government of Iran." He attributed the destruction of the Tehran Point Four office to "huge mobs, fueled by the clever antics of the Tudas [Tudeh]."[119] The Utahns learned through the Tehran grapevine that "the American CIA had somehow overcome the Communist Party."[120]

But those interpretations overstate the role communists played in the upheaval. Dean Peterson did not mention a communist insurrection when he described the events of August 19 to I. O. Horsfall of the University of Utah just days after they happened. Rather, he wrote that the Point Four offices were "demolished when soldiers went to arrest Dr. Mossadegh."[121]

FIGURES 3.2 AND 3.3. Damage done to Point Four vehicles and offices in Tehran on August 19, 1953. *Courtesy,* Richard Welling Roskelley Photograph Collection, Special Collections and Archives, Merrill-Cazier Library, Utah State University, Logan.

Ali Rahnema has recently argued that gangs organized by Ardeshir Zahedi pillaged Mossadegh's home and the adjacent Point Four compound. If true, that presents an ironic twist to the day's bloody events: a USU graduate and great friend of the Point Four Program orchestrated the roughnecks who destroyed its headquarters during the coup's climactic hours.[122] Former Iranian diplomat Darioush Bayandor, in contrast, implies that the crowd was "mosque-driven," probably by Kashani. He argues that Zahedi lacked the time and money necessary to organize a sufficiently large crowd. Bayandor also points out that paid hooligans rarely risked their lives in violent confrontations with the authorities.[123] Finally, many of the items stolen from Mossadegh's residence and the Point Four offices later turned up in local markets, which suggests looting as a motivation.[124] None of these interpretations, however, emphasizes a communist revolution as the primary cause of the violence on August 19.

The 1953 overthrow of the Mossadegh government marked a significant turning point in modern Iranian history and in US-Iranian relations, though that did not become completely apparent for another quarter century. Most Point Four personnel welcomed the regime change because they had come to associate Mossadegh's government with political chaos, economic stagnation, and communist agitation. In contrast, the new cabinet of General Zahedi restored order to the streets and brought a measure of stability to the Iranian government.[125] Warne praised the enthusiasm with which Zahedi's cabinet embraced rural development.[126] Anti-American rhetoric also diminished, at least in the short run. The Utah families discovered that "a whole new attitude had been formed in favor of America" when they returned to Tehran three days after the overthrow of Mossadegh.[127] "Ebullient civilians warmly welcomed them."[128] Point Four education expert Clarence Hendershot noted with some exaggeration that the American advisers felt "the friendship and cooperation of the great majority of Iranians" compensated for the "difficulties and trials" following the "suppression of the communists."[129] Such assessments underscore the relief Point Four personnel felt following Mossadegh's ouster. US-Iranian relations warmed, however, especially after effective control of the Iranian oil industry was returned to an international consortium that included both British and American companies in 1954.[130] The Eisenhower administration showered the Iranian government with unprecedented levels of economic and military aid.[131]

CONCLUSION

The reactions of the Utah families to the disturbances of 1951 through 1953 shed interesting light on how these Point Four pioneers understood Iran and the Cold War. As foreigners who had limited experience in the country, they were understandably confused by the often chaotic political climate of the Mossadegh era. There is no question that their fear of communist insurrection shaped their understanding of events. When asked decades later if she would do it all over again, Helen Milligan replied "yes, because I feel like we got there with enough soon enough that the communists didn't take over."[132] Point Four's agricultural chief similarly concluded that the program "was largely responsible for keeping Iran from going behind the Iron Curtain."[133] Max Berryessa believed communists had been "playing the hand of Mossadegh."[134] "We experienced street disturbances, lived through mob activities and a series of other things," recalled agricultural chief Richard Welling Roskelley, "but we realized that we were actually participating in a struggle for supremacy of two ideologies, i.e., democracy or another way of life."[135] Such assessments reflected the operative American view of the Iranian political crisis for the next quarter century. They helped convince the Utah advisers that the coup was a positive development, not just for Western interests but also for the country itself.

But the Utah families also seem to have largely missed the liberal and nationalist underpinnings of the Mossadegh era. "If Americans could have just supported him [Mossadegh]," recalled USU agricultural adviser Jay Hall in a 1999 interview, "we would really have had a lot of support in Iran."[136] That was a decidedly minority view, however, at least in the summer of 1953. Like most other American observers, the Utahns were much more focused on the Cold War threat than on the National Front's attempt to secure economic independence and constitutional legitimacy for the country. Richard Cottam, a CIA analyst who arrived in Iran just before the coup, later reflected that Americans, "who prided themselves on being the primary proponents of liberal democratic nationalist values," played a decisive role in overthrowing a government that "conceivably could have incorporated those ideals" into Iranian society.[137] Linking Mossadegh's government with the threat of a communist revolution undoubtedly helps explain why many of the Utah advisers cultivated an ambivalent, even hostile attitude toward the prime minister's legacy yet embraced the shah, whose authoritarianism they deemphasized in favor of seeing him as a progressive and stabilizing figure. Louise Hubbard recalled that Americans "preferred the shah to Mossadegh's communist and Russian ties." Her husband, Deon, added that the Iranian people "seemed to be in adoration of the shah," who was "quite cooperative with the agricultural program which our Point Four team was working on."[138]

Divergent American and Iranian views of the coup emerged over the next quarter century. Few American leaders questioned their belief that they helped rescue the country from disaster. Meanwhile, Iranians had to accept the reversal of oil nationalization, the shah's increasing authoritarianism, and an enlarged American presence in their country. Not surprisingly, then, more came to see the coup—and the resultant increase in American influence—as an unwelcome foreign intrusion that sidetracked their country's development as an independent and prosperous nation.

4

TO MAKE THE IRANIAN DESERT BLOOM

The villagers are in the grips of destitution and ignorance . . . they are totally
lacking health and education, and they live for the most part a very hard life.
Mostafa Zahedi, Iranian Ministry of Agriculture

Cooperative effort, well planned and executed, can launch a new era for the
Iranian farmer.
Bruce Anderson, USU adviser in Iran, 1951–54, 1954–56, 1957–60

It was very difficult to change these people from the agriculture of two
thousand years ago into the agriculture of the twentieth century . . . You
don't change things very fast.
Bertis L. Embry, USU adviser in Iran, 1960–62

Most of the Utah projects focused on rural improvement because that was
a major priority of the Iranian government after World War II. Utah State
University (USU) advisers helped the Ministry of Agriculture develop a pro-

DOI: 10.7330/9781607327547.c004

gram of agricultural research and demonstration and assisted in the development of Karaj Agricultural College as a modern institution of higher
learning that would serve the practical needs of Iranian agriculture. The
University of Utah medical team contributed to rural public health initiatives, and advisers from Brigham Young University (BYU) helped train rural
teachers, an important part of rural improvement discussed in chapter 5.
The Utah advisers came to Iran with confidence that their technical expertise could transform that country as completely as it had the American West
during the preceding century. The rural improvement program fell short
of its lofty expectations, however, despite the tenacious efforts of the Utah
advisers and their achievement of some localized successes. The shah might
have dreamed of a rapid transformation of the countryside, but Iran's deep
and pervasive rural poverty and its underdeveloped infrastructure proved to
be formidable barriers. Even as the government devoted more resources to
rural improvement, change did not come quickly.

Point Four championed low modernization for most of its rural improvement initiatives. The approach tried to incorporate local knowledge wherever
possible and resisted technological solutions that were beyond the means of
peasant farmers or that would bring unsettling social change to rural communities. The Utah advisers helped incubate some rural improvements in Iran,
mostly in agricultural research and extension work. Their efforts floundered,
however, once they reached the limits of what the country's traditional social
and economic structures could absorb. Neither the Utah advisers nor their
Iranian partners in the field had the capacity to influence the wider-ranging
reforms that were required to sustain more dramatic development. Moreover,
American officials turned over the primary responsibility for maintaining
technical assistance projects to their Iranian counterparts, a process known
as integration, as soon as possible and often before the latter were ready to
shoulder such burdens. Few projects, therefore, had become self-sustaining
prior to American support phasing out. The net result was that Point Four
rural improvement realized few long-term gains in Iran.

RURAL CONDITIONS IN 1950

Rural poverty ranked among Iran's most acute social problems in the
mid-twentieth century.[1] Peasant farmers accounted for almost 80 percent of

the population, and most lived at or near the subsistence level. A multitude of factors conspired to keep them destitute, including feudal land ownership, little or no access to formal education, and a scarcity of clean water. To illustrate the problem of land tenure, a 1949 government survey of 1,300 villages around Tehran found that 95 percent of families owned fewer than 3 hectares (7.5 acres) of land; most owned none at all. The typical farm family in that region cultivated around 2 hectares (5 acres), from which it could expect to harvest, on average, no more than 200 bushels of wheat per year.[2] Many tenant farmers could claim legal rights to only one-fifth of that yield, however, based on a common system that divided the harvest into fifths and allocated a 20 percent share for each of the five main factors of production: land, seeds, oxen or machinery, water, and labor. Because landlords often controlled the first four factors, they received up to 80 percent of the harvest, which left many peasants with only the 20 percent share due for their labor.[3] In practical terms, that meant tenant farmers in the vicinity of Tehran lived on around $100 per year in 1950, or about one-tenth the annual income of modest landowning families.[4] The situation was generally worse for peasants in the hotter and drier southern provinces of Khuzestan and Kerman.

Agricultural techniques had progressed little for most peasants since ancient times. The Ministry of Agriculture estimated that the country of 17 million had fewer than 1,000 tractors, 100 combines, and just 40 threshing machines in 1950. Few Iranian peasants used even the sturdy metal plows that had become standard in the West during the nineteenth century. Rather, most plowed their fields with a single wooden spike pulled by weak oxen. Seed was usually sown broadcast, an imprecise method that produced a great deal of waste. Harvesting and threshing were also done by hand; it was difficult and time-consuming work. Commercial fertilizers were beyond the means of most farmers, and most animal waste was used for heating and cooking fuel. Much of the cropland therefore had to remain fallow for regeneration. A vast network of irrigation tunnels, qanats, provided water from mountain sources to some dry interior areas, but the country had fewer than 300 deep irrigation wells. Pumps were often antiquated and inadequate; irrigation practices were often inefficient. Farmers who lacked access to water had to rely on dry farming, a risky proposition in most of the country. On top of it all, pests and insects reduced the annual harvest by 15 percent on average. "The soil yields a small quantity of product," sighed one Ministry of Agriculture official, "which is barely enough to keep flesh and bones together."[5]

Unsanitary public health conditions also severely compromised the well-being of rural Iranians. Because most villages lacked deep clean wells, fresh-water had to be brought from distant sources. It was distributed throughout communities in surface channels known as *jubes*, which also carried away wastewater. "Such water is highly contaminated," noted a rural develop-ment specialist who advised the Iranian government between 1945 and 1948. "Many villagers wash in it and dispose of their wastes in it as it flows toward its destination." Disease was also a constant debilitating presence. Medical technicians in the late 1940s found that 82 percent of the population of one village carried the malaria parasite in their blood, and more than 12 percent tested positive for trachoma, a bacterial infection that can cause blindness. Epidemics of diseases such as smallpox, diphtheria, typhoid, and typhus fever were also frequent occurrences.[6] "The villagers are in the grips of destitu-tion and ignorance," Mostafa Zahedi of the Ministry of Agriculture told an audience of American academics. "Although they support the people of our country, they are totally lacking health and education, and they live for the most part a very hard life."[7]

The growth of Iran's petroleum industry made its rural poverty appear much more acute by 1950. While rising national income led to some socioeco-nomic improvements in the cities, Iran's rural population remained among the poorest in the world. The country's preindustrial system of taxation still fell disproportionately on agricultural products.[8] An US Embassy researcher found that "practically none of the financial benefits" that accrued from the petroleum industry "have seeped to the eighty percent of the population which still ekes out an existence from agriculture."[9]

The Iranian government took halting steps to help farmers before 1950, but they bore little fruit in part because Reza Shah, who ruled Iran from 1925 to 1941, put much greater emphasis on urban industrialization and building the army. A 1937 law attempted to increase the amount of land under cultivation and improve water conservation, but provincial officials lacked the will and the means to enforce it. The Allied armies added to the peasants' misery during the war by strong-arming landlords into selling much of the harvest at discounted prices. Prime Minister Ahmad Qavam managed to pass an agri-cultural reform bill in the Majlis in 1946 that raised the peasants' share of the harvest by 15 percent, but that law encountered stiff resistance from landlords, who defeated it the following year. Early attempts at land reform also failed as a result of the government's administrative limitations and because few peasants could secure enough credit to purchase even modest plots.[10] The Ministry of Agriculture offered little assistance to farmers. Almost half of its employees worked in Tehran, far removed from the country's farmers, and few had agricultural training. Accurate maps and cadastral surveys were so sparse that government officials apparently did not know about the existence of many villages.[11] A fledgling agricultural college at Karaj trained students for bureaucratic positions within the ministry rather than to solve practical agricultural problems. Even low-level civil servants considered agricultural fieldwork beneath the dignity of public officials. All told, the standard of living of the average Iranian farmer in 1950 was not significantly better than it had been in 1900.[12]

Improving agriculture and rural health was therefore the natural starting point for rural development in Iran. Agricultural production, after all, still accounted for a larger share of the national economy than did petroleum. Moreover, poor conditions throughout the Iranian countryside had the potential to incubate "stomach communism." Franklin Harris, Luther Winsor, and George Stewart all reported that Soviet propaganda made effective use of the country's ubiquitous rural poverty.[13] But USU livestock specialist Farrell Olson also pointed out that by helping "the people adopt new and better practices," rural development could "instill in them a healthy philosophy of faith in their country."[14]

THE RURAL IMPROVEMENT PROGRAM TAKES SHAPE

Point Four's Iranian rural improvement program took more than two years to become fully functional. Iran became the first country in the world to accept Point Four aid when Prime Minister Ali Razmara signed a small pilot agreement with the newly formed Technical Cooperation Administration in October 1950. Mohammad Mossadegh, who built his political career on opposing foreign influence in Iran, begged the US government to provide more aid in light of the British oil embargo during his visit to Washington the following year.[15] After protracted negotiations, the United States agreed to increase its Point Four commitment to nearly $23.5 million at the end of January 1952.[16] With a new agreement signed, Point Four officials and the Iranian government formed a joint US-Iranian commission for rural improvement that spring. Mossadegh assigned the ministers of health, education, and agriculture along with representatives from the country's central planning organization, commonly known as the Plan Organization, to its steering committee.[17] Point Four had already assigned Roskelley to head its agricultural division. He, along with USU advisers George Stewart and Cleve Milligan, sat on the agricultural committee of the rural improvement commission.[18] None of the Americans spoke Persian and only two of the Iranians were conversant in English, so Point Four hired an Iranian who had recently graduated from Utah State University to serve as an interpreter.[19]

All of the USU advisers found themselves in some form of leadership role by the end of 1952. In addition to overseeing the entire agricultural division, Roskelley also directed the agricultural extension branch. It was a tough assignment. On the one hand, he was a veteran extension agent and had experience training new agents in the United States.[20] But he also found his double responsibilities difficult to manage and did not enjoy unqualified support among the American advisers or their Iranian colleagues.[21] Stewart was named head of the plant science branch, and Milligan, former chair of civil and irrigation engineering at USU, directed the agricultural engineering branch. Three of the original five section heads were also USU men: J. Clark Ballard, A. Glenn Wahlquist, and Hendrik Versluis headed the horticulture, agronomy, and veterinary medicine sections, respectively. Finally, all eight of the first provincial directors were USU team members: Bert Despain, Odeal Kirk, and Melvin Peterson, all of whom arrived in February 1952, directed operations in Azerbaijan near the Soviet border and Mazanderan on the Caspian Sea. J. Glenn Morrill, Verne Oberhansley, and Leroy "Roy" Bunnell, all of whom arrived that October, did the same in Khorasan, Kerman, and Tehran, respectively. Bruce Anderson and Jay Hall jointly led the Shiraz office in Fars. USU had fourteen advisers in Iran at the end of 1952; together, they accounted for all but two leadership positions within Point Four's agricultural division.[22] The success of the agricultural program, then, largely depended on the performance of these men.

It took some persuasion to get Mossadegh and the influential Ayatollah Abol-Ghasem Kashani to accept Point Four's low-modernization principle.

Both initially hoped that the program would provide large scale infra structure improvements. After becoming prime minister, for example, Mossadegh mockingly likened the modest size of the original Point Four agreement to an Iranian tarantula by saying that Point Four "jumps up and down and scares everybody, but it has never been known to bite." It was a characterization William Warne found "grossly unfair." When Warne met with Ayatollah Kashani, the influential speaker of the Majlis, in the summer of 1952, Kashani said he hoped Point Four would do "something substantial" for Iran and suggested a hydroelectric dam on the Karun River to bring rural electrification to Khuzestan. Warne replied that the cost of such a project would be near $250 million and easily exceed the Point Four budget, at which Kashani "appeared amazed and thought that a hundred dams could be built for that amount."[23] American officials countered that Iran's technical problems were more "fundamental in nature" and "needed to be resolved not by automation or high dams, but rather through a grass roots approach to the problems themselves."[24]

Point Four planners could point to the success of a similar community-based rural improvement program the Near East Foundation (NEF) had founded five years earlier in the Varamin region outside Tehran. While "decidedly small" in its geographic scope, the NEF experimented with an ambitious range of projects that included teacher training, adult literacy classes, DDT treatment to reduce disease-transmitting insects, rudimentary water purification, and agricultural demonstrations.[25] NEF rural development deliberately emphasized the low-modernization approach. Its agricultural program stressed "practical instruction carried directly to the people on their primitive farms and in their simple houses in isolated communities."[26] NEF technicians favored techniques that were "simple, easy to apply and adapted to local conditions."[27] Lyle Hayden, one of its demonstration specialists, wrote that the goal was to "evolve practices" villagers could adopt "without doing violence to the general social pattern."[28] Avoiding techniques that required traumatic social change was an important part of the low-modernization philosophy that helped both the NEF and Point Four earn the trust of rural elites and peasants alike. But that same strategy ultimately proved a barrier to significant development in countries such as Iran, where traditional village life stifled social development and prevented upward mobility.

AGRICULTURAL RESEARCH AND DEMONSTRATION

Roskelley attempted to formulate a coherent agenda for agricultural development during the spring of 1952. Improving productivity and developing an extension service were the Iranian government's highest priorities and would therefore command the most attention.[29] Initial research emphasized the development of higher-yield seeds that would resist drought and insects, especially in cereal crops. Grains accounted for almost 95 percent of land under cultivation in 1950; wheat fields alone comprised nearly two-thirds of all farmland.[30] Yet drought conditions around the city of Ardabil near the Caspian Sea destroyed much of the grain harvest in 1951, leaving Azerbaijan, Iran's second-most-populace province, on the brink of starvation. The country's varied climate and geography meant agricultural research would have to be tailored to local conditions. USU scientists therefore tested dozens of cereal, vegetable, and livestock varieties that had thrived under comparable conditions in the American West to see which could profitably be imported into Iran.[31]

Cultivating the trust of rural people was the first task that confronted the USU advisers. Indeed, it proved as important as providing sound technical advice. "The important job," observed Roy Bunnell, who spent nearly five years in Iran, "was to gain the confidence of the people." Progress, he explained, was measured "first by attitudes, followed by confidence, trials, observation, further trials, then eventually by introducing a new practice."[32] Irrigation engineer Bruce Anderson, who spent more than seven years working with Iranian farmers, acknowledged that it was a challenging task because the idea of experimentation was "completely foreign and hard for them to accept." The key, he concluded, was to start small until farmers gained confidence in new approaches. Rural improvement had to emphasize changes that "can be made without causing a burden on the farmer for new equipment and materials."[33] Stanley Andrews, who led the Point Four Program during the final years of the Truman administration, emphasized the need for humility. Even one or two American advisers who appeared haughty or domineering could easily ruin a project and poison the goodwill Point Four was supposed to generate.[34]

One reason farmers were hard to convince was that early efforts produced mixed results. The first major Point Four agricultural initiative involved George Stewart exchanging 60 tons of a drought- and disease-resistant variety of wheat for the smut-infested seeds of tenant farmers in the fall of 1951.

Side-by-side trials the following spring showed the clear superiority of the improved seed under the same cultivation methods.[35] Early experiments on cotton irrigation around Shiraz likewise demonstrated that remarkable gains in yield could be realized with less water when farmers planted their fields in rows and then irrigated the shallow furrows rather than planting seed broadcast and lightly flooding the fields ("karte" irrigation). Sugar beet trials, however, produced much more disappointing results in the summer of 1952. USU advisers had not studied the beet variety sufficiently; further, they did not know enough about local soil conditions and water management before they planted three test fields in different areas of Fars. As a result, none of the fields produced well. Half of the plants in the first field failed to germinate when water had to be diverted into neighboring wheat fields. Local landlords provided the land and water for the beet experiments, but the test fields were a lower priority than their commercial fields. The drying soil in the second field cracked in such a way that it choked off many of the fledgling beet plants, a condition Point Four advisers might have anticipated had they acquired a better understanding of the soil. Things "went nicely" in the third field "until hit with locusts."[36] Early beet trials, then, served as important learning experiences for the USU advisers but did little to convince local farmers to embrace American practices.

Projects designed to improve livestock breeding also required time and modification before they produced consistently good results. Early efforts focused on the introduction of healthier animals to improve breeding. The importation of sturdy Brown Swiss bulls from the United States and Jack donkeys from Cyprus helped breed stronger draft animals in those limited areas into which they were introduced. Point Four also imported tens of thousands of healthy chicks into Iran in 1952 and 1953, but many succumbed to local diseases.[37] Over time, though, the livestock program did make progress. Point Four established a livestock station near Shiraz for diary, sheep, and poultry; cross-bred cows were producing 150 percent–250 percent more milk than native-bred cows by 1957. Roy Bunnell also cooperated with the Ministry of Agriculture in establishing a processing plant that turned beet pulp, a by-product of beet processing that had previously been discarded, into livestock feed. Control of animal diseases made significant strides as the result of an increase of nearly 2,000 Iranians trained in basic veterinarian medicine. The Tehran Veterinary Department, for example, vaccinated more than 11 million farm animals between 1952 and 1956. Anthrax, which posed a serious threat to livestock and could be transmitted to humans, dropped 77 percent during those years.[38] The results of the livestock program were impressive in some areas, but improved breeding and disease control had little impact outside the regions Point Four advisers served.

Agricultural engineering concentrated on irrigation and mechanized agriculture, two areas that stretched the limits of the low-modernization approach. Both required more sophisticated technology and structural changes to Iranian agriculture. Of the two, improving irrigation was the higher priority because the scarcity of water had long limited agricultural production in much of the country. Cleve Milligan was shocked by the water-usage practices he found when he set out to drill twenty deep wells throughout the country in early 1952. "Notwithstanding the great concern" for water scarcity he wrote, "there are many places where [it] is used inefficiently." Iranian agricultural agents had not been trained in water management, and the Ministry of Agriculture had little reliable information on groundwater supplies or usage throughout most of the country. Milligan understood the importance of building better irrigation works for improving agricultural production, but Iranian officials first needed assistance in collecting reliable information on Iranian hydrology and training agents with a basic understanding of irrigation engineering.[39]

Bruce Anderson felt irrigation work was making good progress by the summer of 1956. Demonstration farms illustrated the superiority of shallow-row irrigation over the more common karte system. USU advisers and their Iranian counterparts also designed simple ox-drawn tools to level and corrugate fields. USU advisers began offering short courses on efficient irrigation practices in the summer of 1952.[40] Point Four also sponsored irrigation research around Shiraz and in the Varamin region near Tehran, where it continued to partner with the NEF. "The future looks brighter than ever before," Anderson wrote. The Ministry of Agriculture had employed Point Four–trained Iranian engineers to begin projects for leveling land, topographic mapping, and research into the design of irrigation structures and water drainage.[41]

Yet the irrigation program also illustrated some of the limitations of low modernization. The country lacked sufficient equipment and trained engineers to sustain a program of nationwide irrigation research, not to mention building more efficient water distribution systems. Improving irrigation

FIGURE 4.1. Demonstration of mechanized agriculture. *Courtesy,* Richard Welling Roskelley Photograph Collection, Special Collections and Archives, Merrill-Cazier Library, Utah State University, Logan.

required a major infusion of technology and a fundamental reordering of water control. It also demanded a higher level of cooperation among land-lords and the farmers themselves. "The Persian people do not know what the world 'cooperate' means," lamented Luther Winsor in 1946. "They do not understand how a canal can be built to serve many farms."[42] Improving irrigation would therefore be very difficult to sustain without significant corresponding changes to rural society.

Point Four's attempts to introduce mechanized agricultural practices likewise stretched the limits of low modernization. The mechanization program had to be limited because Point Four's modest budget allowed only for the purchase of equipment to be used in research and demonstration. Mechanized demonstrations and training created an obvious problem, then, if such equipment was not widely available to farmers. Milligan further pointed out that mechanized agriculture would do little good unless Iranians concurrently solved a host of other problems related to the quality of seeds, availability of water, and control of insects.[43] "Only in rare conditions," advised Farrell Olson, "should tractors and accompanying equipment be encouraged in this early stage of improved farming methods in Iran."[44]

FIGURE 4.2. Inspection of irrigation works. *Courtesy*, Richard Welling Roskelley Photograph Collection, Special Collections and Archives, Merrill-Cazier Library, Utah State University, Logan.

Increased mechanization was not always practical or even desirable. The country's transportation system left many areas inaccessible to large-scale machinery, and the small plots many farmers cultivated were often better suited to smaller equipment anyway.[45] The cost of operating tractor-driven equipment was also prohibitive for most farmers. Iran had few domestic suppliers of spare parts and a dearth of trained mechanics. Parts ordered abroad were expensive and had to be bought with dollars or sterling, two commodities that were in short supply, especially during the oil nationalization crisis. Iran also lacked a stable supply of refined fuel and limited means to distribute it, despite its status as a burgeoning oil producer.[46] USU electrical engineering professor Bertis L. Embry observed many cases in which poorly trained operators and mechanics did more harm than good to the machinery.[47] Bruce Anderson reported that "every region is plagued with machinery problems" in the fall of 1954 and noted that several landlords abandoned their tractors or sold them and bought more oxen instead.[48] Finally, tenant farmers did not necessarily embrace mechanization, though it might reduce their work loads.

Some were reluctant to use machinery if they believed landlords would realize most of the benefits. Moreover, machinery increased efficiency, which threatened to deprive peasant families of the traditional gleaning that took place in fields after the harvest was finished.[49] All told, fewer than 10 percent of Iranian farms used tractors for plowing in 1960.[50]

USU advisers nevertheless tried to incorporate a range of mechanized practices where they might be profitable, especially at experiment stations and on demonstration farms. The establishment of a machinery training and repair center in Shiraz was among the first agricultural projects Point Four attempted in the country.[51] Iranian farmers showed interest, but a single shop could make only limited headway. Bruce Anderson advised that it would take "considerable time and effort" to train enough qualified mechanics in Iran's fledgling vocational schools. He therefore urged that "the program should have a long range view." USU advisers also attempted a tractor and machinery operations course in the summer of 1955, but it was not successful. An overabundance of students coupled with a dearth of machinery limited the hands-on work each student received.[52] The introduction of smaller horticultural equipment such as garden planters and ox-pulled cultivators proved more successful. Such equipment was ideal for smaller farms. It was relatively cheap and durable, simple enough for farmers to repair, and helped increase the amount of land under vegetable cultivation.[53]

Difficulties in introducing mechanized agriculture were not unique to Iran. It was easy to see modern technology as a panacea that could rapidly transform agriculture in the developing world, but it rarely worked in practice. The problem was actually much greater than the paucity of spare parts, fuel, and trained mechanics. Mechanization would fundamentally alter both the physical environment of the countryside and its social structure. Iranian rural society, as in much of the developing world, was simply not ready to absorb such sweeping change quickly.[54]

AGRICULTURAL EXTENSION

Creating a modern agricultural extension service that could provide assistance to the country's farmers was a high priority for the Iranian government. Ministry of Agriculture officials had been impressed with extension services in the United States and wanted to replicate them in Iran. Agricultural extension brought out the best in the low-modernization approach and was probably the most successful USU contribution to Iranian agriculture. But an extension program would have to be built almost from scratch, as the small service that did exist in 1950 functioned more as a regulatory agency than an educational body. Its agents were not trained in agricultural research or demonstration. Deputy Minister of Agriculture Mostafa Zahedi organized an extension training seminar in the summer of 1952 with the help of Point Four, NEF, and US Department of Agriculture officials. They also carried out a pilot course for a small group of agricultural engineers at about the same time.[55] Point Four and ministry officials agreed to launch a full-fledged training program in extension work during 1953. It soon became apparent, however, that some members of the ministry staff were having difficulty understanding the extension concept. The ideas of helping people help themselves and "working with villagers to . . . solve their problems were not emphasized in their previous experiences."[56]

Extension work had to employ the low-modernization approach. It engaged villagers on terms they could understand and in ways that would allow them to see how improved techniques would improve their livelihoods. D. C. Purnell, for example, taught farmers how to control the sen bug that ravaged wheat fields around Isfahan and how to apply sulfur spray to control mildew on grapes.[57] Melvin Peterson worked with Qashqai leaders in Fars to develop a pasture rotation system that doubled the amount of grass available to the tribe's horses.[58] Roy Bunnell worked with pistachio growers to create a system for spraying trees to eliminate worms from the nuts.[59] Peasants often showed reluctance to embrace innovation, so the advisers assisted the Ministry of Agriculture in organizing community fairs and field days. These events allowed agents to demonstrate new techniques and local farmers to show off their improved produce and livestock. Some became quite extravagant productions, with hundreds and even thousands of farmers participating. Utah advisers also worked with a team of audiovisual technicians from Syracuse University to produce informational films to assist agents in educating illiterate peasants about insect and disease control.[60] Agents designed programs for women and children as well. The Iranian government initiated a home economics extension program in 1958 to help rural homemakers adopt better practices for food preparation, sanitation, and clothing repair. The home extension program offered one of the few

FIGURE 4.3. A group of agricultural extension agents. Richard Welling Roskelley is third from the left. *Courtesy,* Richard Welling Roskelley Photograph Collection, Special Collections and Archives, Merrill-Cazier Library, Utah State University, Logan.

professional opportunities for rural women. A youth program modeled on the American "4-H" approach taught young people about agriculture, health, and handicrafts.[61]

One aspect of extension work that proved frustrating for the USU advisers was the attempt to nurture cooperative farms. Pooling resources was a common practice among Iranian peasants, who had long shared tools, draft animals, labor, and water in a collective practice known as *boneh*.[62] But having control over how a farm was run was completely new to most peasant families, who still farmed land owned by other people. "It is a far cry for them to change from a position of always being told what to do," observed Bruce Anderson, "to one where they must make the decisions and formulate the policy and operate their own enterprise."[63] Cooperative farms required access to land, the sustained commitment of members, and the ability to reach a consensus—all of which proved difficult to maintain. Social status led wealthier peasants to look down on their poorer counterparts, and mass migration into the cities disrupted continuity in many rural communities. Most cooperatives depended on the Agricultural Bank for funding and therefore came under the control of bank officials. They sometimes assigned farm managers who had more interest in defending the status quo than in increasing production or members' incomes. Mechanization increased yields on some cooperative farms but caused several others to stagnate. Anderson found that on one co-op, for example, only one of four tractors was working properly in the fall of 1954. Lack of trained operators and poor mechanic work had sidelined two, and one was used exclusively to transport kerosene for other machinery.[64] By 1956, it was clear that American advisers had underestimated the amount of time required to make cooperative farms profitable.

Extension advisers also had to cultivate friendly relations with village elders, especially landlords and *mullas* (Shi'i Islamic clerics), who still wielded enormous legal and moral influence in rural life. Most Iranian villages remained under the control of large landlords during the Point Four era, despite government attempts to distribute more land to peasants.[65] Agricultural technician C. David Anderson reported that a villager could only participate in Point Four initiatives "to the extent that his landlord approved of the project."[66] Local landlords exploited for their own uses one of the cooperative farms USU advisers had helped start.[67] Clerics held less direct influence on rural development, but their approval was often an important prerequisite for peasant participation in American projects.[68] Engaging village leaders required an understanding of local customs and politics. Consultations had to begin with the *kadkhoda* (mayor), who was usually appointed by the landlord, and the village council. Discussions were almost always carried out over tea and a meal of meat and rice. The USU advisers learned that following traditional village procedure could help win the cooperation of important elders, but deviations from accepted protocol could jeopardize an entire project.[69]

INTEGRATION

Point Four agricultural programs were making enough progress by the mid-1950s that officials decided it was time to shift greater administrative burdens onto the Ministry of Agriculture through a process that became known as integration. Iranian officials would take greater control of project planning and execution while American advisers shifted their emphasis to training extension agents. This seemed like a natural step to USU dean of agriculture Rudger Walker. "The program must be an Iranian program," he wrote in 1956, "not an American program."[70] James B. Davis, Point Four's chief of agriculture in 1966, added that while extension work had helped Iranian farmers, it was also "dominated by Americans" in its early years.[71] Some USU advisers believed integration made their work more productive. Farrell Olson observed from Kermanshah that the changes created "more time for teaching the technicians, for holding demonstrations, and doing all those things needed for the lasting improvement of agriculture in Iran."[72]

Many Americans, however, felt integration was premature and that it triggered a decline in agricultural projects. Allen C. Hankins, an extension adviser in Kurdistan, observed that integration resulted in the loss of some concepts when Iranian agents assumed responsibilities for which they were not ready. He thought the Ministry of Agriculture created too many "crash programs" instead of fostering the ones that already existed. Political rivalries and frequent turnover within the ministry had "a debilitating effect" on real long-term planning.[73] Others complained that Iranian agents continued to rely on American advisers to make administrative decisions and that the Iranians struggled to use scarce resources efficiently.[74] Odeal Kirk, one of USU's longest-serving extension agents in Iran, wrote in 1958 that he did not believe ministry personnel "had sufficient experience" to keep a demonstration farm "moving ahead."[75] Iranian economist Jahangir Amuzegar noted that nationwide, only two-thirds of the Point Four projects had yet to be completed when integration began in 1956; some had just started. "There hardly seemed any technical or economic reason," he concluded, "for an immediate transfer of these project[s] to Iranian administration."[76]

Watching their Iranian counterparts gain expertise and take over leadership roles nevertheless proved rewarding for many USU advisers. Farrell Olson congratulated Malek Almedi, chief of veterinary medicine, for his "dogged determination" to build a livestock cooperative in Kermanshah. Mahmoud Bahadory, an enterprising young extension agent, almost single-handedly brought agricultural extension to the impoverished and remote desert province of Baluchistan in southeastern Iran.[77] The Ministry of Agriculture congratulated another extension agent, Amir Riazi, for his outstanding work in the field of fruit orchard management. In 1959 Riazi was doing extensive work in 6 villages as well as scattered work in 150 others, and he helped establish 3 cooperative farms. In one year he carried out 83 fertilizer demonstrations, 48 in wheat seed and smut control, as well as 40 poultry demonstrations, and he helped castrate chickens in 40 villages. Such a record would have made any

Iowa extension agent proud, but this was Iran, a nation with few paved roads and little material support for extension agents. Even ordinary laborers benefited from employment on the extension farms.[78] Odeal Kirk spent much of the last of his three assignments supervising the Karaj Demonstration Farm, which he called "an excellent training place for people regardless of status or education." Common laborers who had worked on the farm for even a short while "found themselves quite in demand" and were able to find "more profitable employment" because of their experience.[79]

KARAJ AGRICULTURAL COLLEGE

Utah State University advisers provided assistance to Karaj Agricultural College throughout their fourteen years in Iran. Mohamad Amin Sepehri, the first Iranian graduate of USU, helped found the college's direct predecessor, an agricultural school for boys in Tehran, after World War I.[80] Reza Shah moved the institution to the royal gardens at Karaj, about twenty-five miles west of Tehran, in 1927, and the Majlis joined it to the University of Tehran in 1946. The college was a modest enterprise in 1951, despite being the only institution of higher learning for agriculture in the country.[81] It enrolled about 125 students in a three-year course designed to prepare them for bureaucratic work within the Ministry of Agriculture. According to Roskelley, teaching "was not service oriented," and courses were "not related to the problems of rural people." Bertis L. Embry put it more bluntly: "As far as I was concerned, education in the College of Agriculture was a joke."[82] The campus lacked sufficient student and faculty housing to accommodate growth. There were few laboratories, "practically no library," and no student activities. The dean reported that the college had not supported research since 1940.[83]

The USU advisers were tasked with helping the college develop a teaching and research program that would be more responsive to the country's agricultural needs. They tried to convince Iranian administrators and professors to accept the principles of American land-grant colleges. Roskelley explained that students "will be trained in a practical fashion to recognize the problems in agriculture and how to initiate measures to solve them." They would also learn "the art and science of disseminating this information to farmers."[84] In addition to helping plan and construct an adequate campus and library, the USU advisers also encouraged the Karaj faculty to incorporate practical fieldwork into their courses and to develop a constructive research program. The USU collaboration with Karaj Agricultural College necessarily deviated from low modernization. The American advisers promoted American-style higher education practices that were foreign to most Iranian academics. Perhaps not surprisingly, the Iranian faculty greeted the American proposals with a mixture of enthusiasm, uncertainty, and stiff resistance. They welcomed American financial assistance in developing a more attractive and functional campus, but they often resisted pedagogical innovations that clashed with Iranian tradition.

Karaj Agricultural College figured only marginally in USU's work between 1951 and 1954. Five advisers began collaborating with the college on a part-time basis in the fall of 1951, but most of their attention was directed toward the rural improvement program. Point Four did, however, contribute money for "badly needed physical facilities" during those early years.[85] The college experienced some growth in 1952, but Prime Minister Mossadegh appointed its energetic dean to be minister of agriculture the following summer, just before the coup that removed him from office. The college languished for the remainder of 1953 under the uncertain leadership.[86] Roskelley made little headway in convincing college administrators to adopt American-style curriculum reforms during his three years in Iran (1951–54). Faculty members were "very appreciative of the dollars that were spent" on improving the campus as long as "the expenditure did not represent any threat to them or their concept of how they felt they should operate."[87] USU hired William Carroll, a former Utah State professor of swine husbandry and the retired dean of agriculture at the University of Illinois, to collaborate with Karaj College administrators on a comprehensive plan for the college's development in the fall of 1954.

Carroll proved to be a catalyst for impressive growth at the college. Roskelley recalled that "he established himself in the confidence of the staff," and as a result, "for the first time in the history of the institution, it became evident that change was being made."[88] Mohammad Hassan Mahdavi, who served as dean of the college from 1954 through 1962, added that "he worked hard, he worked with everybody, and they loved him very much." Mahdavi acknowledged that it took three years for the Iranian professors to "learn how to cooperate with Americans, and discuss activities of mutual interest," but relations between the American advisers and the Iranian faculty certainly improved during the two years Carroll spent at Karaj.[89] The master plan Carroll helped develop emphasized the building of new classroom buildings, laboratories, and residences for both students and faculty. The lack of adequate housing proved to be one factor that prevented the college from growing; it also forced many of the professors to live in Tehran, where they spent much of their time away from the students. The college implemented Carroll's plan between 1956 and 1961, aided by more than $1 million of Point Four money.

The building progress created excitement, but it also encountered hiccups. The college "experienced great difficulty in obtaining adequate and timely financing" from the Iranian government, while changes within Point Four contracts and the housing shortage left the USU team without a full complement of advisers in late 1957 and early 1958.[90] Enrollment more than tripled between 1952 and 1958 despite these obstacles. The college added new housing for 500 students and 30 faculty families by 1960. It completed two large classroom buildings equipped with modern laboratories and developed a suitable library. It also expanded an experiment and demonstration farm by leveling new fields, constructing a large new machinery shed, drilling four deep wells, and equipping them with modern irrigation pumps. Despite some frustrating delays, Karaj Agricultural College boasted a modern and aesthetically pleasing campus by the end of 1961.

The college became the USU advisers' main focus by the late 1950s. The majority of USU advisers in Iran were working at the college by 1958, and its development had become their exclusive focus in 1961. The Utah State advisers hoped the new arrangements would allow them to impart more characteristics of an American land-grant institution on the college. Roskelley observed that while William Carroll's plan for the college had transformed the physical campus, "emphasis on improving teaching was conspicuously absent." Following a two-week inspection trip to Iran in the spring of 1958, during which he visited Karaj Agricultural College, USU president Daryl Chase appealed directly to Rudger Walker to lead the effort in curriculum reform. As the university's longtime dean of agriculture, Walker had supported the USU projects in Iran from the beginning. He was also remarkably well versed in agricultural higher education in the United States. Walker advised Dean Mahdavi from mid-1958 until the summer of 1960 before turning the reins over to J. Clark Ballard, who was already a veteran of Point Four

FIGURE 4.4. Students and instructors at Karaj Agricultural College, 1953. *Courtesy*, Eldon J. Gardner Photograph Collection, Special Collections and Archives, Merrill-Cazier Library, Utah State University, Logan.

work in Iran, having directed the horticulture division of the rural improvement program between 1951 and 1953. Mahdavi spoke "extremely [favorably]" of Ballard "and the kind of leadership he gave" during the USU team's final four years at Karaj Agricultural College.[91]

The Utah State attempt to infuse the college with American pedagogical practices nevertheless met with limited success. Roskelley noted that "the personnel at Karaj College were reluctant to change, quite resistant to change." They were "very secure" in their curriculum and teaching methods "and weren't about to make any great change."[92] Mahdavi also acknowledged that Iranian faculty members "did not always indicate that they were interested in having Americans on campus" and conceded that "the only reason the Iranian professors put up with Americans was that they brought so much money with them."[93] Among the most persistent obstacles was getting students and professors to embrace farm labor as an important part of their training and research. Carroll explained that most Karaj professors had been educated in a European system that was "divorced from practical application." Moreover, Iranian social convention eschewed manual work for educated officials. The students, Carroll wrote in 1957, "consider any job that requires them to put down their briefcase, or put on work clothes, or to get their hands soiled, to be beneath the dignity of the educated man."[94] The USU advisers nevertheless made some progress on that front. Ballard pointed out that a cadre of "progressive as well as aggressive faculty members," many of whom had received advanced degrees at Utah State, began to incorporate farm work into their courses and research by 1962.[95]

The USU advisers tried to introduce other reforms they felt would make the college more responsive to the nation's agricultural needs; most of them were based on practices common in American land-grant colleges. They convinced the college to adopt a credit system that would allow students to specialize in a particular area. Previously, all students had taken a uniform schedule of classes; failure in one class would prevent a student from moving on to the next year until the deficiency was corrected. Most of the USU advisers also felt the college would benefit from recruiting more students from rural communities. They encouraged the Ministry of Agriculture to allow graduates of agricultural high schools to compete in the entrance examinations.[96] The college proved unable or unwilling to embrace other American practices. The USU advisers, for example, counseled the college to develop a home economics program. Not only was that emerging field one of the few professional avenues open to Iranian women, it also held promise for raising the standards of living for rural families. College leaders appeared interested and hired a home economist to begin planning the program, but "a great deficiency" in living quarters for female students and a lack of classroom space kept the program grounded.[97] In addition, the college farm appears to have languished after the USU advisers left. Leonard Pollard and A. Glenn Wahlquist worked diligently with Iranian staff members to make it "a blooming enterprise" that "everybody could point to with pride." Mahdavi reported that by the late 1960s, however, the farm was "not so much used anymore as an education tool." Rather, it became a source of revenue for other college activities.[98]

Roskelley returned to Karaj in 1967, three years after the last USU advisers left and thirteen years after his own time in Iran had come to an end. He could not hide his disappointment in what he saw. Mohammad Mahdavi had been replaced as dean by a political appointee who had no background in higher education. The curriculum and teaching showed little evidence of practical application. Staff members told him that "any person who would stoop to drive a tractor, pick up a shovel, dig into the soil . . . was unfit to be a university professor." Roskelley reflected that perhaps the advisers had pushed too hard to impose American agricultural practices on the college without sufficiently explaining how they would improve its educational product. Their efforts, while undeniably well-intentioned, had sparked a backlash. "Practically all of the Iranian professors," he acknowledged, felt that the American presence was "a great threat to their own professional standing." Roskelley also thought that perhaps the Americans had also put too much pressure on the administration to expand enrollment too quickly.[99]

Other commentators took a more positive view of American contributions to Karaj Agricultural College. In his assessment of American technical aid in Iran, Gholam Kazemian wrote that the USU "contribution in reorganizing the curriculum and improving teaching was definitely a positive measure toward the agricultural development of Iran." Utah State's "emphasis on the practical aspects of agriculture," he added, was "of great value" to Iranian students "who previously were not exposed to actual farming practices and field work."[100] Former Point Four director Stanley Andrews visited the college in 1961 and reported that "the rapid development" of the institution "is regarded with some pride by the Iranian government."[101] That affirmation represents considerable praise coming from Andrews, who knew the problems associated with technical assistance well and was generally suspicious of attempts to transplant American agricultural pedagogy into other countries. It is also worth remembering that America's own land-grant colleges required several decades of growth and evolution before they became major assets to rural development in the United States.[102] It was unreasonable to expect a faster rate of return in a country with fewer resources and little experience with practical education.

THE UNIVERSITY OF UTAH AND PUBLIC HEALTH

Franklin Harris's extensive travels throughout Iran had made him keenly aware of the tremendous public health challenges the country faced. Iran had just 1 doctor for every 5,000 citizens (compared to 1 doctor for every 750 citizens in the United States), and most worked in the major cities. Rural public health initiatives were still in their infancy, despite the fact that Iranian peasants battled malnutrition and suffered from a daunting array of debilitating diseases.[103] Point Four officials judged the generally poor health of rural Iranians to be the most "formidable barrier to social and economic development" in the country.[104] The University of Utah, meanwhile, operated a modern medical school that trained doctors and surgeons in the latest practices. It is not surprising, then, that Harris heralded the university's decision to join Point Four's rural improvement program as "very good news" in the summer of 1951. Its initial contribution was modest—just two doctors, two nurses, and two sanitary engineers—but Harris could use all the rural health assistance he could get. "We are very much in need of this personnel," he assured President Ray Olpin. "All . . . you can send here will be well used." Point Four medical technicians were already cooperating with the Ministry of Health on malaria eradication, and "the results are most dramatic and satisfying." But there was much to be done.[105]

In contrast to the major role USU advisers played in agriculture, the University of Utah medical team represented only a small piece of Point Four's public health initiatives. Still, they made some inroads. The nursing program in Azerbaijan was "really rolling along," for example, in the summer of 1953. Ruth Brown, who was among the first Utahns to arrive in the fall of 1951, wrote to I. O. Horsfall, project administrator in Salt Lake City, that "we have been so busy we scarcely have time to breathe." Two nurses worked in the region; Mary Virginia Webb handled classroom teaching in Tabriz, while Brown devoted herself to fieldwork in the outlying rural communities.[106]

But the University of Utah team also encountered an array of difficulties that made the work less than satisfying. Part of the problem was that the University of Utah personnel differed in some important ways from their colleagues on the USU and BYU field teams. The LDS identity and missionary zeal was less deeply embedded in the culture of the University of Utah than was the case at BYU and USU. Franklin Harris likewise had less direct influence there than he did at the other two intuitions. Whereas many of the BYU and USU families knew each other and easily bonded into tight-knit communities in Iran, the University of Utah recruited some of its field team from non-academics in private practice. Moreover, Horsfall wondered how well Dean Peterson, who was managing the Utah contracts in Tehran, represented the University of Utah. He complained that people from his university were "getting the little end on the cost of living allowances" compared to advisers

FIGURE 4.5. Point Four's rural public health initiative, early 1950s. *Courtesy*, Richard Welling Roskelley Photograph Collection, Special Collections and Archives, Merrill-Cazier Library, Utah State University, Logan.

from BYU and USU.[107] Concerning negotiations toward the extension of those contracts the following spring, Horsfall lamented that Peterson "seemed to come here as representative only of the USAC [USU] and the BYU." "Quite extensive programs" had been arranged for those two institutions, "but as of yet [there was] nothing but a bare continuance" for his university."[108]

The University of Utah field team also suffered a number of personal tragedies. William McSwain had to leave Iran to seek medical treatment in the summer of 1953.[109] Sanitary engineer Orrin "Bud" Miller and his wife, Jane, endured a very difficult 1952. They were stationed in Shiraz, but their infant son contracted a serious illness in February that caused them to spend several months in Tehran. The family welcomed another child in December, but that baby was born six weeks prematurely and died before the end of the year.[110] Miller later requested transportation home, apparently confused and frustrated about the nature of his assignment. The experience left both Miller and his wife deeply saddened; he later returned to Tehran to visit the cemetery in which his infant child was buried.[111]

The worst tragedy, however, came on Christmas Day 1952 when Nurse Cecile DeMoisy died in a plane crash outside Tehran. DeMoisy was among the first University of Utah people to arrive in Tehran back in November 1951, and she was stationed in Shiraz, where she shared an apartment with the Millers. She was traveling to Tehran for a holiday vacation when her plane crashed two miles from the airport while attempting to land in heavy fog early in the evening. Three other Americans died in the accident that claimed all but two of the twenty-five people onboard. One of the survivors, an Iranian Point Four engineer, sought help on foot, and local authorities found the wreck by late evening.[112] A local photographer apparently posed DeMoisy's body against the wrecked plane and took a photograph that appeared in a Tehran newspaper. The picture haunted Lula Anderson for a long time afterward.[113] Dean Peterson and William Warne retrieved DeMoisy's body the morning after Christmas. The Point Four community held a memorial service in Tehran; her body was sent home to Ogden for burial. Warne eulogized her as "a valiant worker" who "made a host of friends" and "was admired by Iranians and Americans alike."[114] Edith DeMoisy recalled that her daughter had helped deliver her Iranian gardener's baby just weeks before the crash. She asked that most of Cecile's personal items and medical clothing be donated to that gardener and to the hospital in Shiraz.[115] The accident came almost a year to the date following the one that killed Henry Bennett and Benjamin Hardy at the same airport and under very similar circumstances near the end of 1951.

Finally, the University of Utah struggled to find medical personnel with appropriate expertise to address the health problems common in rural Iran. Alfred Lazarus, a virologist who specialized in trachoma, provided valuable expertise in treating that common and debilitating disease, but his assignment ended in the spring of 1953, leaving Point Four in urgent need of a qualified replacement.[116] His colleague L.H.O. Stobbe, in contrast, accepted a Point Four assignment thinking he would advise Iranian doctors on better medical training, surgery practice, and obstetrical care. He soon found, however, that Point Four actually needed doctors who could work in the field "helping the destitute villagers symptomatically." Stobbe was willing to engage in such "operation grassroots" work because he "want[ed] to be loyal to Point IV," but he expressed a desire for work "on a much higher plane, with more authority and more in the line of a physician and surgeon."[117] Unfortunately, the rural improvement program had few such lofty positions in its public health repertoire. Stobbe did provide much of the primary medical care for the Utah families in Iran, including delivering at least three of their babies.[118] His frustration reflected problems common to using American doctors to tackle public health problems in the developing world: Point Four assignments required that doctors have a working knowledge of diseases that were rare in the United States and that they eschew the modern facilities and prestige that came with practicing medicine in the United States for decidedly more primitive conditions overseas. Most of the University of Utah public health team nevertheless performed well in the field. Horsfall reported that the morale of the field team was generally high throughout 1952.[119] The University of Utah's participation in public health began to taper off a year later, however, and it ended in 1956 as the institution moved on to other projects.

ASSESSING THE RURAL IMPROVEMENT INITIATIVES

The record of Utah accomplishments regarding Iranian agriculture and public health is not easy to evaluate. All American contributions, we must remember, represented only part of the Iranian government's much broader development schemes. The efforts of the Utah advisers, though very substantial in agriculture, were modest when stacked against the country's overall needs. The limited US technical assistance budget and Point Four's emphasis on low modernization meant it could provide little more than a primer for Iranian development. The work of the University of Utah rural health advisers in particular was dwarfed by the Iranian government's much larger and better-known initiatives to vaccinate children and eradicate malaria.[120]

In turning our attention to agricultural advisers, commentators have emphasized that Point Four's significant contributions came not in creating successful programs but rather in nurturing innovation in agricultural research and extension work.[121] Kazemian acknowledged that Point Four "introduced certain revolutionary measures which would have otherwise been very difficult, if not impossible, for the Iranian Government to undertake" and added that its work on the extension service was "the most constructive element of American technical aid."[122] Economist and former cabinet minister Jahangir Amuzegar likewise ranked new research initiatives, especially on disease-resistant seed, among Point Four's most remarkable contributions, though he also noted that work in other areas such as irrigation improvement produced less impressive results.[123] Stanley Andrews also praised the

"really significant progress" USU advisers made in developing both the extension service and Karaj Agricultural College.[124] Mark Gasiorowski has similarly noted that "probably the most effective aspect of US agricultural assistance was its focus on education."[125] Bruce Anderson, in contrast, sensed that
the agricultural program's emphasis on research actually defected attention
away from training between 1952 and 1954.[126]

Still, the rural improvement program fell short of its lofty expectations.
Stark differences between American and Iranian administrative practices presented constant challenges, and frequent turnover of personnel on both sides
made them harder to overcome. Iran had eight different cabinets during the
1950s. Each brought in a new set of ministers, and personal rivalries often led
new ministers to discard the policies of their predecessors. High turnover
was also common among American technical advisers. A normal assignment
was two years, but the effective service of many Utahns was only twenty-two
months because of the common practice of storing leave time for use at the
end of an assignment. Four different USU advisers directed agricultural operations in both Fars and Azerbaijan, two of Iran's most important agricultural
provinces, between 1952 and 1956. Some of the changes reflected reassign-
ment of advisers who were already experienced in Iranian agriculture. Bert
Despain served in Azerbaijan in 1952 and 1953 before moving to Gilan in 1954.
Melvin Peterson made a steady southward journey during his five years in
Iran—from Mazanderan on the Caspian Sea (1952–53) to Isfahan (1953–55) and
finally to Fars (1955–57).[127] Each new assignment, of course, required advisers
to develop an understanding of local problems and build working relations
with local leaders. They also had to learn what their predecessors had been
doing. It could all take months. The process was much more daunting for
those who were just arriving in Iran. "It takes time to learn about this country," Roskelley reminded Madsen in 1953, "to understand the problems, and
to develop patterns of working with the people."[128]

It also appears that the process of integration, coming only four years
after the initiation of most agricultural projects, stunted the effectiveness of
rural improvement. Point Four officials were naturally eager to turn more
administrative and financial responsibility over to the Iranian government as
quickly as possible, but in so doing they truncated the promising starts some
projects had shown. Many of the agricultural programs, especially the extension service, were still in their early developmental phase in the mid-1950s,

and the Ministry of Agriculture lacked the administrative capacity to take full responsibility for their operation.[129] The ministry also lost the services of approximately 3,600 Iranian Point Four technicians when the US government scaled back its support. Kazemian reports that the ministry had agreed to hire these agents but decided that they lacked the necessary qualifications.[130] Bertis Embry complained in 1962 that the United States "seems to want to turn over all [it] can" to Iranians "who neither know how to operate or in many cases [don't] want to know." The predictable result was that "much time, effort, and materials are wasted."[131] Something similar happened at Karaj Agricultural College, where the USU advisers and even some Iranian staff members felt American support should continue beyond the summer of 1964. According to Dean Mahdavi, however, "somebody decided we should be on our own."[132]

In retrospect, it seems clear that the US government overemphasized what technical assistance could do for rural improvement and how quickly it could be accomplished. Economist Demos Hadjiyanis noted in 1954 that "the agrarian structure of the country with the extremely uneven distribution of farm property" limited Point Four's success.[133] Historian Nikki Keddie has likewise observed that unrelenting poverty and the persistent power of landlords diminished the effectiveness of American agricultural assistance.[134] Genuine rural transformation, then, required more than demonstrating improved farming and public health practices. Ultimately, Iranian society had to be fundamentally reordered, and that was beyond the capacity of Point Four's low-modernization projects. Indeed, one Eastern European diplomat criticized small-scale community development projects for "avoiding the basic problems of social reforms."[135] The Iranian government was not insensitive to the need for underlying social transformation. Indeed, the shah embraced rural development in part because he saw it as a golden opportunity to reduce the power of landlords and the religious establishment.[136] But even Iranian attempts to transform the countryside fell well short of meeting expectations. Historians have found that the standards of living for many rural Iranians rose little between the 1950s and the 1970s. Neither the amount of land under cultivation nor overall agricultural productivity increased significantly despite nearly twenty years of foreign aid and more attention from the Iranian government.[137]

The problems the Utah rural improvement advisers encountered were not unique to Point Four operations in Iran. In a 1961 survey of US agricultural assistance to nine countries, former Point Four director Stanley Andrews found that few projects had become self-sustaining before being turned over to host governments. He identified several common factors that blunted their effectiveness, including inadequate programs to train extension agents, administrative shortcomings—especially in local governments—and instability in political and economic institutions.[138] All of these issues were present to some degree in Iran. The difficulties USU advisers encountered in trying to develop cooperative farms, such as interference from landlords and creditors, likewise mirrored similar American efforts in many other countries.[139] Further, Karaj Agricultural College was not the only place where American advisers struggled to introduce American concepts of higher education. Advisers from the University of Nebraska, for example, encountered similar resistance from Turkish professors when they tried to bring the land-grant concept to Ataturk University between 1954 and 1968.[140] Indeed, studies on technical assistance conducted during the early 1960s found that fewer than half of the projects that tried to introduce land-grant education into developing countries showed any positive results, and even when they did, the "land-grant pattern was not accepted in a form anywhere near that which the Americans desired."[141] A team of advisers from the University of Pennsylvania similarly met strong resistance when they attempted to transform Pahlavi University into a comprehensive American-style research institution between 1962 and 1968. An American botany professor captured the frustration of the Penn team when he wrote, "Pahlavi Univ., plain and simple, wishes we would take our concepts, innovations, motives, and so forth and get the hell out—But leave the money, the equipment, the books."[142] From the perspective of that ill-fated venture, the USU experience at Karaj Agricultural College appears much more productive and certainly more cooperative.

CONCLUSION

The Utah advisers came to Iran with high hopes that their expertise would uplift the country's impoverished rural peasants, but the results proved less than glamorous. Concepts that had been beneficial to American agriculture, especially research and extension, needed to be developed almost from scratch. Moreover, socioeconomic conditions in the United States were much more favorable to low-modernization rural development than were those in

Iran. The Utah rural improvement advisers approached their projects with laudable sincerity, and they helped cultivate some modest localized successes. But making the Iranian desert bloom would take much more time and social change than a small foreign technical assistance program could muster. "It was very difficult to change these people from the agriculture of two thousand years ago into the agriculture of the twentieth century," recalled Bert Embry years later. "You don't change things very fast."[143]

5

MODERNIZING IRANIAN EDUCATION

Until the young teachers . . . relate the importance of education to meeting individual, community, and national needs, their educational system will remain impractical and artificial.

    A. Reed Morrill, BYU adviser in Iran, 1953–55, 1959–61

My major concern has been education for the women of the Nation [Iran].

    Malno Reichert, BYU adviser in Iran, 1957–61

Brigham Young University (BYU) supported two Point Four contracts that were designed to help the Iranian government expand and improve public education. The first began in 1951 and provided basic training in American pedagogical practices to Iranian teachers through a series of summer courses and at select demonstration schools. Glen Gagon of the BYU team also helped Iranian educator Mohammad Bahmanbaigi develop mobile tent schools for the nomadic Qashqai and Basseri tribes of Fars in southwestern Iran. Those projects ended amid a controversy with Point Four officials

DOI: 10.7330/9781607327547.c005

during the Eisenhower administration's reorganization of technical assistance in the summer of 1955. BYU's second project focused on improving Daneshsaraye Ali, the teachers' college of the University of Tehran, from September 1957 until September 1961.

The BYU advisers put their hearts into these ventures, but they faced momentous challenges. Public education in Iran dated only from the 1920s, and the majority of children still did not attend school in 1950. Iranian schools suffered from a shortage of teachers at all levels, especially in rural communities, and many elementary school teachers had no more than six or seven years of formal education and little pedagogical training. As with the agricultural and public health initiatives, the scope of the country's educational needs coupled with the relatively brief duration of the BYU projects limited their effectiveness. Moreover, the BYU advisers tried to bring fundamental changes to Iranian education by transplanting more aspects of American school curricula and teaching practices into the country's schools. In attempting to reweave the fabric of education, the Utahns stretched the limits of low modernization and found themselves at odds with Iranians who resented their activities as foreign meddling. Indeed, the advisers' very presence seemed to underscore their sense of American superiority and the inferiority of Iranian schools. Iranian administrators, teachers, and parents embraced what they found useful in the BYU program but discarded concepts that deviated too far from accepted practices. While the tent schools probably did improve the prospects of nomadic children in a rapidly modernizing Iran, they were also part of an Iranian government scheme to blunt tribal identity and, ultimately, to terminate the tribal way of life. In this case, the BYU advisers' progressive sensibilities led them to cooperate with the coercive power of the Iranian state.

IRANIAN PUBLIC EDUCATION IN THE MID-TWENTIETH CENTURY

Nationwide public elementary education was still new to Iran when BYU's Point Four advisers arrived. The Majlis enacted the country's first compulsory public education law in 1911 during the ferment of the constitutional revolution. Deputies celebrated universal elementary education as a "means to achieve greater social and political justice," but the government lacked the resources to implement it.[1] The first serious attempts at creating national primary education came as part of Reza Shah's campaign to modernize and westernize the country during the interwar years. The Iranian government recognized that widespread illiteracy, probably around 85 percent nationwide, represented a serious impediment to national development. They also hoped compulsory state-controlled education would encourage national unity and foster civic-mindedness in the country's youth.[2] The Ministry of Education put increased emphasis on educating girls, who would become "the mothers of the great men of tomorrow." It declared that women should "benefit from all the blessings of science, knowledge, civilization, and education" in order to "form healthy and useful families and to educate the brave patriotic children of the country."[3]

Despite the push to create national public education during the interwar years, fewer than half of all Iranian children were attending school in the early 1950s.[4] Girls still accounted for less than a third of elementary school students because of the reluctance of conservative parents to educate their daughters and a scarcity of female teachers—Iranian schools observed gender segregation after the fourth grade.[5] Educational opportunities were even bleaker outside the major urban areas. Fewer than one in five rural children attended school, and most Iranian villages still lacked even a crude elementary school.[6] Few Iranian children completed more than six years of formal education. A 1953 BYU survey found that only about 13 percent of seventh graders went on to finish high school. Many rural parents saw their children as productive laborers at an early age, which resulted in a high rate of absenteeism at important times in the agricultural cycle. Some parents also placed a low value on education's ability to train children for work.[7]

Students who could attend school often had to do so in conditions that were far less than ideal. Issa Sadiq, an American-educated pioneer of modern Iranian education, reported in 1931 that few Iranian school buildings had been constructed for that purpose. Many lacked basic sanitary facilities.[8] Classrooms were often overcrowded, leaving teachers little time to spend with individual students.[9] Max Berryessa, who directed Point Four demonstration schools in Tehran, recalled elementary school conditions when he arrived in 1951. The single classroom was about the size of an average living room and contained "forty boys, no girls, squatting on a dirt floor." The only light in the room came through a hole in the wooden door. There were no textbooks. Blackboards had been improvised from painted plywood, and teachers made the chalk. There were no paper or pencils. It was clearly a "hard thing for the teachers and a poor educational environment for the students."[10]

Reza Shah viewed public education as a means of consolidating political power and homogenizing the country. The system was therefore highly centralized, with a curriculum designed to promote Persian nationalism and blunt tribal and religious influence.[11] The Ministry of Education pursued an "orderly and fixed program" of precise and uniform instruction; local officials could do little except implement policies handed down from above.[12] The BYU advisers reported that the Ministry of Education even dictated that heating stoves be turned on and off on the same day each fall and spring in all parts of the country, though climate varied greatly.[13] The system discouraged innovation and creativity in the classroom. In the words of Issa Sadiq, it "destroys all initiative and quenches all fire of leadership."[14] Ahmad Fattahipour similarly found that Reza Shah's "authoritarian personality kept progressive ideas repressed."[15] Learning relied on rote memorization as measured in annual examinations.[16] There was little emphasis on practical problem solving and other real-life applications of knowledge that would be helpful to national development. "Scholasticism," according to one prominent Western scholar, "was carried to ridiculous extremes." In botany, for example, students were required to learn the names of vegetables but apparently did not have to distinguish between poisonous and edible mushrooms.[17] A primary purpose of Iranian education was to train obedient public officials, so graduates were taught to carry out instructions without variation. Pioneering social worker Sattareh Farman Farmaian argues that Reza Shah created public education "not to produce discerning members of a free society but to turn out loyal, unquestioning subjects." Schools taught students that "unthinking obedience to authority was a virtue."[18] The educated Iranian, concluded sociologist Norman Jacobs, was "quick to copy and serve those in authority" but could "not operate effectively in a critical environment."[19]

To train more teachers, the Ministry of Education opened its first normal school in 1918. Located in Tehran, it was a modest enterprise that initially employed only six fulltime teachers and accepted students with a ninth-grade education. Its upper-level program became the Dar ul-Moalemine-Ali, or the Teacher's Training College, in 1928, and applicants were required to have a high school diploma. The college therefore became the first university-level institution for training teachers in Iran. It later became known as the Daneshsaraye Ali (House of Higher Knowledge) and was attached to the University of Tehran in 1934.[20] Education reformers likewise sought to make both teaching practices and the subjects taught more reflective of the country's needs. As early as the late 1920s, Issa Sadiq was attempting to replace the reliance on memorization with a more pragmatic approach to teaching, and the government began organizing adult reading classes in 1936 as part of a national campaign against illiteracy.[21] The Near East Foundation (NEF) emphasized practical training in agriculture and vocational skills during the 1940s, and it educated girls to be village teachers and home extension agents. The NEF assisted the Ministry of Education in establishing a teacher training school for girls at Ghaleh Nou outside Tehran in 1954.[22]

But the expansion of Iranian schools and the professionalization of teachers happened very slowly, especially at the elementary level and in the countryside. Public spending on education increased more than tenfold between 1925 and 1939, but it still represented only about 4 percent of the annual budget in an era when the military accounted for the majority of government appropriations.[23] Even more telling, the number of schools and teachers grew only half as much as attendance, which added to the problem of overcrowding.[24] The public's growing demand for schools far outpaced the government's ability to build, staff, and maintain them. Most rural teachers still lacked a high school education in 1950; it was common for elementary school teachers to have as little as six years of formal education. Many had no pedagogical training.[25] Historian David Menashri notes that overall, teacher qualifications actually declined between 1925 and 1945 as the Ministry of Education scrambled to keep pace with increasing demand. Low salaries and social standing, especially for elementary school teachers, coupled with competition from urban-based professions discouraged the brightest high school graduates from becoming teachers.[26]

DEMONSTRATION SCHOOLS AND SUMMER
TEACHER TRAINING COURSES

It was in this educational environment that the BYU advisers began work in late 1951. The initial contract involved six advisers working to improve elementary teaching practices in Tehran and the surrounding provinces. When he took a moment to reflect on his experience in Iran, secondary education

FIGURE 5.1. Rural Iranian school, early 1950s. *Courtesy*, Richard Welling Roskelley Photograph Collection, Special Collections and Archives, Merrill-Cazier Library, Utah State University, Logan.

adviser A. Reed Morrill noted that "many of the present mal-practices and unsound concepts are present because of poor and improper training of the teachers."[27] Morrill's colleagues began by experimenting with two demonstration schools. The BYU team followed Issa Sadiq in emphasizing practices that would cultivate students' love of learning and help them develop practical problem-solving skills. They hoped to illustrate that "school was a place where boys and girls could learn to think, analyze data, and develop procedures necessary in solving problems in life situations."[28]

Isfahanik, a small village outside Isfahan in central Iran, became the site of the first demonstration center. The village had never had a formal school, and many children suffered from malaria brought by mosquitoes in the moats around a nearby discarded fort. An Iranian colleague cleared away the stagnant water and started building a school with sanitary facilities while another created a school garden for use in botany and homemaking classes. BYU advisers and their Iranian partners developed an orchard, started poultry production, and built a new playground at a second demonstration school in Kamalabad, about thirty miles west of Tehran. According to Franklin Harris, the local population in each town showed initial reluctance to participate. They had previously "thought of school as something remote from their interest," but the garden, orchard, and poultry projects captured their interest. Once they saw that school activities could improve their lives, families became more willing to enroll their children.[29] As with the Utah State University (USU) agricultural advisers, BYU educators discovered the importance of winning the confidence of local people.

Point Four expanded the project in 1952 by starting more demonstration schools in Tehran; they added thirteen others around the country the following year. The schools helped American advisers establish relationships with local communities and provided platforms for modeling teaching technique to Iranian teachers. Public reaction was often encouraging, even in areas where the population showed initial skepticism. BYU advisers complained, for example, that the mayor of Rasht on the Caspian Sea assigned low-achieving students to the demonstration school in an attempt to discredit it. But the school earned praise when its students posted the highest marks with the fewest failures in the city on the annual examinations. Some schools soon required a waiting list; the mayor of Rasht even decided to enroll his children.[30] The BYU team opened its first demonstration secondary schools in 1953 and had at least one such school in all provinces by the fall of 1954.[31] These schools also emphasized education in vocational fields such as carpentry and home economics that were not widely taught in Iranian schools. The latter was particularly important for promoting better health in rural communities and for being among the very few professional career options open to rural Iranian women.[32] Advisers in Tehran purchased Persian typewriters to conduct typing classes. The courses proved successful enough that the Ministry of Education requested help in setting up similar courses for its employees. The shah even made a personal visit.[33]

The single largest BYU teacher training project was a series of summer courses for practicing teachers that ran from 1952 until 1955. The courses, taught by both Iranian and American instructors, emphasized the practical over the theoretical because few of the teachers had previous pedagogical training. They encouraged student participation in lessons, demonstrated cost-effective ways to construct visual aids that would enhance the learning environment, and taught teachers how to make basic repairs to school equipment.[34] Like the USU advisers at Karaj Agricultural College, the BYU team had to convince Iranian teachers that performing necessary manual labor was not beneath the dignity of a professional educator. Most were reluctant to break social tradition, but it helped to see American professors wielding hammers and saws. The teachers' objections to working with their hands gradually lessened, replaced by a desire to improve the functionality of their schools. The Ministry of Education selected forty-five of the best-qualified rural elementary school teachers from seven provinces to participate in the first summer course in 1952. These teachers played an invaluable role in passing along what they had learned to their colleagues. The summer training courses relied heavily on such teachers because there were very few American advisers, especially in the most sparsely populated provinces, where illiteracy was highest and access to education lowest.[35]

The first summer program helped build good working relationships between BYU advisers and the Iranian educators who orchestrated the program in the provinces. The cooperation, in turn, allowed the program to grow rapidly. Female teachers and representatives of the Qashqai tribe participated for the first time in 1953.[36] The program began offering similar courses for secondary school teachers the following summer. More than 6,000 teachers were participating by the conclusion of the fourth summer program in 1955.[37] Point Four documents suggest that the courses were generally popular among Iranian teachers, many of whom reported an enhanced outlook on the teaching profession.[38] Several provincial education directors asked for the project to be expanded in their districts; one requested that all 3,000 teachers under his supervision take part.[39] The BYU advisers were cognizant, however, that vocal critics within the teaching profession condemned their work as a thinly veiled tool of imperialism.[40] Education director Hoyt Turner estimated, and no doubt exaggerated, that 80 percent of Iranian teachers sympathized with communism.[41] The Americans were determined to silence these critics by showing that US approaches to education could be beneficial to Iran. Rissa Clarke, who helped organize the training courses in 1954 and 1955, remained popular with her Iranian colleagues when she returned with her husband for a second assignment in 1962. "Wherever she appeared," wrote Alva John Clarke in his memoir, "the word spread of her presence." Former students called on her or sent greetings. Several had since risen to become principals or district administrators. They were "anxious and proud to have her see what they had done with the ideas they had received in summer sessions."[42]

For ten years, the summer in-service training courses remained the most extensive Point Four effort to promote professional teacher education in Iran.

At the end of 1959 the program had held 755 courses, most taught by Iranian educators, and had reached most of the country's practicing elementary school teachers. This was no small feat in a country where dirt roads and travel by horse or mule were still common in many rural areas. The accomplishment underscores the dedication and tenacity of the Point Four team but even more so that of the Iranian teachers who did much of the work in the provinces. By the mid-1950s the Point Four team had also designed courses for principals and county directors as well as for the teachers of the newest educational level in Iran: kindergarten.[43]

Iranian teachers played an essential role in the success of the demonstration schools and summer training programs. Language and culture barriers required translators who could communicate educational concepts that were unfamiliar to most Iranians. Discussions of pedagogical approaches inevitably created disagreements, and they occasionally caused friction or exacerbated personality conflicts. But those cases do not seem to have been the norm. Most BYU advisers appreciated that they could not simply dictate to the Iranians or expect that American practices would translate seamlessly to Iran. Rather, they had to work in an equal partnership with Iranians, listening to the teachers and respecting their views.[44] "If we fail in the development of good personnel relations," observed Morrill, "the key to all accomplishment will be lost."[45] Clarke experienced a similar moment of humility when he returned to Iran in 1962 to advise the Ministry of Education on secondary school curriculum reform. "Could I make them see," he wondered, "that I had no desire to tell them what they must do or to transplant an American Curriculum to Iran?"[46]

Both the demonstration schools and the summer training courses continued after the BYU project ended in 1955, but they appear to have lost much of their steam. Clarence Hendershot, who was education director in Iran when the in-service program terminated in 1961, observed that it languished "due primarily to changes in the Ministry [of Education] which brought into power men who had other interests."[47] It also seems that in attempting to provide modest in-service training for thousands of Iranian teachers, the reach of the BYU advisers exceeded their grasp. Perhaps they would have been better served by providing more concerted training to new teachers and then periodically following up as they progressed in the profession. The demonstration schools, too, showed evidence of having achieved largely ephemeral results. Upon returning to Iran to assist the National Teacher's College in 1959, Morrill lamented that the schools had become "typically Iranian in organization, methods of teaching, and results obtained." Many functioned irregularly.[48] The demonstration schools and the summer teacher training courses illustrate two fundamental realities of Point Four education assistance in developing countries. First, results would necessarily be limited given the program's scope and resources. American advisers had to realize that it was unrealistic to expect dramatic transformation quickly. Second, educators and public officials in the host countries would ultimately determine the long-term impact of education assistance projects; they would determine which concepts took root and which would ultimately be discarded.

TENT SCHOOLS FOR TRIBAL NOMADS

Glen Gagon of the BYU team assisted with an innovative attempt to design portable schools for the nomadic tribes of southwestern Iran. Of these, the most successful effort concerned the Qashqai, a confederation of Turkic-speaking tribes who lived around Shiraz and numbered between 150,000 and 200,000 in the mid-twentieth century. Most Qashqai split their time between summer pastures in the highlands of the Zagros Mountains and winter pastures 300 miles to the southeast at the base of the range. Iran's tribal population enjoyed a large degree of autonomy from weak central governments before the early twentieth century, but the Iranian state embarked on concerted efforts to end nomadism and bring the tribes under state control from the 1920s through the 1970s.[49] The expansion of state power presented a serious threat to the economic foundations of nomadic life, as well as to tribal cohesion and cultural identity. Reza Shah employed crushing military power to bludgeon many tribal communities into cooperation during the 1930s, a process that deliberately wreaked havoc on the livelihoods of nomadic herdsmen. His son, Mohammad Reza Shah Pahlavi, used the country's expanding national education system as a vehicle for settling and Persianizing tribal youth two decades later.[50] Gagon therefore found himself engaged in a project that enhanced the educational outlook for tribal children but also cooperated with a state that often used violence and coercion to marginalize tribal life.

The story of tribal education in Iran begins with Mohammad Bahmanbaigi, who was born in 1920 or 1921 into "a life with guns, and bullets and the sound of horses."[51] He spent his first ten years among kin, where his father was a chief of the Bahmanbaiglu sub-tribe and worked for one of the most powerful Qashqai khans.[52] Though not a powerful figure in his own right, Bahmanbaigi's father nevertheless had to relocate to Tehran during the early 1930s as part of Reza Shah's attempt to impose state control on tribal leaders. The exile threw the family into poverty, but it also allowed the young Bahmanbaigi to attend school, where he established a reputation as a good student. He graduated from the University of Tehran with a law degree in 1942, an accomplishment that earned him "a high level of social respect, popularity, and political influence" within the tribe.[53] Bahmanbaigi briefly practiced law and worked for the Iranian national bank during the 1940s, but his real passion was education.[54] Illiteracy was very high among Iran's tribal population in the mid-twentieth century because formal education offered limited advantages to nomads. A handful of men could read and write well enough to keep important records, but it was far more important for most tribal children to learn skills in horsemanship, hunting, weaving, and caring for livestock.

The experience of the 1930s, however, encouraged more Qashqai to value formal education as a means of improving social mobility in a modernizing and increasingly literate society.[55] Bahmanbaigi's own studies of Iranian nomadism convinced him that the pastoral lifestyle held no future for the tribes of Fars. Years later he admitted, "Except for the teachers, I tell our students, 'Don't go back to your people . . . The real power to help them lies not in black tents [nomadism] but where the money and decisions are made—in government, industry, and the professions.'"[56] The only productive future he saw for tribal children was through education. "The key to our problem," he wrote in 1959, "is to be found in the alphabet."[57] Bahmanbaigi began by teaching his neighbors to read and write in the late 1940s and had established a handful of schools in summer and winter pastures by 1950.[58]

Bahmanbaigi approached the Iranian government in 1951 with a proposal to develop mobile tent schools and a plan to train tribal teachers. The Ministry of Education refused to fund the project, however, because of the poor results it had achieved in earlier attempts at creating tribal schools during the 1940s.[59] After failing to secure financial support from the government, Bahmanbaigi turned to the Point Four Program. Glen Gagon, a Utah teacher and one of Max Berryessa's BYU graduate students, became his main American assistant. The Point Four mission in Iran added Bahmanbaigi to its payroll and worked out an arrangement whereby Point Four would provide supplies and help train teachers, Bahmanbaigi would supervise the schools, and the tribes would pay the teachers' salaries.[60] Their work concentrated on Bahmanbaigi's Qashqai tribe and the neighboring Basseri tribe. Bahmanbaigi conducted the annual examinations during the program's early years. The Point Four staff arranged for Gagon to work out of its Shiraz office, but the April 1953 attack on that facility ruined much of his preliminary data collection.[61]

Gagon's contributions nearly ended before they really began. When delays threatened the teacher training program in May 1953, Gagon appealed directly to a leading Qashqai khan, who was serving in parliament. The minister of education reacted fiercely to such an initiative that had failed to consult his office and requested that Point Four eject Gagon from the country. Only the intercession of a government official who had previously worked with Point Four allowed Gagon to stay. That incident was not the end of Gagon's political difficulties. August 1953 brought the coup that removed Mohammad Mossadegh from power, and the Qashqai leadership supported the prime minister. Reasons included both their profound distrust of the monarchy and their positive view of Mossadegh from his days as governor of Fars thirty years earlier. The Qashqai also supported the prime minister's parliamentary fight to nationalize the Iranian oil industry. Rumors that Mossadegh supporters had fled into Qashqai territory following the coup brought an acute threat of armed conflict to the area during the summer of 1953.[62]

Gagon's first assignment in Iran came to an end in September 1953, and he was forced to return to the United States. It had been a frustrating two years. Bahmanbaigi laid the groundwork for the tent schools, and Point Four started working with teachers, but the political crisis and Gagon's own indiscretion prevented the project from going any further. Gagon returned to Iran in January 1954, this time without his family, as the Department of State would not allow them back into Iran because of concerns about their safety. Through Bahmanbaigi, he learned that the Qashqai had avoided a confrontation with the army when three of its most important khans had accepted exile abroad. The tent school program could finally begin.[63]

The schools Bahmanbaigi devised had to be light and durable. They consisted of a circular white tent, textbooks, notebooks, chalk, pencils, soccer and volleyballs for recreation, and a tent to serve as a sanitary latrine. Few of the children used desks, favoring simple lapboards that would allow them to sit on carpets spread over the ground. Nearly 200 tribal students were enrolled in six such schools by 1956. Clarence Hendershot, Point Four's education director and a frequent visitor to the schools, describes the proceedings of the schools as "orderly informality":

> The boys and girls squat together on colorful rugs, usually facing a small blackboard resting on crude posts like an easel, often with a bag of chalk lying on the ground underneath. The upper classes may be sitting in small groups nearby in the open, or in the shade, if any is to be found. All are intent on their books, or the blackboard. The monitor system is common, the older children teaching the younger, or one child works a problem on the blackboard while the others watch, being quick to raise a hand if an error is noted. The concentration of mind, the alertness to every development, the complete absorption of their minds in the learning situation make for a speed of accomplishment not found in many schools.[64]

The tent schools faced serious shortages of funding and teachers during those early years. The Ministry of Education provided no financial support until sometime between 1955 and 1957.[65] Instead, the Iranian government encouraged tribal children to attend the permanent schools in Shiraz. Bahmanbaigi solicited funds from wealthy tribal families, but that was not a sustainable solution. The ministry apparently did provide non-Qashqai teachers in 1955–56. Unfortunately, few non-tribal Iranians were attracted to the arduous nomadic life.[66] Most of the teachers therefore came from settled, literate Qashqai who spoke the Turkish dialect and shared tribal values. Many were already working as private tutors for well-off Qashqai families.[67] The tribal teachers often lacked the requisite formal education to be paid public school teachers, however, so recruiting properly credentialed teachers remained a problem until the ministry's Bureau of Tribal Education opened a normal school in Shiraz in 1957 to train teachers. Admission was initially based on "literacy and general ability" because few tribal young people could meet the usual admission requirement of six years of formal education. The tribal normal school at Shiraz produced nearly 500 teachers in its first decade and about 8,000 by 1977.[68]

American participation in Iranian tribal education declined rapidly after 1955 when the BYU contract ended. The Iranian Ministry of Education assumed financial responsibility for the schools soon thereafter, and Bahmanbaigi left the Point Four payroll.[69]

Western observers have celebrated the tent schools as a success, especially from the perspective of providing tribal youth with the basic skills necessary to operate in an increasingly modern society. Paul Barker, an American Peace Corps volunteer who worked on nomadic education in Shiraz from 1973 through 1975, noted that tribal children seemed to be healthier than those who lived in villages. A vigorous outdoor life and strict standards for teacher hygiene contributed to a healthful environment.[70] As director of tribal education, Bahmanbaigi meticulously inspected the schools and their teachers. Point Four data indicate that tribal children performed better on national exams than did those who attended urban schools. The failure rate was less than 3 percent for the first two grades, and children with the best attendance often advanced more than one grade in a single year.[71] Bahmanbaigi forbade the use of corporal punishment and encouraged parents to send their daughters to the schools. Almost 30 percent of the nearly 112,000 children who attended the schools between 1953 and 1978 were girls. The tribal normal school first admitted girls in 1962; nearly 300 had graduated by 1975.[72] "Many would argue," Barker concluded, "that it has been the most excitingly successful educational experiment in modern Iranian history," though he described Point Four contributions as "fumbling."[73] James Dunhill of the United Nations Educational, Scientific, and Cultural Organization (UNESCO) called the schools "the most astonishing single feat of education I have ever seen."[74] "With deepest satisfaction," Bahmanbaigi reflected, "I have heard foreign observers praise our tribal schools."[75]

Iranian responses, in contrast, have been more restrained and tend to emphasize formal public education as a means of suppressing tribal identities and culture. Political scientist Abbas Milani, for example, celebrates Bahmanbaigi's "uncanny dedication" to "creating a national commonwealth through a shared alphabet," but he also acknowledges that the schools were a "subtle form of subversive activity" designed to make tribal children loyal citizens of the Iranian state.[76] Anthropologist Soheila Shahshahani is far more direct. She calls tribal education an "oppressive pedagogy" that employed coercion to redirect the identities of tribal children toward the state. She notes that while Western observers praised the tent schools, most tribal schools were sedentary by 1978, which speaks to the government's underlying goal of using education as a vehicle for ending nomadism. One teacher described the tent schools as being "like a military camp"; both teachers and students suspected that government officials used them to keep the tribes "under strict surveillance." Shahshahani also questions the praise Western observers have heaped on the tent schools. "Fear existed between the teacher and the students," she writes, adding that "the teacher did not care if the student really understood the lesson."[77] Mohammad Shahbazi likewise found that some graduates believed the tribal schools were designed to alienate "young nomads from their parents and from their ancestral way of life" to assimilate them into the dominant Persian culture. The use of tribal methods was simply a ploy to encourage cooperation. Shahbazi also found graduates, however, who believed the schools provided an important service to tribal people. According to this view, tribal teachers had a better understanding of nomadic culture and problems than did other public school teachers and tailored their instruction "to benefit, rather than to harm the students."[78]

Did the BYU participation in the tent school project cooperate with the coercive power of the Iranian state? In one sense, the answer has to be yes, given the government's goal of using education to end nomadism and bring the tribes under firmer state control. Bahmanbaigi himself doubted that the tribes could maintain their nomadic way of life, and Point Four provided financial assistance to sedentary tribal schools after its support for the tent schools ended. But it is also important to realize that the BYU advisers did not support the tent schools out of a desire to destroy the nomadic way of life or to extend the power of the state over the tribes. As with all of their educational programs, their goal was to raise the socioeconomic status of rural Iranians. If they wanted to extend assistance to tribal groups, they had to do it within a framework suitable to the Iranian government. Moreover, the BYU role came at the very beginning of formal tribal education. The tent schools were a decidedly low-modernization approach that sought to provide education to tribal children within their familiar way of life rather than by undermining it.

THE CONTROVERSIAL TERMINATION OF BYU'S CONTRACT

Point Four officials abruptly announced the termination of the BYU teacher training contract in the summer of 1955, much to the university's chagrin.

After successfully extending the project in 1953, BYU officials expressed interest in continuing the project further, but government officials declined. John Hollister's reorganization of technical assistance reduced the number of university projects and gave "special emphasis to the improvement of foreign educational and other institutions by arranging special services to be provided by similar institutions in the United States." In effect, that meant most university participation would be restricted to providing direct assistance to postsecondary institutions.[79] BYU president Ernest Wilkinson acknowledged as much, but he also reminded Point Four officials that they had praised BYU's work on teacher training and that the university was prepared to continue its efforts through a new contract it had already negotiated with the University of Tehran.[80] The BYU team in Iran felt betrayed. Dean Peterson wrote that "we are very much disappointed at the termination of our contract," despite BYU's willingness to fit its work into Point Four's new priorities. University officials "had been encouraged" to think that the project would continue, and Peterson had recruited a staff for that purpose.[81]

Officials from the Utah schools were concerned that intolerance toward Mormons among key Point Four leaders factored into the decision to end the project. George Stewart of USU wrote to Wilkinson that "the real difficulty hinges around the fact that the L.D.S. people have been given a much more kindly reception by the Iranians than have the people from [the] eastern United States who drink, smoke and carry on in other ways of having a good time." Stewart went on to explain that in "a series of meetings," Ministry of Agriculture officials had "taken the trouble to explain" that they were "particularly pleased with the way that the Utah people live and the attempt that they make to be of sincere purpose to the Iranians." Such behavior, Stewart remarked, contrasted with other Americans who "haven't any interest except for the amount of salaries that they get." He closed by surmising that "a sort of bitterness" toward the Utah teams had crept into Point Four operations in Iran.[82] Wilkinson thought the situation was even more serious; he charged that religious discrimination was at the heart of the matter. Wilkinson believed that Clark Gregory, Point Four's director in Iran, disliked Mormons and that this attitude helped shape the decision to bring the BYU team home. The most compelling evidence in support of this assertion appears to be an October 1955 letter in which Gregory expressed concerns about the problems he saw as "inherent" in having "too many of any one faith working as a unit in a country predominantly Muslim."[83] Wilkinson also offered to produce evidence that during his previous assignment in Jordan, Gregory had promised to "reduce the number of Mormons" in Iran "if he ever had another assignment there."[84]

Wilkinson traveled to New York in September to seek advice from the US Department of Education. He left dismayed and recorded in his diary, "I found, as usual, interdepartmental warfare in the Government." According to Wilkinson, department officials confirmed that the BYU project "was better than any other [university Point Four] program" and that they also "suspected internal politics because we [the BYU team] have the missionary zeal and by comparison have done a better job than others."[85] He received a measure of resolution in November when he and Dean Peterson represented BYU at a conference sponsored by Michigan State University to discuss problems in university technical assistance contracts. A government representative reiterated that Point Four had cancelled the BYU contract because "we [BYU] did not have a specific program but the work we were doing was the scattered kind of work which was fitted better for government employees." The answer fit with the reprioritization of Point Four that was under way, but Wilkinson felt the meeting was an unsuitable forum to ask any follow-up questions about the allegations of religious discrimination.[86]

The fact that the president of BYU was indignant at the apparent anti-Mormonism of such a prominent Point Four leader as Clark Gregory is entirely understandable. And it does not appear that he ever received a satisfactory response to the question of why BYU could not continue its work on teacher training through its proposed contract with the University of Tehran.[87] The USU team was also entirely Mormon, after all, and it continued to operate in Iran for another nine years, mostly in association with Karaj Agricultural College. Finally, Gregory's curt discussions with BYU officials that summer did little to help the situation.[88] It is with justification, therefore, that Wilkinson concluded "we have not been dealt [with] fairly."[89] But it is also possible that Wilkinson's political views informed his analysis of the situation. Despite his support for BYU's Point Four work in Iran, Ernest Wilkinson was a strong anti-statist conservative who was often vocal in his disagreement with federal policies. Richard Brown remembered that Wilkerson was a "great" and "very unique man" but also that "he didn't know when not to talk sometimes . . . I don't think that he helped."[90] Hollister's reprioritization of the Point Four program and the corresponding reduction of university projects probably explain the termination of the BYU contract in the summer of 1955, but the specter of religious discrimination and the terse treatment university officials received from Point Four made that probability more difficult to accept.

BYU ADVISERS AND DANESHSARAYE ALI, 1957–1961

BYU education advisers returned to Iran in September 1957 when the university entered into a new contract to assist in the improvement of Daneshsaraye Ali, the teacher's college of the University of Tehran. Founded in 1928, the college was attached to the university in 1934 during a national overhaul of higher education. It endured a precarious existence in its early years. The college had only six professors of education and was subordinate to other academic units throughout the 1940s. It gained more administrative autonomy in 1955 but still depended on faculty members from other colleges to teach many of its courses outside of education.[91] Daneshsaraye Ali had its own campus located near the Majlis building in the mid-1950s, but by 1959 it had been reduced to renting "six separate, scattered buildings" that were converted homes and "very inadequate" for classroom use.[92] Its faculty consisted of part-time professors who had "scattered interests" outside the college and brought "various degrees of dedication" to their teaching.[93] Daneshsaraye Ali also struggled for recognition, as professors in the university's more established colleges looked down on subjects such as elementary education, physical education, and home economics as unworthy of inclusion in the university curriculum. Khanbaba Bayani, dean of the college, therefore backed a Majlis bill to separate the college from the University of Tehran so it could pursue its own pedagogical reforms. Passage took eighteen months, but the college became an independent institution in 1959.[94]

The BYU advisers emphasized that a good teacher had to be "a well-educated person in the broad sense of the word." Beyond competence in their teaching fields, teachers had to understand "the facts of human growth and development; the whys of human behavior."[95] They also stressed the importance of creating programs for elementary education, home economics, physical education, and audiovisual education—subjects that mattered a great deal for national development but had not yet been accepted into Iranian higher education. The BYU team ran into difficulties, however, in recommending that the college adopt a "basically American curriculum and academic structure" that included general education requirements for all students. They pressed the administration to embrace features of American higher education, such as replacing the traditional system of year-long courses based on a single final examination with a semester system in which professors would regularly evaluate student progress through periodic exams. The team urged professors to introduce course projects that required students to apply what they were learning. Home economics in particular should include practical training in the care of children, first aid, sanitation, textile and clothing repair, food storage and preparation, and the like. The BYU team also recommended that the college devise a one-year training course for university graduates who wanted to go into teaching. Finally, they stressed the importance of developing a fulltime faculty composed of expert teachers who dedicated their full attention to college teaching and related research.[96]

The BYU advisers could point with satisfaction to genuine accomplishments after four years of collaboration with the college. Whereas the faculty had no fulltime professors in 1957, it had thirty by 1961. "Their untiring efforts and dedication," noted Golden Woolf, head of the BYU team, "constitute the back bone of the school."[97] Home economics adviser Malno Reichert described her Iranian colleagues as "some of the brightest people I have ever met, and some of the most progressive."[98] She applauded the pioneering spirit of two young home economists, Nahid Farzad and Vida Daftari, a USU graduate. Both had formerly been Point Four home extension agents and were responsible for building the home economics department out of a dilapidated basement. Though neither held faculty rank, they took the lead in preparing classrooms and laboratories, developing course materials, ordering necessary equipment, and establishing an outreach program to provide training for extension agents working in the field.[99] Library adviser Royce Flandro likewise reported that most of his Iranian colleagues "have proven themselves as dedicated educators, capable of continuing the excellent work they have thus far advanced."[100] Several BYU advisers noted that academic standards rose between 1957 and 1961 and that the college was doing a better job of attracting students who were interested in teaching as a profession.[101]

Perhaps the biggest improvement, however, was in elementary education. Daneshsaraye Ali founded an elementary education department in 1958, but

it got off to an inauspicious start. BYU adviser John Ord recalled that enthusiasm for elementary school teaching was low among the first class. Many in
that cohort treated the college merely as a means to move into better-paying
and more prestigious positions, either in secondary education or in administration. Three years later, however, Ord reported that the importance of professional elementary school teachers "is slowly being realized by the people
of Iran." A more "favorable attitude toward educating all children is now evident." He noted that improvements in elementary education at Daneshsraye
Ali had accelerated in the two years following the college's administrative
break from the University of Tehran.[102]

Significant obstacles to the college's development nevertheless remained.
Daneshsaraye Ali suffered chronic budget shortages throughout the years
of BYU collaboration, and part-time instructors still outnumbered fulltime
professors by a ratio of 4 to 1 in 1961. Golden Woolf complained that "it has
been like an unwanted child to certain educational vested interest groups in
high places." Low pay still forced many professors to take outside employment, which in turn "weakens the attachment and responsibility of staff
members to their home school."[103] David Geddes noted that the physical
education department had no fulltime teachers or permanent facilities of its
own. Students "received much poor instruction" as a result.[104] Morris Shirts
likewise lamented that his Iranian counterpart "is not worth very much and
knows very little about audiovisual education." Shirts pointed out that the
college had more willing and qualified people in that field, but they lacked
the seniority of his assigned counterpart.[105] Developing adequate instruction
materials also proved an ongoing challenge. Few of the students could read
English well enough to make use of American college textbooks, and Persian
versions were not yet available in the emerging fields of home economics and
physical education. While the college library made great strides, a shortage
of usable textbooks and reference materials remained "a great handicap."[106]

Serious pedagogical differences between American and Iranian higher
education also limited the influence of the BYU advisers. Reichert complained that the continued reliance on annual examinations served as a dis-
incentive for student attendance and participation in vital learning activities.
She also lamented the continuing emphasis on rote memorization: "It is
almost impossible for them [students] to differentiate between essential and
non-essential facts, and therefore they make little effort to retain anything,

except for the examination." Some instructors, she acknowledged, expressed a "willingness to make changes in their courses to make them more mean-ingful." They would have been able to do so, she grumbled, "if they were not so regulated by rules and traditions and older professors who cannot change, and do not want anyone else to change."[107] The BYU advisers had little capacity to change this. "Our group was invited on the campus by the college administration to effect some changes, but the individual professors see us as a threat to their status and refuse to work with us," protested Shirts. "Perhaps this is the reason most Americans appear to be doing nothing."[108] Woolf likewise acknowledged that while the BYU advisers helped foster pos-itive change in individual departments, they had little influence on how the college itself was run.

A. Reed Morrill observed that the BYU team's relationship with both the Ministry of Education and the Daneshsaraye Ali administration seemed to fade over time. He could not tell if "our proposals were too difficult" or if an American "educational philosophy was unacceptable." It seemed possi-ble that enthusiasm for the collaboration had simply run out. "Perhaps," he thought, "they [college administrators] had gotten all the advisement . . . they could digest."[109] Reichert even counseled the college to reappraise its use of all foreign advisers. Input from Europeans and Americans was pulling it in different directions, which produced undesirable consequences for teacher training nationwide. The college "should decide what is the most needed to improve the Iranian schools and concentrate on doing that," even if it meant scaling back American concepts.[110]

BYU advisers expressed mixed feelings when their collaboration with Daneshsaraye Ali ended in the summer of 1961. On the one hand, they took pride in the institution's overall growth and increasing academic rigor. They also celebrated the pioneering work the college undertook to professional-ize fields such as elementary education, physical education, and home eco-nomics. But they also felt the Iranian government had not shown sufficient appreciation for the role of teacher education in the country's development. From the group's final report to the Minister of Education: "It is the firm opinion of the BYU Contract Team that there has been and continues to be inadequate concrete tangible recognition of the *institutions* and *devoted indi-viduals* who have been given responsibility, and leadership to full the critical national need of teacher education on both the elementary and secondary levels. In a large degree also they have not been supported in proportion to their National importance."[111] Malno Reichert's greatest disappointment was that education for girls had not made more progress. "At the end of four years in Iran," she wrote, "my opinions of the educational prospects for the women of the country are not bright." She urged the government to make at least a fourth-grade education available to every Iranian girl, both urban and rural. "Any nation which allows 50% of its citizens (the women) to be illiterate and second class citizens," she warned, "will be in the 'developing' stage for a long time."[112]

CONCLUSION

Assessments of the BYU assistance to Iranian public education have varied, from the very laudatory to the highly critical. William Warne praised the BYU advisers' "pioneering spirit" and credited them with making "a great contribution in up-grading the education of the entire country." He commended "their acceptance of the assignment as a 'mission.'"[113] But Warne was not a disinterested observer. His role as the first director of Point Four operations in Iran and his long-standing support for the Utah advisers sometimes led him to overestimate their accomplishments. Economist and former cabinet minister Jahangir Amuzegar offered similarly high praise in his more detached assessment: "Point Four assistance made many Iranian teachers realize that interest in the capabilities, aptitudes, emotions, and individual problems of their students was no less important than interest in the subject matter which was so close to their hearts. By using real-life experiments . . . the youngsters were taught to regard the school not as separate, but as an integral part of their later living—a somewhat new concept in Iran, where schools were regarded as a kind of purgatory."[114] A. Reed Morrill, in contrast, criticized Point Four for undercutting the work the BYU advisers had done in teacher training when it abruptly terminated the project in 1955. Neither the demonstration schools nor the in-service courses received adequate support after the advisers' departure.[115] Morrill concluded that the Ministry of Education was also responsible for the diminishing returns. It had failed to utilize its American-trained teachers effectively and moved slowly in professionalizing teacher training. Upon leaving Iran in 1961 at the end of his work at Daneshsaraye Ali, Morrill sounded almost despondent: "Until the young teachers are given a sound background of thinking regarding teaching and learning[,] their educational system will remain impractical and artificial."[116] A 1960 report by John Allen Fitz of the University of Southern California echoed Morrill in finding a lack of a "clearly stated, stable program" for curricular improvements, as well as inadequacies in college-level teacher training.[117]

Reza Arasteh, a historian of Iranian education, argues that the projects were built on faulty assumptions and naive American expectations. The Americans were arrogant and unrealistic in thinking they could fundamentally reshape Iranian education. Iranians, he points out, "accept[ed] those practices which were in harmony with their own values and . . . oppose[ed] the disharmonious ones." He notes that Iranian educators and officials nominally accepted American practices, "only to circumvent them by devising their own modifications."[118] That was certainly true. Moreover, Iranian public education continued to show widespread deficiencies after more than a decade of American assistance.[119] Illiteracy still stood between 80 percent and 85 percent nationwide in the early 1960s, and Malno Reichert observed that more than 30,000 villages still lacked a school in 1961: "There are simply not enough village teachers, especially for girls' schools."[120] One in four rural children still could not attend school in the mid-1970s, a significant decrease from twenty years earlier, to be sure, but a large number nonetheless.[121] Finally, the BYU education projects played a role in strengthening an Iranian government that wanted to use public education as a means of blunting the power of religious and tribal leaders. Gagon's work on the tent schools, though progressive and practical, was also part of a larger government initiative to undermine the tribal way of life. Max Berryessa similarly supported the shah's tug-of-war with a clerical establishment that, in Berryessa's mind, "didn't want people to be more educated than they were."[122]

In reality, the BYU advisers did the best they could to contribute something positive to Iranian education. They helped found dozens of new schools and contributed to renovations in more than eighty others. They provided at least the rudiments of pedagogical training to thousands of Iranian teachers, an important early step in their professionalization. They also nourished new fields of teacher training at the Daneshsraye Ali. They introduced hundreds of Iranian girls to home economics—one of the very few professional career options for rural women. But the BYU projects also tell us much about the limited capacity of American technical assistance to shape modernization in developing nations. Advisers could demonstrate techniques that worked well in the United States; they could help train teachers and help develop tribal schools. But they lacked the capacity to make profound social changes in Iran. A more complete transformation of Iranian education required a sustained nationwide effort.

6

LEGACIES

A number of Iranians feel that sooner or later the corrupt ruling circles "and all of their US advisors" will be thrown out of the country by a rising groundswell of public indignation.

Lt. Col. Alexis M. Gagarine, 1961

I have always felt bad that the shah was removed because of what he was doing. Yes, there were some people that were killed under his regime. But I saw the good that he was doing for that country.

Gordon Van Epps, USU adviser in Iran, 1961–64

The last Utah technical assistance advisers left Iran in the summer of 1964 when Utah State University's (USU) final contract with Karaj Agricultural College ended. The Brigham Young University (BYU) team had already concluded its work at Daneshsaraye Ali three years earlier. By that time, Point Four's rural improvement initiatives had faded into the background of Iranian development as the country embarked on more grandiose undertakings.

DOI: 10.7330/9781607327547.c006

The Utah advisers hoped their work would promote social justice and democratic development within Iran. Like many Americans, however, they placed
an unwarranted amount of faith in Mohammad Reza Shah Pahlavi's ability
to lead that change. "The young shah wanted to help his people," recalled
Helen Milligan. "He wanted to help the people in the villages."[1] It was a
common sentiment among the Utah advisers. Iran did experience impressive economic growth from the mid-1950s through the mid-1970s, but that
growth did not produce stability. It was uneven, and government inefficiency
squandered much of the economic aid Iran received. Meanwhile, the shah
consolidated his power and stifled democratic development with the support
of the US government. Over time, many Iranians became embittered toward
the shah and his American patrons. Lieutenant Colonel Alexis M. Gagarine,
an American officer who had served in Iran during the late 1940 and early
1950s, noted prophetically in 1961: "A number of Iranians feel that sooner or
later the corrupt ruling circles 'and all of their US advisors' will be thrown
out of the country by a rising groundswell of public indignation."[2] It would
be unfair to insinuate that the Utah advisers contributed to the coming of
the Iranian Revolution that overthrew the shah in early 1979, but this chapter
situates their work within American policies that did. A more positive legacy
was that participation in Point Four helped internationalize the Utah universities and, in the case of USU and the University of Utah, opened the door for
subsequent overseas development work.

A VISION BEYOND ATTAINMENT

Despite the lofty vision President Truman articulated in his 1949 inaugural
address, Point Four work could do little more than act as a primer for Iranian
rural development. The country's pervasive and severe rural poverty, its rudimentary infrastructure, and deficiencies in its public administration all combined to limit Point Four's effectiveness.[3] Moreover, technical assistance was
never a very high priority for the US government, a reality that caused officials in Iran and many other recipient nations to wonder what the program
could actually accomplish.[4] Political Scientist Mark Gasiorowski has calcu-
lated that the US government spent just under $1.9 billion on foreign aid to
Iran between 1950 and 1967. Of that, around $120 million, or just over half of
1 percent, went to technical assistance. Military grants, in contrast, accounted

for $847 million, approximately 45 percent of the total. Put another way, US military aid accounted for roughly $138 million more than all forms of economic aid combined.[5] The balance sheet reveals, then, that the US government put a higher premium on achieving stability by strengthening the shah's regime than on doing so through socioeconomic development.

Americans and Iranians also brought fundamentally different perspectives to technical assistance. The architects of Point Four envisioned a small-scale, grassroots program that would emphasize training over big financial and material commitments. Iranians, in contrast, wanted tangible evidence of modernization: machines, equipment, and buildings.[6] When William Warne first met Ayatollah Abol-Ghasem Kashani in the summer of 1952, for example, the influential cleric expressed his hope that Point Four would do "something substantial" for Iran and suggested that building a hydroelectric dam on the Karun River would jumpstart development in Khuzestan. Warne protested that such a project would exceed the entire Point Four budget for the country by a factor of ten and concluded that "the Ayatollah was completely unrealistic when confronting technical questions."[7] Jahangir Amuzegar writes that Iranian public officials had become "accustomed to a period of rapid industrialization during 1920–1940 when structures (large buildings, automatic factories, mountain-piercing roads) were considered true symbols of economic progress." Point Four's low-modernization emphasis on fostering basic rural improvements left the officials "somewhat cold." What Iranians really wanted, he continues, "was foreign assistance for [the country's] modernization, westernization, and industrialization," all of which Iranians "considered symbolically progressive."[8] The desire for large and showy projects was ironic in the sense that the Iranian government funded comparatively little of the program, especially during the Mossadegh years when the international embargo crippled the country's finances. The Iranian government provided roughly $15 million worth of land, equipment, and services to Point Four efforts between 1950 and 1954, but its cash support equaled just over $1 million. Iranian contributions grew to around $60 million by 1965, but that was still only half what the US government spent. Henry Hazlitt's prediction that Point Four would be unable to attract private investment proved well-founded in Iran; even after 1953, the Iranian government relied overwhelmingly on oil revenue to fund its development.[9]

Logistical challenges proved formidable as well. Gholam Kazemian notes that in addition to the challenges of working across languages and cultures, both Iranians and American technicians struggled to balance technical and administrative tasks. Instability among senior Iranian government officials, the periodic reorganizations of American foreign aid, and frequent turnover among the American advisers added to the difficulty of maintaining the rural improvement program.[10] The onset of integration in 1956 forced the Iranian government to shoulder more of the administrative burden before it was capable of doing so.[11] Both Point Four and Ford Foundation officials found that Iranian agencies failed to maintain agriculture and education projects amid the subsequent reduction of American technical aid.[12] Many of the gains the Utah advisers helped achieve therefore proved ephemeral. Clarence Hendershot, who directed the education programs in Iran during the early 1960s, recalled that the teacher in-service program languished under full Iranian control after 1961.[13] When he returned to Iran for an assignment at Daneshsaraye Ali in 1959, A. Reed Morrill lamented that the Point Four demonstration schools had become "typically Iranian in organization, methods of teaching, and results obtained."[14] After visiting Karaj Agricultural College in 1967, Richard Welling Roskelley likewise expressed frustration at the lack of progress that had been made since the conclusion of the last Utah State contract three years earlier.[15]

Technical assistance operations in Iran also came under intense scrutiny for widespread waste and misallocation of resources. Clark Clifford, the former Truman aid whose enthusiastic support had helped breathe life into Point Four, candidly acknowledged that much American development aid was either "wasted, lost to corruption and inefficiency," or misapplied Western techniques in recipient countries.[16] A comprehensive investigation by the House Committee on Government Operations in 1956 found that economic aid to Iran was doled out in a "loose, slipshod, and unbusinesslike manner" and that it was "impossible with any accuracy" to tell what specific benefits Iranians had derived from it.[17] Majlis deputy and former mayor of Tehran Arsalan Khalatbari complained that Point Four officials appeared to have "no proper program for spending the money at their disposal" and observed that "a good portion" went to salaries, rents, and the purchase of automobiles for the American staff. He further charged that Point Four indulged in "trivial activities" that had little effect on the population. As a result, "The Iranian people have felt none of its results."[18] Lt. Col. Gagarine noted that many Iranians believed American development aid helped "preserve the current government and all the economic and social inequalities." Foreign aid might be good "in principle," he thought, but it was actually harming the American reputation in Iran because "it is channeled through a notoriously corrupt government and only serves to enrich wealthy contractors and key government officials."[19] *The Nation* reported that "foreign aid" payments of up to $15 million went directly into the bank accounts of royal family members while "teachers were being paid just $25 a month" and "tiny children worked sweatshop hours for 20¢ a day or less."[20] Morris Shirts, a BYU audiovisual adviser at Daneshsaraye Ali, wrote to his parents near the end of 1958 that, "Congress should look into this Foreign Aid program again. There is an awful lot of waste in the program, and I wonder at times just how valuable it really is."[21]

The poor quality of some American advisers further undermined Iranian confidence in the Point Four Program. Respected educator Reza Arasteh complained, probably with some exaggeration, that "the majority of American advisors have not been qualified to do their job and personal problems have often distracted them," though he did not implicate any of the Utahns directly. He also charged that Point Four worked with "irresponsible and corrupt Iranian officials" who were more interested in personal gain than in the betterment of their country.[22] Writer and former teacher Jalal Al-e Ahmad emerged as "Iran's most eminent antiestablishment intellectual and social critic of the 1950s and 1960s."[23] His novel based on his brief career as a public school principal includes a story about a brash American Point Four man who ran over one of the school's teachers with his car and then avoided prosecution by hastily paying off the family of the badly injured teacher. The nameless Point Four adviser showed no concern for either the teacher or the community; indeed, the principal gave no indication that the Point Four man was doing anything productive for Iran.[24] Some of the Utahns likewise expressed disappointment with the caliber of Americans working in the country. Lula Anderson put it this way: "For a lot of the federal employees it was just a job."[25] Morris Shirts wrote to his family that he was "quite disgusted with Americans here," many of whose social lives "seem to be one constant whirl of cocktail parties." Shirts found some of his American colleagues to be "professional near-do-wells [*sic*] who couldn't make a decent living in the States, but here they are really living."[26]

The Utahns do not seem to have indulged in corruption or unseemly personal behavior. According to Max Berryessa, "Point Four officials were pleased with the caliber of people who came from BYU."[27] Lula Anderson agreed that the Utahns "were very serious minded. They had a great desire to do good."[28] Dean Farnsworth added that "there was a missionary attitude" of Christian service among the Utah advisers.[29] It appears that the most egregious offenses any of the Utahns committed involved taking impertinent photographs of locals and making ill-advised jokes about aspects of Iranian life that they found humorous.[30] Several of the former advisers felt their Mormon lifestyle made it easier for Iranians to embrace the Utah families. Berryessa said, for example, "They saw that we didn't smoke. They saw that we didn't drink."[31] Mildred Bunnell added that the Mormon reputation became well-known in Iran and even helped ingratiate the Utah advisers to some conservative clerics who tended to be skeptical of foreign influence.[32] "We were treated so kindly and so sensitively by Iranian folks," remembered Farnsworth, who added that some of Iranians said "we would make good Moslems because we had the Word of Wisdom."[33] Vern Kupfer recalled that "most of the people we dealt with saw that there was something to what we had to offer."[34]

Still, it seems likely that the Utahns mistook the affections of Iranian friends and the plethora of official recognition they received for widespread public acceptance of their goals and methods. While it is no doubt true that they enjoyed the genuine support of some Iranians, especially those with whom they had worked effectively, it is also likely that much of the official gratitude amounted to diplomatic nicety and flattery that belied true feelings. Amuzegar found that overall, the attitude of Iranians toward Point Four was "lukewarm and somewhat suspicious" in both government and the private sector. It seems clear that American tactics contributed to their misgivings. One prominent Tehran newspaper publisher complained that the American propensity to dominate projects resulted in insufficient attention to the consent and cooperation of Iranians.[35] Leftist writer Bahman Nirumand charged that "Americans carried out this process of technological development with no regard for the spiritual and cultural conditions prevailing in Iran."[36] The tendency of American publicists to exaggerate the program's accomplishments rankled many Iranians, as it did officials in other recipient countries.[37]

Point Four technical assistance therefore produced only the most modest success in Iran despite the best efforts of the Utah advisers. The scope of the country's socioeconomic challenges, a scarcity of time and resources, divergent American and Iranian priorities, difficulties caused by shifting policies and frequent personnel turnover, ambiguous support among Iranian leaders—all of these factors rendered the noble dream of Point Four architects Harry Truman, Benjamin Hardy, and Henry Bennett a vision beyond attainment.

FROM LOW MODERNIZATION TO TAKEOFF IN IRAN

Iran's development strategy moved beyond the low-modernization approach of the Point Four rural improvement program in the second half of the 1950s. The country experienced tremendous economic growth following its 1954 acceptance of an agreement to allow an international consortium of Western companies to control the oil industry. The new arrangement fell well short of Mossadegh's nationalization scheme, but it did increase the Iranian government's share of the profits from 20 percent to 50 percent.[38] Petroleum once again flowed out of Abadan, and national income from oil multiplied by a factor of ten over the next seven years, from $34 million in 1954–55 to $358 million by 1961.[39] The US government showed its approval of Iran's capitulation on oil nationalization by increasing its technical assistance—to $85 million in 1954 and $149 million in 1955 and 1956. The Export-Import Bank made an additional $53 million loan available for "politically essential economic development programs."[40]

Point Four technical assistance flourished in 1954 and 1955 with the full blessing of the Iranian government. New projects were started in public administration and in the development of industrial chemicals. Point Four also established a modern new orphanage in Tehran. Initiatives became larger and geared more toward improving the country's infrastructure. Tehran, for example, was one of the largest cities in the world that still lacked a municipal water system in the mid-1950s. Point Four technicians assisted in the construction of a dam on the Karaj River to provide the water and procured the materials necessary to start laying the pipes that would finally rescue Tehran's citizens from their reliance on unsanitary *jubes*. Ayatollah Kashani's dream of building a hydroelectric damn on the Karun River to facilitate development in Khuzestan, which Warne dismissed as extravagant in 1951, became a "major project" in 1955.[41]

The Iranian government also embraced central planning and aspects of modernization theory, both of which became popular zeitgeists among liberal American development strategists during the 1960s.[42] Modernization theory called for controlled economic growth though the initial stages of industrialization, which usually included coordinated planning and economic development aid. Once countries reached "takeoff," the point at which their economies became self-sustaining, aid would be diminished, and they would move toward the free market.[43] Modernization theorists prescribed an important role for Point Four's low-modernization approach in the initial stages of economic development insofar as rudimentary work in agriculture, education, and public health would help establish the necessary preconditions for industrial development. But they were mainly drawn to large-scale projects that employed the latest technology in the hopes of bypassing incremental developmental stages and arriving at takeoff more quickly.[44] President John F. Kennedy embraced this apparent panacea for development; within two months of assuming office, he called on the US Congress to reorganize foreign aid to meet the challenge.[45] Of the $709.7 million in economic aid the US government provided to Iran between 1950 and 1965, about two-thirds was capital assistance for large-scale infrastructure projects such as building roads, hospitals, and dams.[46]

Western development strategies appealed to Iranian leaders insofar as they emphasized "prestige-giving" projects that enhanced the country's outward trappings of modernity.[47] The shah created the Plan Organization in 1949 to coordinate industrialization and the transformation of the countryside. The oil crisis and attending economic fallout largely scuttled Iran's first national development plan, which ended prematurely in 1954. According to Amuzegar, many of the initial Point Four projects were designed to rescue this plan "from a complete collapse."[48] The second plan (1954–62) produced the large-scale Khuzestan rural development and electrification project, a collaboration between the Plan Organization and the Development and Resources Corporation, an international development firm led by former Tennessee Valley Authority (TVA) chairman David Lilienthal.[49] The second plan crashed, however, against political rivalries and government inefficiency, showy projects of questionable utility, an underdeveloped industrial base, and insufficient public investment in agriculture and manufacturing.[50] Homa Katouzian concludes that "hardly anything permanent and useful had been achieved" by 1960.[51] But the third national development plan (1962–68) became the country's "big push into the developed world."[52] It is a testament to how marginal Point Four–style rural improvement had become by the 1960s that the American technical assistance mission was little involved in either the planning or the execution of the country's third development plan.[53] Point Four did, however, continue to support agricultural programs in education, rural development, and land reform.[54]

The 1960s therefore became the decade in which the shah cultivated his mystique as a benevolent modernizer who kept a firm hand on the levers of power while guiding his country through a period of tremendous economic growth. He announced a "White Revolution," or Revolution of the Shah and People, in early 1963 that would move Iran toward economic parity with Western countries. Its headlining initiative was a nationwide land reform aimed at transferring ownership of farmland from large landlords to the peasant families who farmed it. The idea was to promote the gradual conversion of Iran's impoverished peasants into more prosperous commercial farmers while simultaneously blunting landlords' political and economic power. The White Revolution also contained measures designed to highlight the shah's sense of social justice, including profit sharing for factory workers and female suffrage. The latter provoked fierce opposition from conservative clerics, but it pleased liberals within the Kennedy administration who welcomed the appearance of political reform.[55] A tightly controlled referendum officially found support among more than 99 percent of voters.[56]

Iran sustained impressive economic growth during the mid-1960s. Gross domestic product increased by an annual average of just under 10 percent between 1962 and 1967.[57] Oil revenue more than doubled during the decade and reached $791 million by 1969. The shah's prestige soared; the White Revolution forged a "legitimizing myth for the Pahlavi monarchy" that shielded him from internal and external criticism.[58] A few opponents of the regime acknowledged that the White Revolution "seemed to be a resounding success." Sattareh Farman Farmaian, a pioneer Iranian social worker and distant cousin of Mossadegh, recalled that the country was "rushing toward the future at breakneck speed . . . New factories were producing everything from helicopters to textiles." The government was making progress toward building a modern transportation and education infrastructure. Public health conditions improved; infant mortality declined.[59] The US Embassy proclaimed that the shah was "making Iran a show-case of modernization."[60] President Lyndon B. Johnson declared Iran a developed nation in 1966 and closed the last American technical assistance missions in that country the following year.[61]

The former Utah Point Four advisers celebrated the major breakthrough that appeared to be taking place. They referred to the shah as "a benevolent dictator because of the changes that he was in charge of having made throughout the country."[62] Royce Flandro "felt that the shah was doing some wonderful worthwhile things and was blessing the people."[63] Richard Brown recalled that "the shah was quite enlightened in many ways and was making real efforts to upgrade the quality of life."[64] Max Berryessa felt "great sympathy for the shah," who "really wanted his country to be brought up to the standards of the western world."[65] USU advisers especially applauded the shah's enthusiasm for agricultural improvement, land distribution, and women's rights.[66] Gordon Van Epps "saw the good" the shah was doing "in changing the people and getting the women out of their homes and being educated."[67] Horticulturalist Clarence Ashton visited peasant farmers during the initial stages of land reform. Nearly four decades later he still recalled that "you can't imagine the difference it made to them."[68] The Utahns were not the only American technical advisers to heap praise on the shah. David Lilienthal called the shah, whom he met on close to thirty occasions, "one of the most capable, practical and economic leaders . . . anywhere in the world" and confided in his journal that "I really believe in this man."[69]

The economic growth, while remarkable in the aggregate, also proved remarkably uneven. The White Revolution actually compounded the problem of poverty in some sectors of the economy. Formidable technical and organizational problems within the land reform caused widespread disruptions in the countryside.[70] According to Fred Halliday, only about half of eligible peasants had received any land by 1966, and the poorest farmers were the most likely to be excluded. Some relatively small landowners lost their land and along with it their means to a livelihood amid the inexact implementation.[71] The *boneh* system of cooperative peasant cultivation also deteriorated following the breakup of large holdings. Economists have noted that government investment in agriculture lagged behind urban-based industries and that much of it was wasted on large but inefficient state-subsidized agribusinesses. Credit available to small and mid-sized farmers was consequently "erratic and patchy" for much of the 1960s.[72] While industries such as construction and mining grew at an annual rate that exceeded 11 percent during the decade, agricultural growth averaged less than 3 percent, and there was almost no increase in productivity.[73] Agricultural stagnation led many rural families to migrate to the cities, where unskilled workers faced chronic unemployment.[74] All things considered, it appears that the much-celebrated land reform brought more trauma than economic opportunity to rural communities. Lilienthal's Khuzestan development project, once hailed as a Tennessee Valley Authority for Iran, became a "debacle" that displaced tens of thousands of rural families and contributed to environmental deterioration. The province's gross domestic product actually declined by the mid-1970s.[75]

Advances in education were also far from complete. Nearly 80 percent of Iranian adults were still illiterate at the end of the 1960s, despite increased government investment in schools and nearly two decades of foreign assistance.[76] Shortages of schools and teachers in rural communities remained a common barrier to education for girls and tribal children.[77] Urban secondary schools, in contrast, began to produce more graduates than the country's universities could accommodate, even though the government founded sixteen new universities between 1949 and 1977.[78] Iran could not therefore produce enough technologically skilled professionals to maintain the rapid rate of industrialization. Many young people had to seek college degrees abroad.[79] A large number of these expatriate students became vocal critics of the regime, and the talents of those who did not return were lost to the nation's development effort.[80]

While the Utahns celebrated the shah's Western orientation, many Iranians resented the rush to emulate the West. Sattareh Farman Farmaian recalled that "an almost delirious admiration for all things Western had seized the country." She noted that many Iranians "felt that we were not only trying to catch up with the West, but to become the West."[81] Jalal Al-e Ahmad coined the term *gharbzadegi*, or "Western sickness," to describe the phenomenon; it became an important part of Iranian criticism of American influence during the 1960s and 1970s. "The entire local and cultural identity of existence," he wrote, "will be swept away."[82] The mounting Iranian antipathy against American influence was particularly pronounced in education.

Teacher and social critic Samad Behrangi, for example, ridiculed many of the shah's educational policies as *Amrikazadeh*, "imitative of America," and out of touch with Iran's educational needs.[83] Al-e Ahmad argued that westernization produced a new class, the useless "nowhere man," who was neither fully westernized nor able to function productively within Iran.[84] Social scientist Marvin Zonis described Western influence in Iranian education as "a symbiosis of divergent traditions" that was "at best halting."[85] In the wake of the Iranian Revolution, Ayatollah Ruhollah Khomeini decried that American-sponsored education reforms "contaminated" Iranian schools. He charged that universities in particular "were in the hands of a group of Anglophiles and later mere admirers of the Americans" and argued that Iranian education had to "cleanse itself from all western values and influences."[86]

Finally, Iranians came to resent the privileged position American technical advisers and military personnel enjoyed in their country. Political scientist Mehrzad Boroujerdi argues that the presence of such Americans reached "unjustifiable proportions" by the 1960s.[87] Al-e Ahmad likewise lamented the "western advisors who are in control of things" and saw little difference between foreign aid workers and the British and Russian military men who once fought for control over Iran: "If, when western man originally came to the East or Asia, he was master . . . today he is an advisor."[88] Arasteh added that "many genuine public-minded Persians" declined to cooperate with American aid programs that offered "economic aid in exchange for political servitude."[89] Iranian nationalists especially rejected a 1964 Status of Forces Agreement (SOFA) that provided full diplomatic immunity to American military personnel and their families in Iran.[90] Ayatollah Khomeini, then a seminary professor at Qom, compared the agreement to the capitulations of old that surrendered elements of Iranian national sovereignty to the British and Russian governments. He decried the fact that "the government has sold our independence, reduced us to the level of a colony, and made the Muslim nation of Iran appear more backward than savages in the eyes of the world."[91]

A central purpose of technical assistance was to promote goodwill toward the United States within the host country. That goal largely failed in Iran. Point Four's initial low-modernization approach to development became increasingly marginal as the country entered a period of tremendous economic growth beginning in the second half of the 1950s. Yet the process of modernization left much of the population disillusioned. The country was becoming wealthier and more technologically advanced, but the material benefits remained unevenly distributed. The influence of American technical advisers, especially in education and the military, contributed to the growing Iranian resentment toward the United States.

FROM STABILITY THROUGH DEMOCRATIZATION TO STABILITY OVER DEMOCRATIZATION

Richard Welling Roskelley was partially correct when he reflected that the Utah advisers became participants "in a struggle for the supremacy of two ideologies" in Iran: "democracy or another way of life."[92] The men whose vision gave life to the Point Four Program—Benjamin Hardy, Harry Truman, and Henry Bennett—all agreed that improving quality of life in less-developed countries would become a vehicle for advancing democracy and world peace. Truman couched much of his rhetoric about Point Four in the language of "peace, plenty, and freedom" and in the idealism of democracy.[93] In urging his fellow Utahns to support Point Four, USU agronomist George Stewart argued that "those holding the democratic ideology must be more active."[94] There is every reason to believe the Utah families who dedicated a portion of their lives to assisting Iranian development sincerely believed in Point Four's democratic idealism.

But Roskelley and many other Americans erred in assuming that "another way of life" would be a communist dictatorship. Iran instead became a textbook case for how US development policies often nurtured oppressive anti-communist regimes in the Third World instead of fostering democratic allies.[95] Communists were a boisterous part of that country's political landscape between 1951 and 1953, but they were never anything close to a decisive force. Rather, "another way of life" turned out to be monarchical dictatorship, and in Iran it reached levels of repression that matched the worst of the communist regimes. The shah employed an increasingly brutal security apparatus to solidify his dictatorship in the decade following the 1953 coup. American leaders facilitated his consolidation of power by extending foreign aid that helped the shah maintain order at the expense of his political opponents. US policy moved away from the original Point Four approach of achieving stability through democratic socioeconomic development and instead prioritized achieving stability over democratization in Iran. While the Utah advisers were aware of the regime's illiberal qualities, they nevertheless continued to emphasize the shah's accomplishments in education, economic development, and women's rights.

In retrospect, it is clear that the overthrow of Prime Minister Mohammad Mossadegh in August 1953 was the first major step toward monarchical dictatorship. Historians have long debated the democratic and authoritarian currents within his leadership, especially during the chaotic thirteen months between July 1952 and August 1953.[96] There is no doubt, however, that Mossadegh's National Front fought for the comparatively liberal values of national sovereignty and constitutional government. To the shah and most American officials, however, Mossadegh was a dangerous demagogue who tolerated, even relied on, leftist support for a suicidal oil nationalization scheme. His refusal to compromise on the oil question coupled with escalating violence in the streets convinced them that the prime minister was leading Iran down the path of ruin and opening the door for a communist revolution. The Utahns therefore greeted the overthrow of Mossadegh as a positive step toward restoring a stable foundation for democratic development in Iran.

Instead of promoting democracy, however, American policy makers put their faith in a series of pro-Western governments that they hoped would secure internal stability. The National Security Council (NSC) acknowledged in early 1955 that the new regime of General Fazlollah Zahedi "failed to achieve widespread support" but noted that it did possess the "will and ability to put down opposition." At the same time, the NSC expressed confidence in the shah, who appeared to be "profoundly anti-Communist," was "sympathetic to US objectives," and was "clearly determined to use authoritarian means if necessary to maintain stability and carry forward desirable economic and political reforms." The NSC did not, however, specify what desirable political reforms might be brought about through authoritarian means.[97] After some hesitation, the shah went along with the American plans. Iran joined the Baghdad Pact, a Cold War mutual security arrangement in the Middle East later renamed the Central Treaty Organization (CENTO), in 1955 and accepted a military alliance with the United States in 1959.[98] US arms sales to Iran, which had totaled less than $17 million during the Truman years, jumped to $436 million under Eisenhower.[99]

Consistent with the Eisenhower administration's emphasis on improving internal security in friendly Third World countries, Point Four advisers offered assistance to Iranian security agencies almost immediately following the 1953 coup. They conducted a full review of the country's police forces in 1954 and subsequently helped modernize both police practices and training facilities. Much of this technical assistance focused on routine police work: increasing administrative efficiency, collecting and analyzing evidence, detecting forgery, improving traffic safety, and the like.[100] As opposition to the shah began to mount in the second half of the 1950s, however, the focus shifted toward "control of civil disorder." Advisers trained police agencies in methods of surveillance, riot control, and interrogation that the Iranian authorities used to curtail civil liberties and harass the shah's political opponents. Americans also assisted provincial police forces "in breaking up anti-Shah riots" and pacifying rebellions by ethnic minorities. Point Four procured tear gas, projectiles, and leg irons in 1961; the US government provided an additional $500,000 for crowd control equipment following the violent clashes between anti-shah Iranian students and his security guards that broke out in New York City during the shah's April 1962 visit to the United States. The Kennedy administration's new Agency for International Development (AID) developed an Office of Public Safety in 1962 to provide police and paramilitary organizations in "hotspot" countries such as Iran with equipment and training to fight the "enemy within"—a euphemism for leftist agitators.[101] All of this support helped Tehran police "cope with any foreseeable urban civil disturbance short of a national revolution."[102] In practical terms, that meant suppressing all the shah's opponents, sometimes through the use of lethal force.

The National Intelligence and Security Organization, known by its Persian acronym SAVAK, emerged as "by far the most important and effective" component of the shah's repressive apparatus by the mid-1960s.[103] It functioned as the shah's "eyes and ears and, where necessary, his iron fist" in rooting out all disloyalty.[104] The CIA provided vital training in intelligence gathering and psychological warfare to SAVAK agents between 1957 and 1961, though it is not clear if the Americans participated in torture training.[105] The organization effectively turned Iran into a police state over the next two decades. It employed more than 3,500 fulltime agents and maintained a large network of informants; it thrived on the shah's "deep-felt need to insulate himself and his regime from all its potential enemies."[106] Historian Barry Rubin writes that "the entire population was subjected to a constant, all-pervasive terror." SAVAK agents pursued the regime's most militant opposition and its mildest critics. Communists, dissident students, journalists, labor leaders, government bureaucrats, and members of the religious establishment all found themselves ensnared in its ever-expanding web. It employed "horrendous torture" practices "equal to the worst ever devised" to obtain information and often released prisoners only after they had informed on friends and family.[107]

John F. Kennedy brought renewed emphasis on democracy and social justice to the presidency in 1961. As a senator, he had criticized the Eisenhower administration's coziness with authoritarian anti-communist governments by charging that it gave "support to regimes instead of people." Kennedy believed Eisenhower's approach incubated popular resentment that would in turn allow sympathy for communism to grow in the newly emerging nations of Asia and Africa.[108] As president, he sought "controlled revolutions" that emphasized economic development and political liberalization as a more productive alternative to propping up unpopular tyrants.[109] Iran proved an early test case for this liberal vision, as Kennedy recognized the country's strategic importance but had little confidence in the shah, whom the president concluded "was corrupt and not a person we could trust."[110] The assessments of the National Security Council and the Joint Chiefs of Staff offered little reassurance. The former "painted a picture of Iran as an inevitable disaster waiting to happen," while the latter cautioned against placing too much faith in a dictatorial shah.[111]

The Kennedy years did, in fact, coincide with the most serious political unrest in Iran since the summer of 1953. Under mounting pressure from the Iranian public and the new US administration, the shah appointed a versatile and independent politician, Ali Amini, to the premiership in May 1961. Kennedy officials hailed it as a "step toward liberalization" because Amini was a well-known opponent of royal dictatorship who also supported progressive measures such as land reform.[112] But his cabinet lasted just fourteen stormy months. The shah issued a decree in November that allowed the government to rule without a parliament following two fraudulent and widely criticized elections to the Twentieth Majlis. Amini's base of support eroded in the absence of an elected government as he became the focus of increased National Front agitation.[113] Police added to the acrimony when they used brutal force to suppress pro–National Front demonstrations at the University of Tehran in January 1962. Some of the students were "beaten to the point of death," and the chancellor reported that soldiers had "criminally attacked" female students in the classrooms.[114] Unrest flared up again in the spring of 1963 when paratroopers and SAVAK agents killed two seminary students in Qom while arresting Ayatollah Ruhollah Khomeini for preaching against the White Revolution. Nationwide demonstrations in June led to hundreds, perhaps thousands, more fatalities. The shah responded by suppressing all dissent, banning (again) the National Front, and arresting key opposition leaders.[115]

The turmoil in Iran and philosophical differences within his administration stifled any chance that Kennedy would seek meaningful political reforms.[116] US Supreme Court justice and Kennedy confidant William O. Douglas thought that an elected government with National Front representation might restore public confidence and put Iran back on the path toward democracy, but neither the shah nor opposition leaders trusted one another.[117] Historian T. Cuyler Young argued that the shah must at the very least curtail censorship and allow independent political parties.[118] Veteran diplomats showed much less enthusiasm for democracy promotion. Department of State officials and many of Kennedy's foreign policy advisers continued to see the National Front as "radical, dogmatic, and incompetent," a view seared into their minds during the Mossadegh years.[119] John Bowling, State's officer in charge of Iranian affairs, dismissed its leaders as "idealistic and impractical" and urged maintenance of friendly ties with the shah over the encouragement of political reform.[120] Ambassador Julius Holmes agreed. Iranian history and "the character of the Persian people" convinced him that the ideal government would be "one where the people are firmly and resolutely guided by a central authority."[121] Preserving stability had to be the first priority, and that meant backing the shah.[122]

Kennedy did not protest when the shah cracked down on all opposition following the disturbances in June 1963. He regretted the violence in Qom and Tehran but blamed it on "unfortunate attempts" to block the shah's "reform programs." The president reassured the shah that opposition would "gradually disappear" as the people came to "realize the importance of the measures you are taking to establish social justice and equal opportunity for all Iranians."[123] The Kennedy administration therefore threw its lot in with monarchical dictatorship despite the president's rhetorical emphasis on democracy. Historian Roham Alvandi notes the irony that while "Kennedy had hoped to strengthen the shah's regime through reform," the president actually "helped silence the shah's critics and further enrich his dictatorship."[124]

The US government did little to challenge the monarchical dictatorship after 1963. Lyndon Johnson and Richard Nixon respected the shah's toughness and his no-nonsense approach to communism. Both had visited Iran during their vice presidencies and considered the shah a personal friend; neither was willing to press a kindred spirit on such matters as tolerating dissent[125] In any event, recent research emphasizes that Iran's growing oil revenue and Johnson's preoccupation with Vietnam further eroded US leverage in Tehran during the 1960s. As the shah became more secure, he became more assertive; as he became more assertive, American officials stopped trying to nudge him toward democracy.[126] Instead, Johnson and Nixon accepted the shah's view that military power was the source of Iran's strategic value to the United States and should therefore drive relations between the two countries.[127]

Jimmy Carter, in contrast, came to the presidency intent on making democracy and human rights foreign policy priorities. The shah had by that time adopted the language of both, but he preferred to speak about them in terms of broadening opportunity for Iranians rather than expanding political freedom. Carter understood that such rhetoric was deliberately misleading, but he also appreciated Iran's strategic importance to the United States. His emphasis on human rights lacked teeth when it came to Iran.[128] The president celebrated the shah's "enlightened leadership" during the latter's November 1977 visit to the United States.[129] Meanwhile, Washington, DC, police used clubs and tear gas to disperse nearby student protesters. Some of the most enduring images of the shah's failing regime resulted when he and Carter became visibly uncomfortable as tear gas wafted onto the White House lawn. When Carter visited Iran at the end of December, he proclaimed that "the cause of human rights . . . is shared deeply by our people and the leaders of our two nations" and praised Iran as "an island of stability in one of the more troubled areas of the world."[130]

In reality, the mid-1970s were a time of grisly repression in that country. SAVAK agents subjected opponents of the regime to "the most severe forms of torture" with tacit government approval.[131] People "disappeared from their homes without explanation," and political executions "increased sharply."[132] Amnesty International concluded in 1976 that "no country in the world has

a worse record in human rights."[133] The shah dismissed mounting international criticism: "I am working for the good of my country . . . I can't waste
my time on a few young idiots."[134] The former Utah advisers were aware of
the repression, though their reminiscences suggest they did not grasp its full
extent. Horticulturalist Clarence Ashton remembered simply that "President
Carter said the human rights were being violated."[135] Gordon Van Epps also
acknowledged that "yes, there were some people that were killed under his
regime." The Utahns nevertheless tended to emphasize the shah's record
on economic development over his abysmal suppression of political freedom. Van Epps praised "the improvement that was being made throughout
the country."[136] Jay Hall reflected that the shah "wasn't the stinker that the
Persians made him out to be."[137]

The regime of Mohammad Reza Shah Pahlavi collapsed in early 1979 amid
a popular revolution, but the former Utah advisers saw it as a tragic blow
for the country they had served a quarter century earlier. Ashton declared
it "one of the worst things that ever happened." A former student later told
him that the revolutionary government let flounder many of the agricultural programs Point Four helped establish: "They wanted it to fail, and it
did fail."[138] Van Epps agreed that the fall of the shah was "bad for the country.
It was a real setback."[139] "I hate to see what happened after Khomeini came
into power," lamented Hall.[140] Lula Anderson added that the new regime
"tried to stifle" progress. Khomeini "put the country back hundreds of years"
and "put the women back in their chadors and took away their freedoms."[141]
She recalled that many Iranians who worked with Americans had to leave
the country "because they were marked."[142] Hall and Flandro noted that
some Iranians who had ties to Point Four were "executed because they
worked with us."[143]

The Point Four Program was born out of the belief that raising the level of
material prosperity in less-developed countries would lead to peaceful democratic development. The Utah advisers no doubt embraced that vision. But
that idealistic goal failed in Iran, as both the US government and the shah
pursued policies that prioritized the achievement of stability over democratization rather than the achievement of stability through democratization.[144]
Neither Point Four nor the Utah advisers caused that shift in US policy, of
course, but they did generally approve of the main result: the shah's quasi-
westernized dictatorship.

BROADENING HORIZONS

Perhaps the most positive legacy of the Point Four experience was that it helped open the door to more international opportunities for the Utah advisers and their home universities, especially USU. The experience of living and working in Iran left a deep and generally positive impression on most of the advisers and their families. Roskelley called the three years he spent in Iran "some of the most profitable years of my life." The assignment gave his family the opportunity to visit Israel, India, and Pakistan, where they saw some of the great cultural treasures of world history.[145] Bruce and Lula Anderson judged their seven years in Iran "a great cultural experience." Lula later recalled that it was "very enriching and enlightening to see how other people lived."[146] Jay Hall and his family were among the first Utahns to arrive in the fall of 1951; they returned for another two years in the mid-1950s. "It's still something I'm always talking about," he acknowledged more than four decades later.[147] Agricultural economist Deon Hubbard likewise called his time in Iran "a learning adventure, a growing experience," and added that he developed an appreciation for the country's history and culture.[148] Morris Shirts often found his work at Daneshsaraye Ali frustrating, but on the way home he and his wife, Maxine, enjoyed the chance to visit several countries of the Mediterranean region and Western Europe. "I'm glad we went," he recalled, "because how else do you get the experiences?"[149]

Many of the Utah advisers remained active in international development work long after the Point Four contracts ended. Roskelley devoted much of his career to working on rural problems in Asia and Latin America. He worked as an AID research analyst for university-based projects in Southeast Asia and later joined USU's Institute for International Rural and Community Development.[150] Bruce Anderson became the executive director of the Consortium for International Development (CID), an organization of universities in western states that coordinated work on food problems in developing nations. He went back to Iran in 1975 to oversee technicians from the US Department of Agriculture.[151] Dean Peterson worked on AID irrigation projects in India and later directed the agency's Office of Water for Peace.[152] Bertis L. Embry spent a summer working on agricultural problems in Venezuela and several years in Guatemala near the end of his career. Max Berryessa and his family spent three years in Thailand working on an education contract for the Department of State between 1961 and 1963. Berryessa went back to Thailand for a second assignment in 1973 as an education adviser for the United Nations Educational, Scientific, and Cultural Organization (UNESCO).[153] Leah Hart, who taught at the American School in Tehran between 1959 and 1961, later lived in Afghanistan for five years when her husband accepted an AID assignment in that country.[154]

Agricultural engineer Richard Griffin had already completed one two-year Point Four irrigation assignment in Brazil before he arrived in Iran with his wife and two sons in the spring of 1955. After Iran, Griffin took engineers to China and the Soviet Union on agricultural study tours designed to improve the image of American science and technology in communist countries as part of President Eisenhower's People-to-People Program. He and his wife later accepted an LDS mission assignment in Nigeria that included providing agricultural assistance; he worked on a water management assignment in Yemen through the CID during the 1980s.[155]

Jim Wood accepted a Peace Corps assignment in India in the late 1960s, and he and his wife, Imogene, lived in New Delhi for five years, until 1972. Jim took another assignment in Uganda with the Near East Foundation, and the couple lived in Bolivia for two years during the 1970s while Jim worked on a CID project. Imogene Wood later recalled that Jim enjoyed the assignments because "he felt like he was doing something for other people."[156] There were other Utahns who continued Point Four's adventurous idea of applying American expertise to the problems of developing nations.

Point Four work also helped internationalize the Utah universities, especially USU, an institution that sponsored an impressive array of international development programs from the 1950s through the 1980s. Dean Peterson and Bruce Anderson helped the university become a charter member of the CID in 1967. USU faculty contributed to a host of CID-affiliated agricultural development projects throughout the 1970s and into the 1980s in Bolivia, Cape Verde, Egypt, Gambia, Kenya, Mali, Mauritania, Niger, Senegal, Sudan, and Tanzania. The university opened an Institute for International Rural and Community Development in 1984 to coordinate its various development efforts; Richard Welling Roskelley, who had become professor emeritus of sociology, was one of its affiliated experts. USU and the Iranian Ministry of Agriculture formed an International Sheep and Goat Institute in 1974, and the university once again sent agricultural advisers to Iran. They helped improve livestock production and dry-land crops as well as training farm managers.

That project was similar in purpose to Point Four's agricultural program of twenty years earlier but more modest in scope.[157]

The University of Utah also rekindled ties with Iran when it announced a ten-year plan to partner with several Iranian universities in 1974. Recognizing that "over the years there have been close ties between Iran and Utah," President David Gardner pledged to increase exchanges of professors and students with the medical schools at the University of Tehran and Pahlavi University in Shiraz. The university also promised support for a new technical institution, Aryameher University, which, according to Gardner, was "really a major modern university . . . of special interest to the Shah."[158] At least one faculty member, however, questioned the wisdom of establishing closer ties to Iranian universities because the country's "political directions" had become "most unappealing."[159]

The upheaval of the Iranian Revolution and the subsequent severing of US-Iranian diplomatic relations ended these cooperative ventures. USU scientists Thomas Cox and Paul Daniels had to suspend their work with the International Sheep and Goat Institute in late 1978 because of the mounting unrest. Cox reported that "like other Americans," he and Daniels had been "accosted on the streets" by Iranians and told to go home. He added, with more confidence than foresight, that the USU scientists were "planning on returning to Iran by popular demand."[160] USU scientists tried to continue work on other projects through the early stages of the revolution. Bruce Anderson pitched a USU proposal to cooperate with the Ministry of Agriculture in developing a new Center for Agricultural Management in early 1979, and the ministry indicated interest in continuing CID water conservation projects that summer.[161] None of these projects survived the revolution. The government of the new Islamic Republic stopped paying CID contract obligations and froze the organization's assets in Iranian bank accounts in 1981. The CID, in turn, brought a suit against Iran to recover the money at the Iran–United States Claims Tribunal at The Hague.[162] The University of Tehran and Pahlavi University—renamed Shiraz University during the revolution—also terminated their relationships with the University of Utah.[163]

Point Four work also added diversity to the Utah campuses. The limits of Iranian higher education forced thousands of its young people to study abroad during the 1950s and 1960s, and Franklin Harris used his contacts to steer many of them toward Utah. Dean Farnsworth recalled that "excellent

FIGURE 6.1. USU president Daryl Chase presents Ardeshir Zahedi, Iranian ambassador to the United States, with an honorary doctorate, 1961. *Courtesy*, Daryl Chase Photograph Collection, Special Collections and Archives, Merrill-Cazier Library, Utah State University, Logan.

Iranian students" came to BYU, though he also remembered that some who brought lax attitudes toward cheating and sexual morality "caused quite a bit of trouble."[164] Iranian student enrollment also increased at the University of Utah, from just 8 in 1949 to more than 100 by the mid-1970s, which made Iranians the largest international student group at that school.[165] Only 5 Iranians were enrolled at USU in 1946, but that number reached 18 in the spring of 1952 and 74 in 1961. A total of 261 Iranian students enrolled at USU between 1951 and 1961, while another 132 visited the university to participate in shorter courses on subjects ranging from agriculture to international banking and trade. One in 5 international students at USU was an Iranian by the early

1960s. The university awarded its most famous Iranian alumnus, Ardeshir Zahedi, an honorary doctorate in 1961 in recognition of his work as "diplomat, promoter of international friendship, ambassador of good will and staunch proponent of peace."[166] Zahedi graduated from the college in 1950 and went back to Iran to join William Warne's Point Four staff. He served as ambassador to the United States from 1960 to 1962 and again from 1973 until the Iranian Revolution in 1979. He was also foreign minister from 1966 until 1971.

The Iranian students helped make Utah State's campus in Logan a more cosmopolitan place. While many understandably struggled with culture shock and homesickness, a number became active in campus life. They hosted Norooz celebrations to mark the Persian New Year on the first day of spring and presented the university with carpets, vases, and other pieces of Iranian art. USU designated a "Persian Room" to display the pieces. Mohammad Moghadam, a University of Tehran linguist, taught a series of courses on Middle East culture and civilizations during the 1960–61 school year, while another Iranian professor taught Persian to a group of USU students. Jalil Mahmoudi, former dean of Karaj Agricultural College, pursued both master's and doctorate degrees at Utah State. He helped train Peace Corps volunteers for work in Iran and offered a course on Problems in the Middle East during his time in Logan.[167]

The Iranian student enrollment at USU began to decline in the second half of the 1960s. One foreign student adviser complained of having "more difficulty with Iranian students than with any other group," especially after an anti-shah movement began to form among the "politically minded" Iranian students. While some administrators pushed to limit the number of Iranians at USU, the drop in enrollment also reflects the university's lack of direct connections with Iran between 1964 and 1973. The USU student body remained remarkably internationalized during the 1960s and 1970s, in part because of the university's other overseas commitments. USU ranked tenth nationally in the percentage of international students among the total student body in the spring of 1968, but by that time only one in ten such students was an Iranian.[168]

Life became more precarious for the few remaining Iranian students at USU, many of whom had turned vocally against the shah, during the Iranian Revolution. The seizure of the US Embassy in Tehran by radical students in November 1979 and the ensuing hostage crisis provoked a strong backlash in Logan as throughout the United States.[169] Hamid Salehi, who was among the last Iranian students to come to Utah State before the revolution, recalled that a group of local residents beat up some Palestinians they had mistaken for Iranians and added that "no one would hire an Iranian." Despite finding himself ostracized, Salehi completed his degree at USU and made the town his home. He still owned a popular sandwich shop on Main Street in the summer of 2014.[170] One reader of the *Utah Statesman* railed against the revolutionary regime, claiming that "the zealous Moslems cannot be dealt with in a rationable [*sic*] fashion." He argued that the US government should not "bow down to terrorism and blackmail" by returning the deposed shah to Iran "for certain death."[171] Another reader expressed disappointment that Iranian students failed to condemn the embassy seizure and instead blamed the American media for its negative portrayal of Iran.[172]

Still, the situation at USU appears to have remained more civil than was the case on other American campuses, where Iranian students reported being subjected to insults, intimidation, and sometimes physical abuse. An anti-Iranian poster at one North Carolina university sneered "Nuke 'em till they glow. It worked in Japan, it'll work in Iran"; another that appeared on a mountain adjacent to BYU demanded "Deport Iran."[173] "Iranian students at the University of Arkansas reported receiving threatening phone calls, while a local shop sold Iranian flags "just right for burning." Hundreds protested the presence of Iranians at Lamar University in Texas by burning an effigy of Khomeini and shouting "deport, deport. Go to hell Iran. Camel jockeys go home."[174]

Discussion of the hostage crisis in the *Utah Statesman* remained remarkably calm by comparison. Most writers seemed to respect the rights of Iranians students, and the editorial staff condemned the tactics of federal immigration agents who came to interview Iranian students and check their papers. The editors argued that the agents threatened academic freedom when they queried Iranian students about their political loyalties. They also charged that a federal agent had "threatened with physical violence" one of the student editors who was taking pictures of the scene.[175] The *Utah Statesman* defended legal due process when it ran a cartoon titled "Your Papers, Please," which depicted aggressive masked federal agents chasing frightened Iranian students.[176] One reader commented, "Since all the chaos started, I have started to ask myself several questions, putting myself into someone else's shoes. How many times have I disagreed with what the US government has done?"[177] A representative of the Baptist Student Union acknowledged that Americans' "bitterness and anger" was understandable in the wake of the embassy seizure but urged the USU community to "be Christian toward Iranians." He noted that Iran "has been in turmoil for a long time and there are deep hurts relating to this continuing conflict in which thousands have died."[178]

Participation in Point Four technical assistance helped broaden the horizons of the Utah advisers and their home universities. It offered an opportunity to travel the world and helped attract more Iranian students to Utah. The Point Four experience also fostered interest in a wide range of international activities, from agricultural development to academic exchanges. USU in particular developed a remarkable range of international development projects, but the University of Utah also built on its Point Four experience by expanding academic links with Iran during the mid-1970s. None of those links, however, survived the Iranian Revolution. The hostage crisis deepened the animosity between the two countries, and the last of the Utah universities' associations with Iran came to an end.

CONCLUSION

The Utah advisers who worked in Iran embarked on a noble pursuit. But their understanding of that country's development was flawed by a misplaced faith in the shah's ability to lead productive change. Point Four touted democratic development through grassroots citizen participation, but the US government abandoned that goal in the 1950s in favor of strengthening the shah's authoritarian regime and embracing larger-scale infrastructure modernization. The Utahns generally applauded these strategies because they appeared to bring progress in economic growth, educational improvements, and women's rights. They rightly saw themselves as sincere friends of Iran, but they largely missed the mounting Iranian resentment that exploded at the end of the 1970s. As the Utahns lamented the overthrow of the shah as a setback for Iranian development, they could at least take some comfort in the cultural enrichment Point Four work brought to both themselves and their home institutions.

AFTERWORD

Not long after the Iranian Revolution, someone produced a brief reflection on USU's development work in that country. "The United States must learn to accept the realities of development around the world," the anonymous author wrote. "Development means change—and the disruption of status quo is fraught with dangers and disturbances. When it is controlled and happens somewhat under peaceful conditions then we are fortunate indeed." Change was "controlled" in Iran, but it did not lead to the peaceful democratic development Point Four envisioned. The author nevertheless took solace in claiming small successes: "US trained Iranians will be better for the training we gave them, and we can expect no more." Furthermore, the university's ongoing work on agricultural problems around the world would "continue to contribute to the well-being of all mankind."[1] It was a remarkably hopeful observation, given the immediate context of the Iranian Revolution and hostage crisis, which also expressed a sober wisdom wrought from decades of experience.

The reality that the Utah universities' projects failed to produce impressive results places them on par with most international development schemes

DOI: 10.7330/9781607327547.c007

during the 1950s and 1960s. In country after country, from India and the Philippines to Nigeria and Ethiopia, the abundant optimism that American expertise would eradicate the scourge of mass poverty gave way to underwhelming results. Development failures in high-profile countries such as Iran and South Vietnam contributed to a cooling of US government support for technical assistance during the 1970s. Free trade and market liberalization emerged as the new zeitgeists for solving the world's poverty problems over the next three decades. Yet nearly a third of the world's population still subsisted on less than two dollars per day at the close of the twentieth century, and many nations of what is now called the Global South still struggled to provide basic education and healthcare to their citizens.[2] Historians have found little reason to celebrate the fruits of President Truman's adventurous idea or most other attempts to incorporate economic development into US foreign policy. Some emphasize the hubris inherent in the American belief that it can remake the world in its image; others criticize US aid policy for creating and sustaining brutal dictatorships.[3] To be sure, much of the blame must fall on leaders of those countries, including Iran. Iranian leaders often failed to make effective use of US development aid, either because of inefficiency and corruption or because they emphasized showy projects that gave the appearance of modernity.

But the shortcomings also reflect faulty American assumptions, planning, and execution. Attempts to transplant what worked in the United States to other countries rarely went as planned. Progress was slow and marginal; the much-vaunted American "expertise" produced more frustration than success. American Cold War strategy increasingly prioritized achieving stability *over* democratic development in countries like Iran while subordinating Point Four's vision of achieving stability *through* democratic development. Technical assistance for rural improvement enjoyed only ambivalent support among career diplomats. In the 2012 movie *Argo*, based on the international rescue of six American diplomats who escaped from the US Embassy in Tehran at the beginning of the hostage crisis, a Department of State officer briefly suggests that the rescue operation could pose the Americans as Canadian agricultural technicians—whom he belittles as "do-gooders." The conversation was fictitious, but the dismissive sentiment was real. American leaders also found it difficult to settle on a consistent development strategy. The ebb and flow of domestic politics and disagreements over priorities and methods—which are, of course, natural parts of the policy-making process—nevertheless stifled coherence.

On January 21, 2009, six decades and a day after Harry Truman first announced his Point Four proposal, a new president, Barack Obama, used his own inaugural address to tell "the people of poor nations" that "we pledge to work alongside you to make your farms flourish and let clean waters flow; to nourish starved bodies and feed hungry minds."[4] The sentiment echoed Truman, but it did not lead to anything like a revival of the Point Four experiment. The new administration's attention was focused on recovery from the Great Recession, and there was little appetite within the United States to expand foreign aid amid costly ongoing conflicts in Iraq and Afghanistan. That is not to say that the grassroots, localized approach to technical assistance the Point Four architects championed has disappeared from the development landscape. But in the early twenty-first century it is carried out mostly by nongovernmental organizations (NGOs) and universities, many of which got their start in international development more than half a century ago by participating in what was then a bold new idea.

NOTES

HSTL	Harry S. Truman Library and Museum, Independence, MO.
IRIPRIPF	Iranian Rural Improvement Program Records, Iran Project Files 1951–56, ACC 209, University of Utah, Salt Lake City.
JFKL	John F. Kennedy Presidential Library and Museum, Boston, MA.
MSU	University Archives and Historical Collections, Michigan State University, East Lansing.
PFPF	Point Four Program Files, MSS SC 2993, BYU.
PPNSF	Papers of John F. Kennedy, Presidential Papers, National Security File, JFKL.
UPI	University Participation in Iran, 23.5, USU.
UPICA	University Participation, International Cooperation Administration, 23.14/1, USU.
USFAA	Records of United States Foreign Assistance Agencies 1948–61, Record Group 469, National Archives II, College Park, MD.
USU	Special Collections and Archives, Merrill-Cazier Library, Utah State University, Logan.
Utah	Archives/Records Management, J. Willard Marriott Library, University of Utah, Salt Lake City.
UUIOHP	Utah Universities in Iran Oral History Project, MSS 7752 Series 35, Subseries 1, BYU. Jessie Embry conducted these interviews for the Charles Redd Center at Brigham Young University.
VPHSR	University of Utah Vice President for Health Sciences Records, 1945–90, ACC 475, University of Utah, Salt Lake City.

INTRODUCTION

1. Lula Anderson, interviewed by Jessie Embry, March 1, 1999, UUIOHP, BYU.

2. Untitled document dated July 7, 1957, folder 1, box 7, UPICA, USU.

3. Anderson interview, March 1, 1999, UUIOHP, BYU.

4. Jonathan Bingham, *Shirt Sleeve Diplomacy: Point Four in Action* (New York: John Day, 1954); Merle Curti and Kendall Birr, *Prelude to Point Four: American Technical Missions Overseas, 1838–1938* (Madison: University of Wisconsin Press, 1954), 7; Stephen Macekura, "The Point Four Program and US International Development Policy," *Political Science Quarterly* 128 (March 2013): 129, 137.

5. Henry Bennett, Memorandum by the Technical Cooperation Administrator to the Director of the Management Staff, April 20, 1951, *FRUS 1951*, vol. 1, 1644.

6. Jess Gilbert, "Low Modernization and the New Deal: A Different Kind of State," in *Fighting for the Farm: Rural America Transformed*, ed. Jane Adams (Philadelphia: University of Pennsylvania Press, 2003), 131; Amanda McVety, "Pursuing Progress: Point Four in Ethiopia." *Diplomatic History* 32 (2008): 385.

7. Walt Rostow, *The Stages of Economic Growth: A Non-Communist Manifesto* (New York: Cambridge University Press, 1960), 10–11.

8. David Ekbladh, *The Great American Mission: Modernization and the Construction of an American World Order* (Princeton, NJ: Princeton University Press, 2011); Nils Gilman, *Mandarins of the Future: Modernization Theory in Cold War America* (Baltimore: Johns Hopkins University Press, 2003); Michael Latham, *The Right Kind of Revolution: Modernization, Development, and US Foreign Policy from the Cold War to the Present* (Ithaca, NY: Cornell University Press, 2011). Roland Popp has questioned the extent to which American policy in Iran remained true to modernization theory in "An Application of Modernization Theory during the Cold War? The Case of Pahlavi Iran," *International History Review* 30 (March 2008): 76–98.

9. See also Daniel Immerwahr, *Thinking Small: The United States and the Lure of Community Development* (Cambridge, MA: Harvard University Press, 2015).

10. Larry Grubbs, *Secular Missionaries: Americans and African Development in the 1960s* (Amherst: University of Massachusetts Press, 2009), 8–10.

11. Figures for Point Four spending quoted in Thomas G. Paterson, *Meeting the Communist Threat: Truman to Reagan* (New York: Oxford University Press, 1988), 151; and "Point Four Program Costs for Fiscal Year 1953," Stanley Andrews Papers, folder 1953, Status of Point IV Activities, box 10, HSTL. Figure for military assistance quoted in Michael Hogan, *A Cross of Iron: Harry S. Truman and the Origins of the National Security State, 1945–1954* (New York: Cambridge University Press, 1998), 324. Figure for the Marshall Plan quoted in Latham, *The Right Kind of Revolution*, 31.

12. Mark Gasiorowski, *US Foreign Policy and the Shah: Building a Client State in Iran* (Ithaca, NY: Cornell University Press, 1991), 102–3.

13. I borrowed the phrasing from Victor Nemchenok, " 'That So Fair a Thing Should Be So Frail': The Ford Foundation and the Failure of Rural Development in Iran, 1953–1964," *Middle East Journal* 63 (Spring 2009): 262. Nemchenok was writing about the Ford Foundation's work in rural improvement, but the dichotomy is applicable to Point Four.

14. Iran had become the world's fourth largest producer of petroleum by 1950. Wladimir S. Woytinsky and Emma S. Woytinsky, *World Population and Production: Trends and Outlook* (New York: Twentieth Century Fund, 1953), 899.

15. James Goode, "A Good Start: The First American Mission to Iran, 1883–1885," *Muslim World* 74 (April 1984): 100–18; Mark Hamilton Lytle, *The Origins of the Iranian-American Alliance, 1941–1953* (New York: Holmes and Meier, 1987), xv, 10.

16. Touraj Atabaki, "The First World War, Great Power Rivalries, and the Emergence of a Political Community in Iran," in *Iran and the First World War: Battleground of the Great Powers*, ed. Touraj Atabaki (New York: I. B. Tauris, 2006), 1; Firuz Kazemzadeh, *Russia and Britain in Persia, 1864–1914: A Study of Imperialism* (New Haven, CT: Yale University Press, 1968), 15–36; Rouhollah Ramazani, *The Foreign Policy of Iran, 1500–1941* (Charlottesville: University of Virginia Press, 1966), 20–80.

17. Daniel Yergin, *The Prize: The Epic Quest for Oil, Money, and Power* (New York: Simon and Schuster, 1991), 136–37, 148–49, 161.

18. Geoffrey Jones, "The Imperial Bank of Iran and Iranian Economic Development, 1890–1952," *Business and Economic History* 16 (1987): 69–81.

19. Edward Brown, *The Persian Revolution of 1905–1909* (London: Frank Cass, 1966 [1910]), 121–25, 260–90; Ali Gheissari and Vali Nasr, *Democracy in Iran: History and the Quest for Liberty* (New York: Oxford University Press, 2006), 32.

20. Yergin, *The Prize*, 269–71.

21. Ervand Abrahamain, *Iran between Two Revolutions* (Princeton, NJ: Princeton University Press, 1982), 113–16, 126–32. See also Cosroe Chaqueri, "Communism in Persia: 1920–1941," in *The Left in Iran, 1905–1940*, ed. Cosroe Chaqueri (Pontypool, UK: Merlin, 2010), 83–97.

22. *A Century of Mission Work in Persia, 1834–1934* (Beirut: American Press for the Presbyterian Church in the USA, Iran Mission, 1936); J. Arthur Funk, "The Missionary Problem in Persia," *Muslim World* 10 (1920): 138–39.

23. Margaret A. Frame, *Passage to Persia: Writings of an American Doctor during Her Life in Iran, 1929–1957* (Stanford, UK: Summertime, 2014).

24. Robert Daniel, *American Philanthropy in the Near East, 1820–1960* (Athens: Ohio University Press, 1970), 91.

25. Samuel Jordan, "Constructive Revolutions in Iran," *Muslim World* 24 (1934): 348.

26. Michael Zirinski, "Harbingers of Change: Presbyterian Women in Iran, 1883–1949," *American Presbyterians* 70 (Fall 1992): 173–86.

27. Monica Ringer, *Education, Religion, and the Discourse of Cultural Reform in Qajar Iran* (Costa Mesa, CA: Mazda, 2001), 137–38.

28. James Bill, *The Eagle and the Lion: The Tragedy of American-Iranian Relations* (New Haven, CT: Yale University Press, 1988), 17.

29. W. Morgan Shuster, *The Strangling of Persia: A Record of European Diplomacy and Oriental Intrigue* (New York: Century, 1912).

30. Bill, *The Eagle and the Lion*, 24–25.

31. James L. Barton, *The Story of Near East Relief (1915–1930): An Interpretation* (New York: Macmillan, 1930); Paul Monroe, R. R. Reeder, and James I. Vance, *Reconstruction in the Near East* (New York: Near East Relief, 1924), 1–18.

32. Harold Allen, "The Rural Factor," *Muslim World* 44 (1954): 171–80; Harold Allen, *Rural Reconstruction in Action: Experience in the Near and Middle East* (Ithaca, NY: Cornell University Press, 1953), 1–24; "Near East Foundation Report on Activities in Iran," March 31, 1954, box 11, entry 576, USFAA, Archives II.

33. Bruce Kuniholm, *The Origins of the Cold War in the Near East: Great Power Conflict and Diplomacy in Iran, Turkey, and Greece* (Princeton, NJ: Princeton University Press, 1980), 137–42; Lytle, *Origins of the Iranian-American Alliance*, 21–32.

34. John Jernegan, "American Policy in Iran," January 23, 1943, in *The United States and Iran: A Documentary History*, ed. Yonah Alexander and Allen Nanes (Frederick, MD: University Press of America, 1980), 94–99.

35. "The Tripartite Declaration of 1943," *FRUS* 1943, vol. 4, 413–14.

36. Kuniholm, *Origins of the Cold War*, chapter 5; Lytle, *Origins of the Iranian-American Alliance*, chapter 9.

37. T. Cuyler Young, "The Race between Russia and Reform in Iran," *Foreign Affairs* 28 (January 1950): 278–89.

38. McGhee quoted in Sara Ehsani-Nia, " 'Go Forth and Do Good': US-Iranian Relations during the Cold War through the Lens of Public Diplomacy," *Penn History Review* 19 (Fall 2011): 7.

39. Young, "Race between Russia and Reform," 282.

CHAPTER 1: FORGING A PARTNERSHIP FOR DEVELOPMENT

1. Harry Truman, "Inaugural Address," January 20, 1949, *Public Papers of the Presidents*, Harry S. Truman, 1949 (Washington, DC: GPO, 1964), 112–15.

2. Truman, "Inaugural Address," 112–15.

3. Walter Adams and John A. Garraty, *Is the World Our Campus?* (East Lansing: Michigan State University Press, 1960), ix.

4. Roberts and *Time* quoted in Joseph Goulden, *The Best Years: 1945–1950* (New York: Atheneum, 1976), 211. On Truman's early presidency and the 1948 election, see Robert J. Donovan, *Conflict and Crisis: The Presidency of Harry S Truman, 1945–1948* (New York: W. W. Norton, 1977); Alonzo Hamby, *Man of the People: A Life of Harry S. Truman* (New York: Oxford University Press, 1995), 361–466; David McCullough, *Truman* (New York: Touchstone, 1992), 467–722; Merle Miller, *Plain Speaking: An Oral Biography of Harry S. Truman* (New York: G. P. Putnam's Sons, 1973), 249–66.

5. Hardy quoted in Samuel Butterfield, *US Development Aid—an Historic First: Achievements and Failures of the Twentieth Century* (Westport, CT: Praeger, 2004), 2–3. See also Thomas G. Paterson, "Foreign Aid under Wraps: The Point Four Program," *Wisconsin Magazine of History* 56 (Winter 1972–73): 120–21.

6. Clark Clifford, *Counsel to the President: A Memoir* (New York: Random House, 1991), 249–51.

7. Harry S. Truman, *Years of Trial and Hope* (Garden City, NY: Doubleday, 1956), 231–32. See also Hamby, *Man of the People*, 107–12; McCullough, *Truman*, 162.

8. Both newspapers quoted in Benjamin H. Hardy, "Point IV: Dynamic Democracy," 20, box 1, Benjamin H. Hardy Papers, HSTL. For more on press responses, see McCullough, *Truman*, 731.

9. John Kenneth Galbraith, "Making 'Point 4' Work: Some Unsolved Problems in Aiding Backward Areas," *Commentary* (September 1950), accessed June 2, 2016, https://www.commentarymagazine.com/issues/1950-september/.

10. Lilienthal quoted in Hardy, "Point IV," 9.

11. Clifford, *Counsel to the President*, 251.

12. Julius Krug to Dean Acheson, January 25, 1949, DHTP, 8.

13. Truman, *Years of Trial*, 230.

14. Raymond Geselbracht, "Introduction: An Important, Enduring, Complex, and Imperfectly Known Foreign Aid Legacy," in *Foreign Aid and the Legacy of Harry S. Truman*, ed. Raymond Geselbracht (Kirksville, MO: Truman State University Press, 2015), 2. Other major Truman-era foreign aid initiatives included Truman Doctrine aid to Greece and Turkey, the Marshall Plan, and the Military Assistance Program.

15. Capus M. Waynick, "Progress on Point Four," *DSB* 23, no. 586 (September 25, 1950), 493.

16. Amanda McVety, *Enlightened Aid: US Development as Foreign Policy in Ethiopia* (New York: Oxford University Press, 2012), 85.

17. Truman, *Years of Trial*, 232.

18. Clifford, *Counsel to the President*, 252.

19. Dean Acheson, *Present at the Creation: My Years in the State Department* (New York: W. W. Norton, 1969), 265.

20. Brown quoted in Paterson, *Meeting the Communist Threat*, 149.

21. "The President's News Conference of January 27, 1949," *Public Papers of the Presidents*, Harry S. Truman, 1949, 118–19.

22. "Transcription of Extemporaneous Remarks by Secretary of State Dean Acheson, Concerning Point 4 of the President's Inaugural Address, at His Press Conference," January 26, 1949, *FRUS* 1949, vol. 1, 758–59.

23. "Major Foreign Policy Questions Facing the Department Arising out of Point 4 of the President's Inaugural Address," February 3, 1949, *FRUS 1949*, vol. 1, 762–64.

24. "Basic Policies Governing Organizational and Financial Arrangements for Implementing an Expanded Program of Technical Assistance through the United Nations and the Specialized Agencies," February 7, 1949, *FRUS 1949*, vol. 1, 764–68.

25. "Objectives and Nature of the Point IV Program," *FRUS 1949*, vol. 1, 779; "Special Message to the Congress Recommending Point Four Legislation," June 24, 1949, *Public Papers of the Presidents*, Harry S. Truman, 1949, 332–33. See also Paterson, "Foreign Aid under Wraps," 123.

26. Robert E. Wood, *From Marshall Plan to Debt Crisis: Foreign Aid and Development Choices in the World Economy* (Berkeley: University of California Press, 1986), 45–46.

27. Department of State, *The Point Four Program*, Publication 3347, December 1949, accessed April 1, 2017, https://babel.hathitrust.org/cgi/pt?id=umn.31951p010925273; view=1up;seq=2.

28. "Objectives and the Nature of the Point Four Program," *FRUS 1949*, vol. 1, 776–83. See also Macekura, "The Point Four Program," 141–43.

29. Randolph Jones, "Otto Passman and Foreign Aid: The Early Years," *Louisiana History* 26 (Winter 1985): 53–59.

30. Bernard Lemelin, "An Internationalist Republican in a Time of Waning Bipartisanship: Congressman Christian A. Herter of Massachusetts and the Point Four Program, 1949–1950," *New England Journal of History* 58 (Fall 2001): 61–90. Wherry quoted on page 61; Herter quoted on page 67.

31. Hamby, *Man of the People*, 510; Paterson, *Meeting the Communist Threat*, 151.

32. William H. Hardin, "John Kee and the Point Four Compromise," *West Virginia History* 41 (Fall 1979): 50–51.

33. Christian Herter, "A Legislator's View," in *The Point Four Program*, ed. Walter M. Daniels (New York: H. W. Wilson, 1951), 107–10. It is an excerpt from an address Herter gave to the Economic Club of New York on March 24, 1950.

34. "Section by Section Comparison of H.R. 5615 and H.R. 6026," July 1949, DHTP, 113–25. See also Lemelin, "Internationalist Republican," 66–69; Vernon Ruttan, *United States Development Assistance Policy: The Domestic Politics of Foreign Economic Aid* (Baltimore: Johns Hopkins University Press, 1996), 51.

35. Hardin, "John Kee and the Point Four Compromise," 51–55.

36. "Legislative Background of Point Four Program," June 20, 1950, *FRUS 1950*, vol. 1, 846–48. See also Lemelin, "Internationalist Republican," 70.

37. McVety, *Enlightened Aid*, 103.

38. Taft quoted in Paterson, "Foreign Aid under Wraps," 122. See also Colin Dueck, *Hard Line: The Republican Party and US Foreign Policy since World War II* (Princeton, NJ: Princeton University Press, 2010), 72–75. On Taft's attempts to limit

US foreign aid commitments, see Hogan, *A Cross of Iron*, 92–94; Arnold Offner, *Another Such Victory: President Truman and the Cold War* (Stanford, CA: Stanford University Press, 2002), 235.

39. *Executive Sessions of the Senate Foreign Relations Committee*, vol. 2, 81st Congress, 1949–50 (Washington, DC: GPO, 1976), 327–60.

40. *Chicago Daily Tribune* quoted in Hardy, "Point IV," 24. *Wall Street Journal* quoted in Daniels, *Point Four Program*, 66–67. The editorial originally appeared in the *Wall Street Journal* on September 29, 1949.

41. Henry Hazlitt, *Illusions of Point Four* (Irving-on-Hudson, NY: Foundation for Economic Education, 1950). The quotations are on pages 4, 41, and 42.

42. Galbraith, "Making 'Point 4' Work."

43. "Legislative Background," *FRUS* 1950, vol. 1, 849–50.

44. Memorandum, July 12, 1950, DHTP, 421–26.

45. Paterson, *Meeting the Communist Threat*, 151.

46. McVety, *Enlightened Aid*, 85.

47. Congress authorized the president to send American technical advisers to Latin America in 1939 in response to growing Axis influence. The Roosevelt administration set up the Office of the Coordinator of Inter-American Affairs in 1940, and Nelson Rockefeller helped establish the Institute of Inter-American Affairs (IIAA) in 1942. Both were small but direct predecessors of the Point Four Program. See Philip Glick, *The Administration of Technical Assistance: Growth in the Americas* (Chicago: University of Chicago Press, 1957); 8–19; *History of the Office of the Coordinator of Inter-American Affairs* (Washington, DC: GPO, 1947).

48. Mary Renda, *Taking Haiti: Military Occupation and the Culture of US Imperialism, 1915–1940* (Chapel Hill: University of North Carolina Press, 2001), chapter 3. See also Stanley Karnow, *In Our Image: America's Empire in the Philippines* (New York: Random House, 1989), 139–266; Walter LaFeber, *Inevitable Revolutions: The United States in Central America*, 2nd ed. (New York: W. W. Norton, 1993), 34–85.

49. *Executive Sessions of the Senate Foreign Relations Committee*, vol. 2, 328.

50. Stanley Andrews, "How Could We Make More Effective Use of Our Moral Resources," folder Speech File 14/16m, Principia College of Liberal Arts, box 12, and "Agricultural Technical Assistance and the American Image," folder 1960 Report, box 14. Both are in the Stanley Andrews Papers, HSTL.

51. Milton Eisenhower, "Education for International Understanding," April 29, 1954, folder 1954 speeches, articles (2 of 2), box 5, Milton S. Eisenhower Papers, DDEL.

52. Truman to Rockefeller, January 13, 1951; Charles Murphy to David Lloyd, February 28, 1951, DHTP, 466–42.

53. According to the Morrill Act of 1862, each state could claim federal land to build an agricultural college or enhance agricultural and mechanical programs

within an existing institution. The Agricultural College Act of 1890 extended the land-grant concept to historically black institutions in states with segregated higher education. Henry S. Brunner, *Land Grant Colleges and Universities, 1862–1962* (Washington, DC: GPO, 1962).

54. Wayne D. Rasmussen, *Taking the University to the People: Seventy-Five Years of Cooperative Extension* (Ames: Iowa State University Press, 1989), 1–40. See also Milton Eisenhower, "Democracy and the Land-Grant Colleges," folder Speeches, October 1944–45, box 1, Milton S. Eisenhower Papers, DDEL.

55. For the text of Hannah's letter to Truman, see Richard O. Niehoff, *John A. Hannah: Versatile Administrator and Distinguished Public Servant* (Lanham, MD: University Press of America, 1989), 216–18.

56. "Digest of Committee Reports to the Conference on Agricultural Services to Foreign Areas," folder Agriculture 1951, box 4, entry 1399, Subject Files, 1948–56, Records of the United States Foreign Assistance Agencies, 1948–61, Archives II.

57. "The Participation of American Colleges and Universities in Technical Cooperation Programs Abroad," folder 7, box 2, Dean Peterson Collection, BYU.

58. "Truman Names Bennett Point 4 Chief," *Daily Oklahoman* [Oklahoma City], November 15, 1950, folder Newspaper Clippings, box 1, Henry Bennett Papers, HSTL.

59. Bingham, *Shirt Sleeve Diplomacy*, 13.

60. Paul William Bass, *Point Four: Touching the Dream: A Bold, New US Foreign Policy* (Stillwater, OK: New Forums, 2009), 17–20.

61. Memorandum with Attachment, DHTP, 432–33; "A&M's Great Progress Credited to Dr. Bennett," *Stillwater [OK] News-Press*, November 19, 1950, folder Newspaper Clippings, box 1, Henry Bennett Papers, HSTL.

62. "Dr. Bennett off to Advise Addis Ababa," March 29, 1950; "Noted American Educator Arrives in City," April 10, 1950, both in folder Newspaper Clippings, box 1, Henry Bennett Papers, HSTL; *The Agriculture of Ethiopia*, January 1958, folder World Trip, Ethiopia, box 14, Stanley Andrews Papers, HSTL.

63. "The Point 4 Program and the Contribution of Home Economics," March 21, 1951, folder Speeches and Articles, box 1, Henry Bennett Papers, HSTL.

64. "Excerpts from Remarks by Dr. Henry G. Bennett, Administrator, Technical Cooperation Administration, Department of State, before the American Society for Engineering Education, Michigan State College," June 28, 1951, folder Speeches and Articles, box 1, Henry Bennett Papers, HSTL.

65. "The Point Four Program and the Negro Land Grant Colleges," October 18, 1951, folder Speeches and Articles, box 1, Henry Bennett Papers, HSTL.

66. "The Human Side of Point Four," November 15, 1951, folder Speeches and Articles, box 1, Henry Bennett Papers, HSTL.

67. "Point 4: Philosophy of Plenty," November 12, 1951, folder Speeches and Articles, box 1, Henry Bennett Papers, HSTL.

68. John M. Richardson Jr., *Partners in Development: An Analysis of AID-University Relations, 1950–1966* (East Lansing: Michigan State University Press, 1969), 18.

69. "US Technical Aid Enlists Colleges," *New York Times*, October 7, 1953, 18, accessed March 6, 2018, newyorktimes.com.

70. Harold Stassen to William H. Rand, October 9, 1953, folder Use of University Contracts (1 of 2), box 101, John Ohly Papers, HSTL.

71. Quoted in Ruttan, *United States Development Assistance*, 205.

72. Edward W. Weidner, *The World Role of Universities* (New York: McGraw-Hill, 1962), 158.

73. Richardson, *Partners in Development*, chapters 2 and 3; *Technical Cooperation through American Universities* (Washington, DC: International Cooperation Administration, undated); Weidner, *World Role of Universities*, 154–62.

74. *Technical Cooperation through American Universities*; Weidner, *World Role of Universities*. See also *Building Institutions to Serve Agriculture: A Summary Report of the C.I.C.-A.I.D. Rural Development Research Project* (West Lafayette, IN: Purdue University, 1968).

75. *Technical Cooperation through American Universities*.

76. Matthew Shannon, unpublished manuscript shared with the author, October 2015.

77. Ralph Smuckler, *A University Turns to the World* (East Lansing: Michigan State University Press, 2003), 7–18, 36–40; John Ernst, *Forging a Fateful Alliance: Michigan State University and the Vietnam War* (East Lansing: Michigan State University Press, 1998).

78. "Summary of Point Four Activities in 35 Countries," July 14, 1953, folder 1953 Status of Point Four Activities, box 10, Stanley Andrews Papers, HSTL.

79. *Technical Cooperation through American Universities*, 35–41.

80. David Bell, "The University Contribution to Developing Nations," folder Education and World Affairs, October 11, 1963, East Lansing, Michigan, box 25, David E. Bell Personal Papers, JFKL. See also Robert Freeman Butts, *American Education in International Development* (New York: Harper and Row, 1963), 27.

81. Lynton K. Caldwell, "The University-Government Relationship," and Walter H.C. Laves, "University Leadership in Transnational Educational Relationships," both in *Universities . . . and Development Assistance Abroad*, ed. Richard A. Humphrey (Washington, DC: American Council on Education, 1967), 19, 28–37.

82. William Warne, "Report of the Contributions Made by Brigham Young University in the Development of the Point Four Program in Iran," folder 1, PFPF, BYU.

83. William C. Paddock to Milton Eisenhower, November 6, 1952, folder 43, box 80, Office of the President, Papers of John Hannah, MSU.

84. Fayette Parvin to Milton Eisenhower, November 21, 1952, folder 43, box 80, Office of the President, Papers of John Hannah, MSU.

85. John Hannah, "Universities' Expectations of Government," in *University Projects Abroad: Papers Presented at the Conference on University Contracts Abroad* (Washington, DC: American Council on Education, 1956), 53.

86. "Reorganization of Foreign Aid and Information Programs," *DSB* 28, no. 729, June 15, 1953, 849–56.

87. Sergey Y. Shenin, *America's Helping Hand: Paving the Way for Globalization, Eisenhower's Foreign Aid Policy and Politics* (New York: Nova Science, 2005); Richardson, *Partners in Development*, 34–36, 43–46; Weidner, *World Role of Universities*, 158.

88. Rudger Walker to Cedric Seager, September 16, 1953, folder 3, box 2, UPICA, USU.

89. Richard Welling Roskelley to Rudger Walker, January 26, 1954, folder 1, box 26, Richard Welling Roskelley Papers, USU.

90. Michael R. Adamson, "'The Most Important Single Aspect of Our Foreign Policy'? The Eisenhower Administration, Foreign Aid, and the Third World," in *The Eisenhower Administration, the Third World, and the Globalization of the Cold War*, ed. Kathryn C. Statler and Andrew Johns (Lanham, MD: Rowman and Littlefield, 2006), 47–49. Humphrey quoted on page 49.

91. John Hollister, Memorandum from the Director of the International Cooperation Administration to the Secretary of State, August 29, 1956, *FRUS* 1955–57, vol. 9, 90–92.

92. John Hollister, "An Outline of the Mutual Security Program for 1957," *DSB* 34, no. 876, April 9, 1956, 605–7.

93. Edwin Arnold to John B. Hollister, November 15, 1956, folder University Contracts (1 of 2), box 101, John Ohly Papers, HSTL.

CHAPTER 2: UTAHNS IN IRAN

1. Jessie Embry, "The Church Follows the Flag: US Foreign Aid, Utah Universities, the LDS Church, and Iran, 1950–1964," *Journal of Mormon History* 32 (Fall 2006): 148. Taggart was then with the Office of Foreign Agricultural Relations.

2. Harris to Rudger H. Walker, July 15, 1951, folder 3, box 30, Louis Madsen Papers, USU.

3. *Deseret News* [Salt Lake City] and Henry Bennett quoted in Jessie Embry, "Utah Universities in Iran, 1950–1964," *Journal of the Utah Academy of Sciences, Arts, and Letters* (2002): 166.

4. "Point Four Agreement Signed with Utah Colleges," *DSB*, July 16, 1951, 111.

5. Gwen Haws, ed., *Iran and Utah State University: Half a Century of Friendship and a Decade of Contracts* (Logan: Utah State University, 1963), 7.

6. Bob Parson, "International Students and Programs," folder 16, box 4, University History Materials, USU.

7. William Warne, *Mission for Peace: Point Four in Iran* (Bethesda, MD: IBEX, 1999), 39.

8. Abbas Milani, *Eminent Persians: The Men and Women Who Made Modern Iran, 1941–1979* (Syracuse, NY: Syracuse University Press, 2008), 331.

9. Haws, *Iran and Utah State University*, 7.

10. Janet Jenson, *The Many Lives of Franklin S. Harris* (Provo, UT: Brigham Young University Press, 2002), 110–14, 142–43, 174–83; Brigham Young University, *Franklin Stewart Harris: Educator, Administrator, Father, Friend: Vignettes of his Life* (Provo, UT: Brigham Young University Press, 1965), 36–38, 44–49, 50. See also Benjamin Hardy, "Point IV: Dynamic Democracy," 40–42, box 1, Benjamin Hardy Papers, HSTL.

11. Franklin Harris Diaries, 1908–54, vol. 4, 1061–1161, MS 1611, Church History Library, Salt Lake City, UT.

12. Franklin Harris Diaries, 1908–54, vol. 4, 1083–84.

13. Franklin Harris Diaries, 1908–54, vol. 4, 1127.

14. Franklin Harris Diaries, 1908–54, vol. 4, 1086–87.

15. According to his diary, Harris visited Persepolis, the capital of the classical-era Persian Empire; the tomb of King Cyrus at Pasargadae; Shi'i Islamic shrines in Qom; the former capital of the Safavid Dynasty (1501–1722) at Isfahan; and the tombs of medieval poets Hafiz and Sadi at Shiraz.

16. Parson, "International Students and Programs," University History Collection, USU; Haws, *Iran and Utah State University*, 8.

17. See the photos in folder 18, box 15, Luther Winsor Collection, USU.

18. Luther Winsor, "Iran (Persia) a Land of Opportunity," and "Iran's Most Urgent Problem," both in folder 13, box 15, Luther Winsor Collection, USU.

19. Luther Winsor, "What Can America Do to Help Iran?" folder 13, box 15, Luther Winsor Collection, USU.

20. George Stewart, "Iran: Pathway of the Middle East," *Improvement Era*, October 1950, 790–92.

21. Franklin Harris to Rudger Walker, February 14, 1951, folder 2, box 2, UPICA, USU.

22. Franklin Harris to Louis Madsen, February 25, 1951, folder 2, box 2, UPICA, USU.

23. Franklin Harris to Lois Madsen, April 11, 1951, folder 3, box 30, Papers of Louis Madsen, USU.

24. Bennett quoted in Embry, "Utah Universities in Iran," 166.

25. Program in Iran, May 1, 1951, folder 2, box 2, Dean Peterson Collection, BYU.

26. William Warne, "Report of Contributions Made by Brigham Young University in the Development of the Point Four Program in Iran," folder 1, PFPF, BYU.

27. Embry, "Utah Universities in Iran," 166.

28. A photograph on the front page of the May 12, 1951, edition of the *Deseret News* [Salt Lake City].

29. "Point Four Agreement Signed," 111.

30. Embry, "Utah Universities in Iran," 167.

31. Handwritten notes on telephone conversation, May 18, 1951, folder 3, box 30, Papers of Louis Madsen, BYU; Ernest Wilkinson to Hoyt Turner, March 2, 1955, folder 3, box 2, Dean Peterson Collection, BYU; Ernest Wilkinson to Joseph Stokes, January 3, 1956, folder 8, box 2, Dean Peterson Collection, BYU.

32. Rudger Walker to Louis Madsen, July 27, 1951, folder 3, box 30, Papers of Louis Madsen, USU.

33. Walter Olson to D. A. Burgoyne, May 15, 1952, folder 3, box 2, UPICA, USU.

34. Of the first dozen Utah advisers to arrive in Iran, Bruce Anderson and Jay Hall were recent USAC graduate students, while public school teacher Glen Gagon was a graduate student at BYU. See Embry, "The Church Follows the Flag," 150–51.

35. Gordon Macgregor to Rudger Walker, December 6, 1951, folder 3, box 2, UPICA, USU.

36. Helen Milligan, interviewed by Jessie Embry, June 23, 1998, UUIOHP, BYU.

37. Harris to Walker, July 15, 1951, Papers of Louis Madsen, USU.

38. Franklin Harris to Ray Olin, July 18, 1951, folder 1, box 1, IRIPRIPF, Utah.

39. Imogene Wood, interviewed by Jessie Embry, March 1, 1999, UUIOHP, BYU.

40. Gordon Van Epps, interviewed by Jessie Embry, June 2, 1999, UUIOHP, BYU.

41. Bertis Lloyd Embry, interviewed by Jessie Embry, undated; Dean Burton Farnsworth, interviewed by Jessie Embry, November 6, 1998; Milligan interview, June 23, 1998; Van Epps interview, June 2, 1999, all in UUIOHP, BYU.

42. Untitled speech to an LDS audience, folder 5, box 26, Papers of Richard Welling Roskelley, USU.

43. A. Reed Morrill to Dean Peterson, August 19, 1955, folder 8, box 2, Dean Peterson Collection, BYU.

44. J. Richard Brown, interviewed by Jessie Embry, November 10, 1998; Farnsworth interview, November 6, 1998; Milligan interview, June 23, 1998, all in UUIOHP, BYU.

45. "Personnel of the College to Be Given Additional Study and Consideration by the Board of Trustees," April 18, 1953; Minutes of the June 27, 1953, USAC Board of Trustees meeting, both in folder 4, box 14, Papers of Louis Madsen, USU.

46. L.H.O. Stobbe to William Warne, September 13, 1952, folder 24, box 5, Dean Peterson Collection, BYU.

47. George Stewart to Rudger Walker, August 11, 1951, folder 1, box 1, IRIPRIPF, Utah.

48. Post Report, Isfahan, March 27, 1951, folder 3, box 2, IRIPRIPF, Utah.

49. Rudger Walker to Dale Clark, December 12 and December 20, 1951, folder 3, box 2, UPICA, USU.

50. E. Reeseman Fryer to I. O. Horsfall, October 9, 1951, folder 3, box 2; Bruce Anderson to Dean Peterson, June 12, 1952, folder 4, box 2, both in UPICA, USU.

51. Anderson interview, March 1, 1999, UUIOHP, BYU.

52. Nola and Vern Kupfer, interviewed by Jessie Embry, June 21, 1999, UUIOHP, BYU.

53. Cleve Milligan, Termination Report, January 7, 1954, folder 17, box 7, UPICA, USU.

54. Max Berryessa and Janet Berryessa, "Our Life Together: A Personal History of the Max and Janet Berryessa Family," 62, MSS SC 2954, BYU; Richard Welling Roskelley, "Three Years in Iran," folder 6, box 26, Richard Welling Roskelley Papers, USU.

55. Anderson interview, March 1, 1999, UUIOHP, BYU.

56. Berryessa and Berryessa, "Our Life Together," 62.

57. A. Reed Morrill to Ernest Wilkinson, October 9, 1953, folder 4, box 4, A. Reed Morrill Papers, BYU.

58. Franklin Harris to Louis Madsen, November 14, 1951, folder 2, box 2, UPICA, USU.

59. Warne, "Report of the Contributions Made by Brigham Young University," PFPF, BYU.

60. Haws, *Iran and Utah State University*, 12.

61. Harris Diaries, vol. 6, 1750, 1752.

62. John Evans to Rudger Walker, October 7, 1951, folder 1, box 1, IRIPRIPF, Utah.

63. I. O. Horsfall to John G. Evans, November 3, 1951, folder 3, box 2, IRIPRIPF, Utah.

64. Harris Diaries, vol. 6, 1752.

65. Morrill to Wilkinson, October 9, 1953, A. Reed Morrill Papers, BYU.

66. Louise and Deon Hubbard, interviewed by Jessie Embry, February 28, 1999, UUIOHP, BYU.

67. Maxine Shirts, interviewed by Jessie Embry, June 21, 1999, UUIOHP, BYU.

68. Van Epps interview, June 2, 1999, UUIOHP, BYU.

69. Louise and Deon Hubbard interview, February 28, 1999, UUIOHP, BYU.

70. Milligan interview, June 23, 1998, UUIOHP, BYU.

71. Jessie Embry has done extensive work on the Utah Point Four advisers and the LDS in Iran. See Jessie Embry, "The LDS Church and Iran: The Dilemmas of an American Church," *John Whitmer Historical Quarterly* 21 (2001): 51–59; Embry "The Church Follows the Flag," 165–69. She reports that all of the Utah State and BYU families were Mormon and many of those from the University of Utah were as well. See also Roskelley, "Three Years in Iran," Richard Welling Roskelley Papers, USU.

72. Harris Diaries, vol. 6, 1753.

73. Max Berryessa, interviewed by Jessie Embry, November 3, 1998; Jay Hall, interviewed by Jessie Embry, March 19, 1999, both in UUIOHP, BYU.

74. Kupfer interview, June 21, 1998, UUIOHP, BYU.

75. Embry, "The LDS Church in Iran," 52–54. McAffee quoted on page 54.

76. Roskelley, "Three Years in Iran," Richard Welling Roskelley Papers, USU.

77. Anderson interview, March 1, 1999, UUIOHP, BYU.

78. Milligan interview, June 23, 1998, UUIOHP, BYU.

79. Embry, "The Church Follows the Flag," 163–64.

80. Milligan interview, June 23, 1998, UUIOHP, BYU.

81. Joseph T. Bentley to Harvey L. Taylor, October 22, 1954, folder 7, box 3, Dean Peterson Collection, BYU. Iranian converts to the LDS faith came primarily from among Armenian Christians.

82. Anderson Interview, March 1, 1999; Farnsworth interview, November 6, 1998, both in UUIOHP, BYU.

83. Mildred Bunnell, interviewed by Jessie Embry, June 17, 1999, UUIOHP, BYU.

84. Leah Hart, interviewed by Jessie Embry, June 18, 1999, UUIOHP, BYU.

85. Bunnell interview, June 17, 1999, UUIOHP, BYU. Pioneer Day: a Utah holiday celebrated on July 24 that commemorates the arrival of Brigham Young's party in the Salt Lake Valley in 1847.

86. Berryessa interview, November 3, 1998, UUIOHP, BYU.

87. Elizabeth Cobbs Hoffman, *All You Need Is Love: The Peace Corps and the Spirit of the 1960s* (Cambridge, MA: Harvard University Press, 1998), 60; William J. Lederer and Eugene Burdick, *The Ugly American* (New York: W. W. Norton, 1958).

88. Berryessa interview, November 3, 1998, UUIOHP, BYU.

89. Bunnell interview, June 17, 1999, UUIOHP, BYU.

90. Richard E. Griffin, interviewed by Jessie Embry, March 23, 1999, UUIOHP, BYU.

91. Iranian schoolteacher and public intellectual Jalal Al-e Ahmad addressed the problem in his novel *The School Principal*, trans. John K. Newton (Minneapolis: Bibliotheca Islamica, 1974).

92. Farnsworth interview, November 6, 1998, UUIOHP, BYU.

93. Anderson interview, March 1, 1999, UUIOHP, BYU; Gregory quoted in Embry, "The LDS Church in Iran," 53–54.

94. Embry, "The Church Follows the Flag," 162.

95. Shirts interview, June 21, 1999, UUIOHP, BYU.

96. Anderson interview, March 1, 1999, UUIOHP, BYU.

97. Hall interview, March 19, 1999, UUIOHP, BYU.

98. McSwain quoted in Embry, "The Church Follows the Flag," 165.

99. Embry, "The Church Follows the Flag," 166; Kupfer interview, June 21, 1999, UUIOHP, BYU.

100. Bunnell interview, June 17, 1999, UUIOHP, BYU.

101. Wood interview, March 1, 1999, UUIOHP, BYU.

102. Anderson interview, March 1, 1999; Milligan interview, June 23, 1998; Wood interview, March 1, 1999, all in UUIOHP, BYU.

103. Bunnell interview, June 17, 1999, UUIOHP, BYU.

104. Shirts interview, June 21, 1999, UUIOHP, BYU.

105. Anderson interview, March 1, 1999, UUIOHP, BYU.

106. Bunnell interview, June 17, 1999, UUIOHP, BYU.

107. Bunnell interview, June 17, 1999, UUIOHP, BYU.

108. Shirts interview, June 21, 1999, UUIOHP, BYU.

109. Wood interview, March 1, 1999, UUIOHP, BYU.

110. Haws, *Iran and Utah State University*, 110–11.

111. Parson, "International Students and Programs," 11, University History Collection, USU.

112. Avery Johnson to Ray Olpin, July 31, 1952, folder 2, box 1, IRIPRIPF, Utah.

113. Glen Gagon to William Warne, September 13, 1952, folder 24, box 5, Dean Peterson Collection, BYU.

114. Stobbe to Warne, September 13, 1952, Dean Peterson Collection, BYU.

115. I. O. Horsfall to Avery Johnson, September 9, 1952, folder 2, box 1, IRIPRIPF, Utah.

116. Warne quoted in Embry, "Utah Universities in Iran," 171.

117. Avery Johnson to I. O. Horsfall, September 22, 1952, folder 2, box 1, IRIPRIPF, Utah. See also, Embry, "Utah Universities in Iran," 171.

118. "Basic FOA Policy on University Contracts," June 13, 1955, folder 7, box 2, Dean Peterson Collection, BYU.

119. George Stewart to Ernest Wilkinson, undated, folder 7, box 2,; Wilkinson to Stokes, January 3, 1956, folder 8, box 2, both in Dean Peterson Collection, BYU.

120. Enshalah: "God willing," an expression of hope that something will happen.

121. Jube: a public water source, often polluted, flowing through canals or gutters. Coolie: low-wage manual laborer.

122. Balie: a polite positive response given to a request when the actual answer is no.

123. Kurdahfez: probably from a Persian expression for goodbye.

124. Mahst and chi: yogurt and tea.

125. Fardah: an expression that describes an uncertain future event.

126. "Dr. Shirts Addition to Terminal Report," a handwritten copy is in folder 1, PFPF, BYU.

127. See chapter 4 for a discussion of the death of nurse Cecile DeMoisy on Christmas Day, 1952.

CHAPTER 3: POINT FOUR AND THE IRANIAN POLITICAL CRISIS OF 1951–1953

1. An enormous scholarly literature exists on the Mossadegh era, Iranian oil nationalization, and its impact on international relations. Works that have informed my understanding include Ervand Abrahamian, *Iran between Two Revolutions* (Princeton, NJ: Princeton University Press, 1982), 242–80; Ervand Abrahamian, *The Coup: 1953, the CIA, and the Roots of Modern US-Iranian Relations* (New York: New Press, 2013), chapter 1; Fakhreddin Azimi, *Iran: The Crisis of Democracy from the Exile of Reza Shah to the Fall of Musaddiq* (New York: I. B. Tauris, 2009), 218–55; Bill, *The Eagle and the Lion*, chapter 2; James Bill and William Roger Louis, eds., *Musaddiq, Iranian Nationalism, and Oil* (Austin: University of Texas Press, 1988); Richard Cottam, *Iran and the United States: A Cold War Case Study* (Pittsburgh: University of Pittsburgh Press, 1988), chapter 2; Mostafa Elm, *Oil, Power, and Principle: Iran's Oil Nationalization and Its Aftermath* (Syracuse, NY: Syracuse University Press, 1994); Mary Ann Heiss, *Empire and Nationhood: The United States, Great Britain, and Iranian Oil, 1950–1954* (New York: Columbia University Press, 1997); Nikki Keddie, *Modern Iran: Roots and Results of Revolution* (New Haven, CT: Yale University Press, 2003) 121–30; Stephen Kinzer, *All the Shah's Men: An American Coup and the Roots of Middle East Terror* (Hoboken, NJ: John Wiley and Sons, 2008), chapters 3 and 4; Sepehr Zabih, *The Mossadegh Era: Roots of the Iranian Revolution* (Chicago: Lake View, 1982), 5–32.

2. On the development of Mossadegh's political career, see Milani, *Eminent Persians*, 237–38; Mohammad Musaddiq, *Musaddiq's Memoirs*, trans. Homa Katouzian (London: National Movement of Iran, 1988), chapters 1–24; Christopher Bellaigue, *Patriot of Persia: Muhammad Mossadegh and the Tragic Anglo-American Coup* (New York: Harper Perennial, 2012), chapters 1–9.

3. The Sixteenth Parliament, convened in February 1950, was the first to contain a Senate. The shah had the right to appoint half of its sixty members. It therefore tended to be more strongly royalist than the Majlis.

4. Elm, *Oil, Power, and Principle*, 82 (parliamentary votes in support of nationalization), 92 (vote in favor of Mossadegh).

5. Habib Ladjevardi, "Constitutional Government and Reform under Musaddiq," in *Musaddiq, Iranian Nationalism, and Oil*, ed. Bill and Louis, 70.

6. William Roger Louis, *The British Empire in the Middle East, 1945–1951* (Oxford: Oxford University Press, 1984), 651–54; Yergin, *The Prize*, chapter 23.

7. Shepherd quoted in Louis, *The British Empire*, 651–52.

8. Louis, *The British Empire*, 662–69.

9. Figures quoted in Yergin, *The Prize*, 464.

10. American proposals included a 50/50 profit sharing with the Iranian government, increasing transparency within AIOC operations, and giving Iranians more responsibility in running the company. See Abrahamian, *The Coup*, 47, 62, 95; Cottam, *Iran and the United States*, 95–96.

11. Ian Cole Lear-Nickum, "Mossadegh in America: A Turning Point, October 9, 1951–November 18, 1951 (MA thesis, North Carolina State University, Raleigh, 2013).

12. Memorandum of Conversation with President Harry S. Truman, Prime Minister Mohammad Mosaddeq of Iran, and Lieutenant Colonel Walters, October 23, 1951, Secretary of State File, Dean G. Acheson Papers, HSTL electronic document, accessed May 27, 1915, http://www.trumanlibrary.org/whistlestop/study_collecti ons/achesonmemos/view.php?documentVersion=transcript&documentid=69 -6_36&documentYear=1951.

13. Acheson, *Present at the Creation*, 504.

14. Berryessa quoted in Kira Cluff, "Serving Iran," *Daily Universe*, July 27, 2003, accessed September 17, 2015, http://universe.byu.edu/2003/07/27/serving-iran/.

15. Telegram from the Embassy in Tehran to the Department of State, November 28, 1951, *FRUS* 1952–54, Iran 1951–54, 160, document 56. See also Abrahamian, *The Coup*, 173.

16. "Probable Developments in Iran in 1952 in the Absence of an Oil Settlement," February 4, 1952, *FRUS* 1952–54, Iran 1951–54, 176, document 63; Memorandum from Director of Central Intelligence Dulles to President Eisenhower, March 1, 1953, *FRUS* 1952–54, Iran 1951–54, 469, document 169. See also Acheson, *Present at the Creation*, 507; Heiss, *Empire and Nationhood*, 77–78; Robert J. McMahon, *Dean Acheson and the Creation of an American World Order* (Washington, DC: Potomac Books, 2009), 158–59; David S. Painter, *Oil and the American Century: The Political Economy of US Foreign Oil Policy, 1941–1954* (Baltimore: Johns Hopkins University Press, 1986), 175.

17. Memorandum of Conversation, October 23, 1951, Secretary of State Files, Dean G. Acheson Papers, HSTL.

18. "Man of the Year: Challenge of the East," *Time*, January 7, 1952, 18–21.

19. Ed Haroldson, "Iran Resists Red Menace, Utahn Reports," *Deseret News* [Salt Lake City], May 12, 1951. A copy of this article is in folder 3, box 30, Papers of President Louis Madesen, USU.

20. Dorman H. Smith, "His Favorite Chef," *Herald Journal* [Logan, UT], September 11, 1952. A copy is in folder 1, box 26, Papers of Richard Welling Roskelley, USU.

21. Winsor, "What Can America Do to Help Iran?" Luther Winsor Collection, USU.

22. Stewart, "Iran: Pathway of the Middle East," 790–92.

23. Maziar Behrooz, "The 1953 Coup in Iran and the Legacy of the Tudeh," in *Mohammad Mosaddeq and the 1953 Coup in Iran*, ed. Mark Gasiorowski and Malcolm Byrne (Syracuse, NY: Syracuse University Press, 2003), 102; Abrahamian, *Iran between Two Revolutions*, 318–19.

24. Telegram dated May 12, 1951, folder 3, box 30, Papers of President Louis Madesen, USU.

25. Zabih, *The Mossadegh Era*, 29. Kermit Roosevelt, one the chief CIA architects of the 1953 coup, later wrote that at least some of the violence was the work of Iranians in the CIA's employ. See Kermit Roosevelt, *Countercoup* (New York: McGraw-Hill, 1979), 98.

26. Zabih, *The Mossadegh Era*, 30–31.

27. Warne, *Mission for Peace*, 34.

28. Ervand Abrahamian, "Communism and Communalism in Iran: The *Tudah* and the *Firqah-I Dimukrat*," *Middle East Studies* 1 (1970): 291–316; Keddie, *Modern Iran*, 111.

29. Abrahamian, *Iran between Two Revolutions*, 321–22; Behrooz, "The 1953 Coup," 109–10. Homa Katouzian argues that the Tudeh Party remained staunchly opposed to Mossadegh throughout the crisis in *The Political Economy of Modern Iran: Despotism and Pseudo-Modernism, 1926–1979* (New York: New York University Press, 1981), 166–68.

30. Cosroe Chaqueri, "Did the Soviets Play a Role in Founding the Tudeh Party in Iran?" *Cahiers du Monde Russe* 40, no. 3 (1999): 523–25; Sepehr Zabih, *The Communist Movement in Iran* (Berkeley: University of California Press, 1966), 166.

31. Abrahamian, *Iran between Two Revolutions*, 283.

32. Byrne, "The Road to Intervention," in *Mohammad Mossadegh and the 1953 Coup*, ed. Gasiorowski and Byrne, 217.

33. Hakimeh Saghaye-Biria, "United States Propaganda in Iran: 1951–1953" (MA thesis, Louisiana State University, Baton Rouge, 2009), 49–54.

34. Maziar Behrooz, *Rebels with a Cause: The Failure of the Left in Iran* (London: I. B. Tauris, 2000), 32–33; Zabih, *The Mossadegh Era*, 50–52. Maleki was an early

member of the Tudeh Party who rejected its subordination to the Soviet Union. He helped found the non-communist Toiler's Party in 1951 and remained a staunch supporter of Mossadegh. His Third Force Party advocated independence from both the West and the Soviet Union.

35. Zabih, *The Communist Movement*, 167.

36. Memorandum of Discussion at the 135th Meeting of the National Security Council, March 4, 1953, *FRUS* 1952–54, Iran 1951–54, 474, document 171.

37. Abrahamian, *The Coup*, 176.

38. Behrooz, "The 1953 Coup in Iran," in *Mohammad Mosaddeq and the 1953 Coup*, ed. Gasiorowski and Byrne, 106.

39. Harris to Walker, February 14, 1951, UPICA, USU.

40. Franklin Harris to Ray Olpin, July 18, 1951, folder 1, box 1, IRIPRIPF, Utah.

41. Berryessa and Berryessa, "Our Life Together," 65–66, MSS SC 2954, BYU.

42. Warne, *Mission for Peace*, 49. The quotation is Warne's paraphrase of multiple articles.

43. Keddie, *Modern Iran*, 125–26.

44. Jessie Embry's notes to "Incidents in the Lives of Bruce Holmes and Lula Ellis Anderson," 44. I am grateful to Ms. Embry for sharing this material with me.

45. Kupfer interview, June 21, 1999, UUIOHP, BYU.

46. Cleve Milligan, Termination Report, UPICA, USU.

47. Milligan interview, June 23, 1998, UUIOHP, BYU.

48. Anderson, "Incidents in the Lives," 38.

49. Kupfer interview, June 21, 1999, UUIOHP, BYU.

50. Zabih, *The Mossadegh Era*, 39–42. Qavam had skillfully negotiated the Soviet withdraw from Azerbaijan in 1946 based on granting an oil concession he knew the Majlis would not ratify. Royalists believed Qavam would resolve the oil dispute without pressing for Mossadegh's political reforms.

51. Warne, *Mission for Peace*, 88–89.

52. Ala quoted in Telegram from Embassy of Iran to the Department of State, July 21, 1952, *FRUS* 1952–54, Iran 1951–54, 282, document 92.

53. Warne, *Mission for Peace*, 93. Henderson quoted in Telegram from Embassy, July 21, 1942, *FRUS* 1952–54, Iran 1951–54, 282, document 92. For more on reaction of American officials in Iran to the events of July 21, see documents 94 and 98.

54. Zabih, *The Mossadegh Era*, 63.

55. Warne, *Mission for Peace*, 88.

56. Warne, *Mission for Peace*, 96–100.

57. Anderson, "Incidents in the Lives," 73.

58. Anderson, "Incidents in the Lives," 81.

59. Dean Peterson to I. O. Horsfall, February 4, 1952, folder 2, box 1, IRIPRIPF, Utah.

60. Darioush Bayandor, *Iran and the CIA: The Fall of Mosaddeq Revisited* (Houndmills, GB: Palgrave Macmillan, 2010), 57–58; Albion Ross, "Iranian Deputies Rebuff Mossadegh over Martial Law," *New York Times*, August 11, 1952.

61. Abrahamian, *Iran between Two Revolutions*, 320–21.

62. Ali Rahnema, *Behind the 1953 Coup in Iran: Thugs, Turncoats, Soldiers, and Spooks* (Cambridge: Cambridge University Press, 2015), 22–26.

63. Telegram from the Embassy in Iran to the Department of State, October 30, 1952, *FRUS 1952–54, Iran 1951–54*, 390, document 137.

64. Bunnell interview, June 17, 1999, UUIOHP, BYU.

65. Anderson quoted in Embry, "The Church Follows the Flag," 154.

66. Anderson interview, March 1, 1999, UUIOHP, BYU.

67. Haws, *Iran and Utah State University*, 30.

68. Telegram from the Embassy in Iran to the Department of State, February 28, 1953, *FRUS 1952–54, Iran 1951–54*, 462–66, document 166. See also Bayandor, *Iran and the CIA*, 76.

69. Rahnema, *Behind the 1953 Coup*, 49; Mussadiq, *Memoirs*, 272–74.

70. Kashani quoted in Zabih, *The Mossadegh Era*, 97–98. See also Katouzian, "Mosaddeq's Government in Iranian History, 14–15.

71. Mossadegh, *Memoirs*, 302. See also Rahnema, *Behind the 1953 Coup*, 50.

72. Berryessa and Berryessa, "Our Life Together," 65; Bunnell interview, June 17, 1999, UUIOHP, 13–14.

73. Warne, *Mission for Peace*, 125–27.

74. Rahnema, *Behind the 1953 Coup*, 50.

75. William Warne to Louis Madsen, March 4, 1953, folder 3, box 1, IRIPRIPF, Utah.

76. Warne, *Mission for Peace*, 127.

77. Glen Gagon, "A Study of the Development and Implementation of a System of Elementary Education for the Ghasghi and Basseri Nomadic Tribes of Fars Ostan, Iran" (Master's thesis, Brigham Young University, Provo, UT, 1956), 77; Anderson interview, March 1, 1999, UUIOHP, BYU.

78. Warne, *Mission for Peace*, 127.

79. Anderson interview, March 1, 1999, UUIOHP, BYU.

80. Anderson interview, March 1, 1999, UUIOHP, BYU; Warne, *Mission for Peace*, 129–30.

81. Anderson interview, March 1, 1999, UUIOHP, BYU.

82. Berryessa and Berryessa, "Our Life Together," 71.

83. Warne, *Mission for Peace*, 131.

84. Dean Peterson to I. O. Horsfall, April 22, 1953, folder 3, box 1, IRIPRIPF, Utah.

85. Warne, *Mission for Peace*, 128.

86. Gagon, "Study of the Development," 77.

87. "The Iran Situation," April 21, 1953, *FRUS* 1952–54, Iran 1951–54, 541, document 194.

88. Simin Daneshvar's famous 1969 novel, *Savushun*, chronicles the suffering of the people of Shiraz during the British occupation.

89. Gheissari and Nasr, *Democracy in Iran*, 53; Abrahamian, *Iran between Two Revolutions*, 279. Though British nationals had to leave Iran when the government severed diplomatic relations with the United Kingdom in October 1952, British intelligence nevertheless maintained an impressive network of anti-Mossadegh operatives, especially three brothers of the Rashidan family in Tehran. See Abrahamian, *The Coup*, 152.

90. Byrne, "Road to Intervention," in *Mohammad Mossadegh and the 1953 Coup*, ed. Gasiorowski and Byrne, 217.

91. Amin Saikal, *The Rise and Fall of the Shah* (Princeton, NJ: Princeton University Press, 1980), 43–44.

92. Mossadegh quoted in Abrahamian, *Iran between Two Revolutions*, 274.

93. Abrahamian, *The Coup*, 170.

94. Warne, *Mission for Peace*, 241–42.

95. "Prospects for Survival of the Mossadegh Regime in Iran," October 14, 1952, *FRUS* 1952–54, Iran 1951–54, 367–70, document 32.

96. Gasiorowski, "The 1953 Coup d'État against Mosaddeq," in *Mohammad Mossadegh and the 1953 Coup in Iran*, ed. Gasiorowski and Byrne, 227–32.

97. Gasiorowski, *US Foreign Policy and the Shah*, 75; Saghaye-Biria, "United States Propaganda in Iran," 65–68.

98. "Iran: Reds Taking Over," *Newsweek*, August 10, 1953, 36–38. Gasiorowski notes that the article was a CIA plant in "The 1953 Coup," 245.

99. Wilbur quoted in Gasiorowski, "The 1953 Coup," in *Mohammad Mossadegh and the 1953 Coup*, ed. Gasiorowski and Byrne, 245.

100. "Discussion with Minister Akhavi," May 20, 1953, *FRUS* 1952–54, Iran 1951–54, 569–70, document 207; "Conference with Dr. Akhavi and Mr. Zanganeh Regarding Tudeh Party," August 6, 1953, *FRUS* 1952–54, Iran 1951–54, 653–55, document 258.

101. Memorandum from the Chief of the Near East and Africa Division, Directorate of Plans, to Director of Central Intelligence Dulles, July 17, 1953, *FRUS* 1952–54, Iran 1951–54, 628–29, document 243; Memorandum from the Deputy Director for Plans to the Chief of the Near East and Africa Division, Directorate of Plans, Central Intelligence Agency, July 28, 1953, *FRUS* 1952–54, Iran 1951–54, 639–40, document 253.

102. Telegram from the Central Intelligence Agency, August 18, 1953, *FRUS 1952–54, Iran 1951–54*, 682, document 277. American operatives, especially Kermit Roosevelt, argue that the August 14 decree constituted a legal dismissal of Mossadegh from office. They argue that by refusing to step down, it was Mossadegh who carried out a coup against the shah's constitutional authority. That is why Roosevelt calls the subsequent removal of Mossadegh from office on August 19 a "counter-coup."

103. Ali Rahnema surmises that Zahedi spent most of the next three days in the basement of the home of Theodore Hotchkiss, a member of the US Embassy staff who lived near the embassy. Rahnema, *Behind the 1953 Coup in Iran*, 111.

104. "Whose Oil? An Abbreviated History of the Anglo-Iranian Oil Dispute, 1949–1953," C–5; Scott A. Koch, "'Zenbebad, Shah!' The Central Intelligence Agency and the Fall of Iranian Prime Minister Mohammad Mossadegh, August 1953," 50, June 1998. Both are declassified CIA histories that are available online via the National Security Archive, CIA Confirms Role in 1953 Iran Coup, accessed June 10, 2015, http://nsarchive.gwu.edu/NSAEBB/NSAEBB435/.

105. Donald Wilbur, *Overthrow of Premier Mosaddeq of Iran: November 1952–August 1953* (Washington, DC: Central Intelligence Agency, March 1954), 26. The National Security Archive, CIA Confirms Role in 1953 Iran Coup, accessed June 9, 2015, http://nsarchive.gwu.edu/NSAEBB/NSAEBB28/5-Orig.pdf.

106. Warne, *Mission for Peace*, 246–47.

107. Bayandor, *Iran and the CIA*, 129; Rahnema, *Behind the 1953 Coup in Iran*, 109, 147–48.

108. The Ambassador in Iran (Henderson) to the Department of State, August 20, 1953, *FRUS 1952–54*, vol. 10, 752.

109. Wilbur, *Overthrow*, 63.

110. Henderson to State, August 20, 1953, *FRUS 1952–54*, vol. 10, 752; Koch, "*Zenbebad, Shah!*" 62; "Whose Oil," C–6, C–10.

111. Henderson to State, August 20, 1953, *FRUS 1952–54*, vol. 10, 752.

112. Rahnema, *Behind the 1953 Coup*, 125, 139–45.

113. Warne, *Mission for Peace*, 251; Wilbur, *Overthrow*, 71.

114. Warne, *Mission for Peace*, 246–53.

115. Dean Peterson to I. O. Horsfall, undated letter received in Salt Lake City on September 8, 1953, folder 4, box 1, IRIPRIPF, Utah.

116. Berryessa and Berryessa, "Our Life Together," 65; Cluff, "Serving Iran."

117. Berryessa and Berryessa, "Our Life Together," 68; Peterson to Horsfall, received in Salt Lake City September 8, 1953, IRIPRIPF, Utah.

118. Bayandor, *Iran and the CIA*, 138; Bunnell interview, June 17, 1999, UUIOHP, BYU; Milani, *Eminent Persians*, 246; Warne, *Mission for Peace*, 253.

119. Berryessa and Berryessa, "Our Life Together," 65.

120. Berryessa quoted in Cluff, "Serving Iran."

121. Peterson to Horsfall, received in Salt Lake City September 8, 1953, IRIPRIPF, Utah.

122. Rahnema, *Behind the 1953 Coup*, 138–39.

123. Bayandor, *Iran and the CIA*, 138, 145.

124. Author's personal correspondence with Ervand Abrahamian, June 18, 2016.

125. NSC 5504, "Statement of Policy by the National Security Council on US Policy toward Iran," January 15, 1955, *FRUS 1955–57*, vol. 12, 690.

126. Warne, *Mission for Peace*, 256–57.

127. Berryessa and Berryessa, "Our Life Together," 68.

128. Cluff, "Serving Iran."

129. Clarence Hendershot, *Politics, Polemics, and Pedagogs: A Study of United States Technical Assistance in Education to Iran, Including Negotiations, Political Considerations in Iran and the United States, Programming, Methods, Problems, Results, and Evaluations* (New York: Vantage, 1975), 42–43.

130. Bill, *The Eagle and the Lion*, 105–10.

131. Memorandum by the Joint Chiefs of Staff for the Secretary of Defense on the MDA Program for Iran, October 12, 1954; "FOA Announces Program of Aid to Iran," November 1954; "FOA Loan to Iran, 1955," April 25, 1955, all in *The United States and Iran*, ed. Alexander and Nanes, 270–71, 276–78.

132. Milligan interview, June 23, 1998, UUIOHP, BYU.

133. M. J. Regan quoted in Embry, "The Church Follows the Flag," 156.

134. Berryessa interview, November 3, 1999, UUIOHP, BYU.

135. Roskelley, "Three Years in Iran," Richard Welling Roskelley Papers, USU.

136. Hall interview, March 19, 1999, UUIOHP, BYU.

137. Cottam, *Iran and the United States*, 109.

138. Hubbard interview, February 28, 1999, UUIOHP, BYU.

CHAPTER 4: TO MAKE THE IRANIAN DESERT BLOOM

1. Luther Winsor provides two accounts of Iranian rural conditions based on his observations in that country between 1941 and 1946 in "What Can America Do to Help Iran" and "Iran and Her Problems." Both are in folder 13, box 15, Luther M. Winsor Papers, USU. See also Rudger H. Walker, interviewed by Mark K. Allen, October 13, 1978, UA OH 34, BYU.

2. Gideon Hadary, "The Agricultural Reform Problem in Iran," *Middle East Journal* 5 (Spring 1951): 185–86.

3. Variations within this basic system were common. Better-off peasant families might own some land or draft animals, which increased their share of the harvest.

Ownership of smaller livestock such as sheep, goats, or chickens also supplemented the income of some families, though disease could nullify the benefit. Regionally divergent crops and access to water also created variations within the system. Finally, some landlords were more generous toward peasants than were others. See M. Nasseri, "Notes on Land Tenure in Iran and Suggestions for Increased Yield of Crops," folder 1, box 26, Richard Welling Roskelley Papers, USU.

4. Lyle Hayden, "Living Standards in Rural Iran," *Middle East Journal* 3 (Spring 1949): 143.

5. Gholam Hossein Kazemian, *Impact of US Technical Aid on the Rural Development of Iran* (New York: Theo Gaus's Sons, 1968), 8; Hadary, "Agricultural Reform Problem," 183; Haws, *Iran and Utah State University*, 25–26. Ziauddin Behravesh quoted in Andrew J. Nichols, "Development of the Iranian Agricultural Extension Service," May 1957, folder 9, box 26, Richard Welling Roskelley Papers, USU.

6. Hayden, "Living Standards in Rural Iran," 144–45.

7. Mostafa Zahedi, "Problems and Difficulties Facing Extension Work in Iran," folder 19, box 6, UPI, USU.

8. Zahedi, "Problems and Difficulties," UPI, USU.

9. Hadary, "Agricultural Reform Problem," 181.

10. Hadary, "Agricultural Reform Problem," 190–91.

11. Keith McLachlan, *The Neglected Garden: The Politics and Ecology of Agriculture in Iran* (London: I. B. Tauris, 1988), 39, 105–6.

12. Richard Welling Roskelley, "Program of the Agricultural Division of TCI (Point IV in Iran)," April 1952, folder 4, box 26, Richard Welling Roskelley Papers, USU.

13. Ed Haroldson, "Iran Resists Red Menace, Utahn Reports," *Deseret News* [Salt Lake City], May 12, 1951; Winsor, "What Can America Do to Help Iran," and "Iran and Her Problems," both in Luther M. Winsor Papers, USU; Stewart, "Iran: Pathway of the Middle East," 790–92.

14. Farrell Olson, Completion of Tour Report, undated, folder 3, box 7A, UPI, USU.

15. Memo of Conversation between Ambassador Henry F. Grady and Prime Minister Mohammad Mosadeq—May 2, 1951, folder Point IV–Iran, box 5, Country Files 1950–53, USFAA, Archives II.

16. Loy Henderson, US ambassador to Iran, Memorandum to State Department, January 29, 1952, *FRUS* 1952–54, vol. 10, 343.

17. "Expansion of Point Four Activities in Iran," January 21, 1952, in *The United States and Iran*, ed. Alexander and Nanes, 243.

18. Nichols, "Development of the Iranian Agricultural Extension Service," Richard Welling Roskelley Papers, USU.

19. Haws, *Iran and Utah State University*, 32–33.

20. Rudger Walker to Dale Clark, September 18, 1951, folder 2, box 2, UPICA, USU.

21. Parson, "International Students and Programs," University History Collection, USU.

22. Haws, *Iran and Utah State University*, 12–14.

23. "My Visit with Seyed Abdol Ayatollah Kashani," August 12, 1952, *FRUS* 1952–54, Iran 1951–52, 318–19, document 115.

24. Kazemian, *Impact of US Technical Aid*, 18.

25. Hayden, "Living Standards in Rural Iran," 147–49.

26. Harold Allen, *Rural Reconstruction in Action: Experience in the Near and Middle East* (Ithaca, NY: Cornell University Press, 1953), 19.

27. Harold Allen, "The Rural Factor," *Muslim World* 44 (1954): 175, 177.

28. Hayden, "Living Standards in Rural Iran," 146.

29. Roskelley, "Program of the Agricultural Division of TCI," Richard Welling Roskelley Papers, USU.

30. Figures quoted in Kazemian, *Impact of US Technical Aid*, 10.

31. Roskelley, "Program of the Agricultural Division of TCI," Richard Welling Roskelley Papers, USU.

32. LeRoy Bunnell, "Utah State Agricultural College—ICA Contract," folder 11, box 7, UPICA, USU.

33. Bruce Anderson, Terminal Report, November 5, 1951–March 15, 1954, folder 10, box 7, UPICA, USU.

34. Stanley Andrews, "Agricultural Technical Assistance and the American Image," folder 1960 Report, box 14, Stanley Andrews Papers, HSTL.

35. Haws, *Iran and Utah State University*, 35–36; Nichols, "Development of the Iranian Agricultural Extension Service," Richard Welling Roskelley Papers, USU.

36. Anderson, Terminal Report, UPICA, USU.

37. William Warne describes the chick project in a more favorable light in *Mission for Peace*, chapter 6.

38. Bunnell, "Utah State Agricultural College—ICA Contract," UPICA, USU.

39. Cleve Milligan, Termination Report, UPICA, USU.

40. Anderson, Terminal Report, UPICA, USU.

41. Bruce Anderson, Terminal Report, July 1954–May 1956, folder 3, box 6, Bruce Anderson Papers, USU.

42. Luther Winsor, "Iran's Most Urgent Problem," folder 13, box 15, Luther Winsor Papers, USU.

43. Milligan, Termination Report, UPICA, USU.

44. Olson, Completion of Tour Report, UPI, USU.

45. "Ostan Agricultural Programs," draft, May 16, 1960, folder 5, box 7A, UPI, USU.

46. Jahangir Amuzegar, *Technical Assistance in Theory and Practice: The Case of Iran* (New York: Praeger, 1967), 246.

47. Embry interview, undated, UUIOHP, BYU.

48. Anderson to Rudger Walker, November 11, 1954, folder 3, box 3; Anderson, Terminal Report, 1954, both in UPICA, USU.

49. Haws, *Iran and Utah State University*, 27.

50. Fatemeh E. Moghadam, *From Land Reform to Revolution: The Political Economy of Agricultural Development in Iran 1962–1979* (London: I. B. Tauris, 1996), 52.

51. Roskelley, "Program of the Agricultural Division of TCI," Richard Welling Roskelley Papers, USU.

52. Anderson, Terminal Report, 1956, Bruce Anderson Papers, USU.

53. Haws, *Iran and Utah State University*, 70–72.

54. Stanley Andrews presented a thoughtful appraisal of the technology transfer problem in "An Off Shoulder Look at Foreign Aid and Its Administration," folder School for Advanced International Studies, Johns Hopkins University, box 19, Stanley Andrews Papers, HSTL. For another thoughtful analysis that focuses on uses of technology in developing high-yield drought-resistant rice in Asia, see Nick Cullather, "Miracles of Modernization: The Green Revolution and the Apotheosis of Technology," *Diplomatic History* 28 (April 2004): 227–54.

55. "Summary of USAID Agricultural Activity in Iran, 1951–1967"; Ray Johnson, "Johnson Cites Impressive Record in Agriculture Development in Iran," undated, both in folder 1, box 116, entry 617, AID, Archives II.

56. Nichols, "Development of the Iranian Agricultural Extension Service," Richard Welling Roskelley Papers, USU.

57. D. C. Purnell, Terminal Report, undated, folder Isfahan Agricultural Reports, box 14, entry 486, AID, Archives II.

58. Melvin Peterson, Completion of Tour Report, August 1, 1957, folder 1, box 7A, UPI, USU.

59. Bunnell interview, June 17, 1999, UUIOHP, BYU.

60. *Technical Cooperation through American Universities*, 12–13.

61. Government of Iran, Ministry of Agriculture, *Agricultural Extension in Iran* (Tehran, 1959), 8–15.

62. Eric Hooglund, *Land Reform and Revolution in Iran, 1960–1980* (Austin: University of Texas Press, 1982), 23–28; McLachlan, *Neglected Garden*, 126; Moghadam, *From Land Reform to Revolution*, 9.

63. Anderson, Terminal Report, 1956, Bruce Anderson Papers, USU.

64. Present State of Cooperatives, folder 6, box 2, UPI, USU; Anderson to Walker, November 11, 1954, UPICA, USU; Van Epps interview, June 2, 1999, UUIOHP, BYU.

65. For descriptions of Iranian land reform schemes, see Hooglund, *Land Reform and Revolution in Iran*; Afsaneh Najmabadi, *Land Reform and Social Change in Iran* (Salt Lake City: University of Utah Press, 1987). For an account of how land reform affected Point Four work during the early 1950s, see Warne, *Mission for Peace*, 190–204.

66. C. David Anderson, End of Tour Report, undated (tour ended January 1964), folder 1, box 116, entry 617, AID, Archives II.

67. Present State of Cooperatives, UPI, USU.

68. Bunnell interview, June 17, 1999, UUIOHP, BYU.

69. Berryessa interview, November 3, 1998; Brown interview, November 10, 1998, both in UUIOHP, BYU.

70. Walker quoted in Embry, "Utah Universities in Iran," 172.

71. James B. Davis, End of Tour Report, April 30, 1966, folder 1, box 116, entry 617, AID, Archives II.

72. Olson, Completion of Tour Report, UPI, USU.

73. Allen C. Hankins, End of Tour Report, February 9, 1965, folder 1, box 116, entry 617, AID, Archives II.

74. Leonard Williams, Completion of Tour Report, undated (tour ended August 6, 1961), box 118, entry 617, AID, Archives II; Embry, "Utah Universities in Iran," 173.

75. Odeal C. Kirk to Harry A. Brenn and Ray G. Johnson, April 8, 1958, folder 8, box 3, UPI, USU.

76. Amuzegar, *Technical Assistance*, 238–40. The quotation is on page 238.

77. Olson, End of Tour Report, UPI, USU.

78. Ministry of Agriculture, *Agricultural Extension in Iran*, 6–7.

79. Odeal C. Kirk, Completion of Tour Report, 1960, folder 5, box 2, UPI, USU.

80. Haws, *Iran and Utah State University*, 89.

81. A second agricultural college was founded at Ahwaz as part of the University of Ghondi–Shapour in 1956. That institution received support from the Near East Foundation in its early years. See William Fuller, "From Village School to Agricultural College in Iran," in *Bread from Stones: Fifty Years of Technical Assistance*, ed. John Badeau and Georgiana Stevens (Englewood Cliffs, NJ: Prentice-Hall, 1966), 60.

82. Richard Welling Roskelley, "Some Notes on Institution Building at Karaj Agricultural College, 1951–1967," folder 16, box 26, Richard Welling Roskelley Papers, USU; Embry interview, undated, UUIOHP, BYU.

83. Roskelley, "Some Notes on Institution Building," Richard Welling Roskelley Papers, USU.

84. Roskelley, "Program of the Agricultural Division," Richard Welling Roskelley Papers, USU.

85. William Carroll, Terminal Report, March 26, 1957, folder 13, box 7, UPICA, USU.

86. Richard Welling Roskelley, "A Development of Karaj Agricultural College," folder 15, box 26, Richard Welling Roskelley Papers, USU.

87. Roskelley, "Some Notes on Institution Building," Richard Welling Roskelley Papers, USU.

88. Roskelley, "A Development of Karaj Agricultural College," Richard Welling Roskelley Papers, USU.

89. "Interview with Dr. M. Mahdavi," June 12, 1967, folder 16, box 16, Richard Welling Roskelley Papers, USU.

90. J. Clark Ballard, Completion of Tour Report, June 3, 1962, folder 1, box 3; Ernest Jacobson, Monthly Report, April 1958, folder 3, box 7; Lee Stenquist, Monthly Report, November 1957, folder 5, box 7, all in UPICA, USU.

91. "Interview with Dr. M. Mahdavi," Richard Welling Roskelley Papers, USU; Bruce Anderson, Monthly Report, March 1958, folder 1, box 7, UPICA, USU.

92. Roskelley, "A Development of Karaj Agricultural College," Richard Welling Roskelley Papers, USU.

93. "Interview with Dr. M. Mahdavi," Richard Welling Roskelley Papers, USU.

94. Carroll, Terminal Report, UPICA, USU.

95. Ballard, Completion of Tour Report, UPICA, USU.

96. Carroll, Terminal Report; Ballard, Completion of Tour Report, both in UPICA, USU.

97. J. Clark Ballard, Monthly Report, April 1963, folder 1, box 3, UPICA, USU.

98. "Interview with Dr. M. Mahdavi," Richard Welling Roskelley Papers, USU.

99. Roskelley, "Some Notes on Institution Building," Richard Welling Roskelley Papers, USU.

100. Kazemian, *Impact of US Technical Aid*, 83.

101. Stanley Andrews, "University Contracts: A Review and Comment on Selected University Contracts in Africa, the Middle East, and Asia," 1961, folder University Contracts, box 16, Stanley Andrews Papers, HSTL.

102. *Building Institutions to Serve Agriculture*, 207.

103. Warne, "Report of Contributions," PFPF, BYU.

104. Technical Cooperation Administration, "Point 4 Technical Cooperation Program for Fiscal Year 1953: Iran," October 7, 1952, folder Iran—Point IV, box 20, Iran Subject Files 1951–61, USFAA, Archives II.

105. Franklin Harris to Ray Olpin, July 18, 1951, folder 1, box 1, IRIPRIPF, Utah.

106. Ruth K. Brown to I. O. Horsfall, August 10, 1953, folder 1, box 5, Dean Peterson Collection, BYU.

107. I. O. Horsfall to Dean Peterson, February 4, 1952, folder 2, box 1, IRIPRIPF, Utah.

108. I. O. Horsfall to Orrin T. Miller, February 25, 1953, folder 15, box 5, Dean Peterson Collection, BYU.

109. Dean Peterson to I. O. Horsfall, July 19, 1953, folder 14, box 5, Dean Peterson Collection, BYU.

110. Anderson interview, March 1, 1999, UUIOHP, BYU.

111. Dean Peterson to I. O. Horsfall, January 2, 1952, folder 2, box 1; I. O. Horsfall to William Warne, December 24, 1952, folder 2, box 1; William Warne to I. O. Horsfall, January 20, 1953, folder 3, box 1, all in IRIPRIPF, Utah; Anderson interview, March 1, 1999, UUIOHP, BYU.

112. Dean Peterson to Mr. and Mrs. Charles DeMoisy, December 27, 1952, folder 3, box 1, IRIPRIPF, Utah.

113. Anderson interview, March 1, 1999, UUIOHP, BYU.

114. William Warne to I. O. Horsfall, January 3, 1953, folder 3, box 1, IRIPRIPF, Utah.

115. Edith DeMoisy to George Stewart, December 28, 1952, folder 4, box 5, Dean Peterson Collection, BYU.

116. Cedric Seager to I. O. Horsfall, April 28, 1953, folder 3, box 1, IRIPRIPF, Utah.

117. L.H.O. Stobbe to William Warne, September 13, 1952, Dean Peterson Collection, BYU.

118. Anderson interview, March 1, 1999, UUIOHP, BYU.

119. I. O. Horsfall to Dean Peterson, February 4, 1952; I. O. Horsfall to Johnston Avery, September 9, 1952, both in IRIPRIPF, Utah.

120. For a complete overview of Point Four public health initiatives in Iran during the 1950s, see United States Operations Mission/Iran, "A Ten Year Summary of the United States and Iran—a Joint Effort in Public Health, 1951–1960," accessed June 27, 2016, http://pdf.usaid.gov/pdf_docs/PNABI618.pdf.

121. McLachlan, *Neglected Garden*, 49.

122. Kazemian, *Impact of US Technical Aid*, 20, 23.

123. Amuzegar, *Technical Assistance*, 10.

124. Andrews, "University Contracts," Stanley Andrews Papers, HSTL.

125. Gasiorowski, *US Foreign Policy and the Shah*, 107.

126. Anderson to Walker, November 11, 1954, UPICA, USU.

127. Haws, *Iran and Utah State University*, 48.

128. Roseklley quoted in Parson, "International Students and Programs," 12.

129. Amuzegar, *Technical Assistance*, 238.

130. Kazemian, *Impact of US Technical Aid*, 26–27.

131 Embry quoted in Jessie Embry, "Point Four, Utah State University Technicians, and Rural Development in Iran, 1950–1964," *Rural History* 14 (2003): 106.

132. "Interview with Dr. Mahdavi," Richard Welling Roskelley Papers, USU.

133. Demos Hadjiyanis, "Point Four in Iran" (MA thesis, Ohio University, Athens, 1954), 186.

134. Keddie, *Modern Iran*, 117.

135. Quoted in Immerwahr, *Thinking Small*, 166.

136. Ali Ansari, "The Myth of the White Revolution: Mohammad Reza Shah, 'Modernization,' and the Consolidation of Power," *Middle Eastern Studies* 37 (July 2001): 11–15; Latham, *Right Kind of Revolution*, 148–50; Matthew K. Shannon, "American-Iranian Alliances: International Education, Modernization, and Human Rights during the Pahlavi Era," *Diplomatic History* 39 (September 2015): 675–76.

137. Fred Halliday, *Iran: Dictatorship and Development* (Harmondsworth: Penguin, 1979), 106, 126–27, 130–31; Ann Lambton, *The Persian Land Reform, 1962–1969* (Oxford: Clarendon, 1969), 350; Moghadam, *From Land Reform to Revolution*, 6, 94–97; Najmabadi, *Land Reform and Social Change*, 99; Bahman Nirumand, *Iran: The New Imperialism in Action*, trans. Leonard Mins (New York: Modern Reader Paperbacks, 1969), 122–27.

138. Andrews, "Off Shoulder Look at Foreign Aid and Its Administration," Stanley Andrews Papers, HSTL. See also Benjamin Higgins, "The Evaluation of Technical Assistance," *International Journal* 25 (March 1970): 40–41.

139. Henry F. Dobyns, "Sociological and Anthropological Approaches to Engineering Successful Economic Organizations"; Jerry Foytik and Edwin Faris, "Agricultural Cooperatives in Chile"; Marvin D. Miracle, "An Evaluation of Attempts to Introduce Cooperatives and Quasi-Cooperatives in Tropical Africa," all in *Agricultural Cooperatives and Markets in Developing Countries*, ed. Kurt Anshel, Russell Brannon, and Eldon Smith (New York: Praeger, 1969), 163–83, 249–73, 308–13.

140. Richard Garlitz, "Land-Grant Education in Turkey: Ataturk University and American Technical Assistance, 1954–1968," in *Turkey in the Cold War: Ideology and Culture*, ed. Cangül Örnek and Çağdaş Üngör (Houndmills, UK: Palgrave Macmillan, 2013), 177–97.

141. Adams and Garraty, *Is the World Our Campus*, 132–33; Weidner, *World Role of Universities*, 249–50.

142. Quoted in Richard Garlitz, "US University Advisors and Education Modernization in Iran, 1951–1967," in *Teaching America to the World and the World to America: Education and Foreign Relations since 1870*, ed. Richard Garlitz and Lisa Jarvinen (New York: Palgrave Macmillan, 2012), 206.

143. Embry interview, undated, UUIOHP, BYU.

CHAPTER 5: MODERNIZING IRANIAN EDUCATION

1. Iraj Ayman, *Educational Innovation in Iran* (Paris: UNESCO Press, 1974), 2; David Menashri, *Education and the Making of Modern Iran* (Ithaca, NY: Cornell University Press, 1992), 77–78. The quotation is on page 77.

2. Menashri, *Education and the Making of Modern Iran*, 93–104. See also Halliday, *Iran*, 13.

3. Ministry of Education, Pious Endowments and Fine Arts Provincial [Departments of] Education, Memorandum 51561/17224, December 16, 1935. Cited in Camron Michael Amin, Benjamin C. Fortna, and Elizabeth B. Frierson, eds., *The Modern Middle East: A Sourcebook for History* (New York: Oxford University Press, 2009), 202.

4. Government of Iran, Ministry of Education, Bureau of Statistics, *Educational Statistics in Iran* (Tehran, 1965), 2–3, box 124, entry 617, AID, Archives II.

5. Reza Arasteh, *Education and Social Awakening in Iran, 1950–1960* (Leiden: E. J. Brill, 1962), 57.

6. Ayman, *Educational Innovation in Iran*, 3. See also Alva John Clarke, interviewed by Marsha C. Martin, December 7, 1982, LDS Family Life Oral History Project, BYU.

7. A. Reed Morrill, "A Brief Report of Secondary Education in Iran, under the B.Y.U. Contract, 1953–1955," folder 4, box 4, A. Reed Morrill Papers, BYU.

8. Issa Sadiq, *Modern Persia and Her Educational System* (New York: Columbia University Press, 1931), 61.

9. Brigham Young University Contract Team, *Technical Aid: An Investment in People: The Point Four Program in Iran* (Provo, UT: Brigham Young University, 1960), 86.

10. "Point 4 Project Description for Iran Village Development and Rural Improvement Program," folder 2, box 2, Dean A. Peterson Collection, BYU.

11. Arasteh, *Education and Social Awakening*, 55–58; Menashri, *Education and the Making of Modern Iran*, 94–98.

12. Ministry of Education, Memorandum 51561/17224, 202.

13. Brigham Young University Contract Team, *Technical Aid*, 119.

14. Sadiq, *Modern Persia and Her Educational System*, 88.

15. Ahmad Fattahipour, "Educational Diffusion and Modernization of an Ancient Civilization: Iran" (PhD dissertation, University of Chicago, 1964), 59.

16. Ali Mohammad Kardan, *L'Organisation Scolaire en Iran* (Geneva: Imprimerie Reggiam et Jacond, 1957), 99–100.

17. Joseph S. Szyliowicz, *Education and Modernization in the Middle East* (Ithaca, NY: Cornell University Press, 1973), 235.

18 Sattareh Farman Farmaian, *Daughter of Persia: A Woman's Journey from Her Father's Harem through the Islamic Revolution* (New York: Anchor Books, 1993), 212.

19. Norman Jacobs, *The Sociology of Development: Iran as an Asian Case Study* (New York: Praeger, 1966), 159.

20. Arasteh, *Education and Social Awakening*, 88; Manuchehr Afzal, "The Cultural Setting of the Problems of Teacher Training in Iran" (PhD dissertation, Columbia University, New York City, 1956), 222. Name changes cited in "About the College of Science," accessed September 21, 2015, http://science.ut.ac.ir/en/Pages/College.of .Science/Detail-882.aspx.

21. Fattahipour, "Educational Diffusion," 59.

22. William Fuller, "From Village School to Agricultural College in Iran"; Ezzat Aghelvi, "Rural Home Welfare in Iran," both in *Bread From Stones*, ed. Badeau and Stevens, 43–47, 56, 60–61, 77–80; Near East Foundation, "2002 Annual Report," accessed September 21, 2015, http://www.neareast.org/download/annual_reports /2002_AR.pdf.

23. On budget increases for education during the interwar years, see Arasteh, *Education and Social Awakening*, 57. On education spending as opposed to military spending, see Fattahipour, "Educational Diffusion," 59.

24. Arasteh, *Education and Social Awakening*, 57.

25. Afzal, "Cultural Setting," 198–200; Arasteh, *Education and Social Awakening*, 92.

26. Menashri, *Education and the Making of Modern Iran*, 121–22.

27. A. Reed Morrill, End of Tour Report, 1961, folder 1, PFPF, BYU.

28. Brigham Young University Contract Team, *Technical Aid*, 94.

29. Franklin S. Harris, "The Beginnings of Point Four Work in Iran," *Middle East Journal* 7 (1953): 224–26.

30. Luanna Bowles, "The Role of Education in Point IV," December 6, 1953, 17–19, 22, box 13, entry 576, USFAA, Archives II.

31. Hoyt Turner, "The Training Program in Iran," August 5, 1953, 13, box 13, entry 576, USFAA, Archives II; Morrill, "Brief Report of Secondary Education in Iran."

32. Warne, "Report of Contributions," PFPF, BYU. See also Brigham Young University Contract Team, *Technical Aid*, 88–90.

33. Brigham Young University Contract Team, *Technical Aid*, 99–101.

34. Bowles, "Role of Education in Point IV," 11.

35. Hoyt Turner and Stewart Hamblen, "In-Service Education for Iranian Rural Teachers," October 8, 1958, box 13, entry 576, USFAA, Archives II.

36. Glen S. Gagon, "Report of the Educational Activities in the Fars Ostan for the Period November 19, 1951 through September 6, 1953," September 15, 1953, box 13, entry 576, USFAA, Archives II.

37. Turner and Hamblen, "In-Service Education for Iranian Rural Teachers," USFAA, Archives II.

38. Hoyt Turner, Completion of Tour Report, January 16, 1957, box 124, entry 617, AID, Archives II.

39. Turner and Hamblen, "In-Service Education for Iranian Rural Teachers," USFAA, Archives II.

40. Brigham Young University Contract Team, "Technical Aid," 145; Harry W. Kerwin, "An Analysis and Evaluation of the Program of Technical Assistance to Education Conducted in Iran by the Government of the United States from 1952 to 1962" (PhD dissertation, American University, Washington, DC, 1964), 115–16; Warne, *Mission for Peace*, 116–23.

41. Hendershot, *Politics, Polemics, and Pedagogs*, 21

42. Alva John Clarke, "Personal Histories, 1977," folder 1, Alva John Clarke Collection, BYU.

43. Hendershot, *Politics, Polemics, and Pedagogs*, 84–85.

44. Clarke, "Personal Histories," Alva John Clarke Collection, BYU.

45. Morrill, "Brief Report of Secondary Education in Iran."

46. Clarke, "Personal Histories," Alva John Clarke Collection, BYU.

47. Hendershot, *Politics, Polemics, and Pedagogs*, 84.

48. A. Reed Morrill, "Appendix A" to End of Tour Report, Daneshsaraye Ali, 1961, folder 1, PFPF, BYU.

49. On the Qashqai confederation, see Lois Beck, *The Qashqa'i of Iran* (New Haven, CT: Yale University Press, 1986); Lois Beck *Nomads in Postrevolutionary Iran: The Qashqa'i in an Era of Change* (London: Routledge, 2015).

50. Thomas J. Barfield, "Turk, Persian, and Arab: Changing Relationships between Tribes and State in Iran along Its Frontiers," in *Iran and the Surrounding World: Interactions in Culture and Cultural Politics*, ed. Nikki Keddie and Rudi Matthee (Seattle: University of Washington Press, 2002), 61–86; Stephanie Cronin, *Tribal Politics in Iran: Rural Conflict and the New State, 1921–1941* (London: Routledge, 2007), 22–49.

51. Quoted in Milani, *Eminent Persians*, 954. Milani writes that Bahmanbaigi was born in January 1921. Mohammad Shahbazi puts his birth in 1920. See Mohammad Shahbazi, "The Qashqa'i Nomads of Iran (Part II): State-Supported Literacy and Ethnic Identity." *Nomadic Peoples* 6 (2002): 96.

52. Shahbazi, "Qashqa'i Nomads of Iran (Part II)," 96.

53. Shahbazi, "Qashqa'i Nomads of Iran (Part II)," 97. See also Milani, *Eminent Persians*, 955.

54. Muhammad Bahmanbaigi, "Hardy Shepherds of Iran's Zagros Mountains: Qashqai Build a Future through Tent-School Education," in *Nomads of the World*, ed. Gilbert N. Grosvenor (Washington, DC: National Geographic Society, 1971), 100.

55. Shahbazi, "Qashqa'i Nomads of Iran (Part II)," 97.

56. Bahmanbaigi quoted in William Graves, "Iran: Desert Miracle," *National Geographic Magazine*, January 1975, 40.

57. Bahmanbaigi quoted in Ehsan Shahghasemi, "Mohammad Bahmanbaigi," Ezine Articles, March 31, 2011, accessed May 3, 2014, http://ezinearticles.com /?expert=Ehsan_Shahghasemi.

58. Bahmanbaigi, "Hardy Shepherds," 100.

59. Shahbazi, "Qashqa'i Nomads of Iran (Part II)," 97. See also "Education," *Encyclopedia Iranica*, accessed June 28, 2016, http://www.iranicaonline.org/articles/ed ucation-xiii-rural-and-tribal-schools; Milani, *Eminent Persians*, 958.

60. Clarence Hendershot, *White Tents in the Mountains: A Report on the Tribal Schools of Fars Province* (Tehran: United States Agency for International Development, 1965), 8; Shahbazi, "Qashqa'i Nomads of Iran (Part II)," 98.

61. Gagon, "Study of the Development," 77–79, 89–90.

62. Gagon, "Study of the Development," 77–79, 89–90.

63. Gagon, "Study of the Development," 77–79, 89–90.

64. Hendershot, *White Tents in the Mountains*, 17.

65. Discrepancies exist in the sources concerning when the Iranian government began to support the tent schools. Gagon writes that the Ministry of Education agreed to pay teacher salaries after Bahmanbaigi arranged a successful demonstration of the tent schools in 1955. See Gagon, "Study of the Development," 92–93. Abbas Milani and Pierre Oberling write that the Iranian government allocated a modest sum equivalent to about $21,400 to the project in 1956. See Milani, *Eminent Persians*, 958; Pierre Oberling, *The Qashqa'i Nomads of Fars* (Paris: Mouton, 1974), 207. Mohammad Shahbazi writes that state support for the tent schools began in 1957. See Shahbazi, "Qashqa'i Nomads of Iran (Part II)," 96–97.

66. Charles Dove to Stewart Hamblen, September 17, 1959, folder Tribal Normal School, box 10, entry 486, AID, Archives II.

67. Shahbazi, "Qashqa'i Nomads of Iran (Part II)," 98.

68. A discrepancy exists over the number of teachers trained at the tribal normal school in Shiraz. The Iranian government cites 477 teachers trained in the first seven years. See Government of Iran, *Tribal Education in Iran* (Tehran: Kayhan, 1965). Hendershot puts the number at 465 trained in twelve years in *White Tents in the Mountains*, 14. *Encyclopedia Iranica* cites the number of graduates as "about 8,000" between 1957 and 1977. See "Education," *Encyclopedia Iranica*.

69. Caseel Burke, Completion of Tour Report, undated, folder 1, PFPF, BYU.

70. Paul Barker, "Tent Schools of the Qashqai: A Paradox of Local Initiative and State Control," in *Modern Iran: The Dialectics of Continuity and Change*, ed. Michael E. Bonine and Nikki Keddie (Albany: State University of New York Press, 1981), 155.

71. Gagon, "Study of the Development," 121–26.

72. Hendershot, *White Tents in the Mountains*, 28.

73. Barker, "Tent Schools of the Qashqai," in *Modern Iran*, ed. Bonine and Keddie, 139–40, 144.

74. Dunhill quoted in Farian Sabahi, "The White Tent Programme: Tribal Education under Mohammad Reza Shah," in *Tribes and Power: Nationalism and Ethnicity in the Middle East*, ed. Faleh Abdul-Jabar and Hosham Dawod (London: Saqi, 2003), 247.

75. Bahmanbaigi, "Hardy Shepherds," 100.

76. Milani, *Eminent Persians*, 958.

77. Soheila Shahshahani, "Tribal Schools of Iran: Sedentarization through Education," Commission on Nomadic Peoples, *Nomadic Peoples* 36–37 (1995): 147–52. The quotations are on pages 153 and 152.

78. Shahbazi, "Qashqa'i Nomads of Iran (Part II)," 99–100.

79. "Basic FOA Policy on University Contracts," Dean Peterson Collection, BYU.

80. Ernest Wilkinson to William Warne, February 14, 1955, folder 7, box 3; Ernest Wilkinson to Hoyt Turner, March 2, 1955, folder 3, box 2, both in Dean Peterson Collection, BYU.

81. Dean Peterson to George Stewart, September 15, 1955, folder 2, box 7, Dean Peterson Collection, BYU.

82. Stewart to Wilkinson, undated, Dean Peterson Collection, BYU.

83. Gregory to Fitzgerald, Seager, Holmgreen, October 15, 1955, quoted in Embry, "Utah Universities in Iran," 174.

84. Wilkinson to Stokes, January 3, 1956, Dean Peterson Collection, BYU.

85. Ernest Wilkinson Diary, September 11, 1955, folder 3, box 99, Papers of Ernest Wilkinson, BYU.

86. Wilkinson Diary, November 17, 1955, Papers of Ernest Wilkinson, BYU.

87. Wilkinson Diary, December 12, 1955, Papers of Ernest Wilkinson, BYU.

88. Dean Peterson to Glen Gagon, September 2, 1955, folder 5, box 5, Dean Peterson Collection, BYU.

89. Wilkinson Diary, September 11, 1955, Papers of Ernest Wilkinson, BYU.

90. Brown interview, November 10, 1998, UUIOHP, BYU.

91. Arasteh, *Education and Social Awakening*, 88–89; Afzal, "Cultural Setting," 222.

92. Morrill, End of Tour Report, folder 1, PFPF, BYU; Farnsworth interview, November 6, 1978, UUIOHP, BYU.

93. Brigham Young University Contract Team, "Evaluation and Recommendation for Daneshsaraye Ali Prepared by a Committee of Iranian Professors and the Brigham Young University Contract Team, 1960–1961," 11.

94. Edith Bauer, Completion of Tour Report, 1959, folder 1, PFPF, BYU. BYU advisers referred to the institution as the National University of Teachers Education, or NUTE, after its separation from the University of Tehran.

95. "Education in Iran with Special Reference to Teacher Education and to *Daneshsaraye Ali*," July 29, 1961, folder 1, PFPF, BYU.

96. "Recommendations for Teacher Education Program at National Teachers College," April 1958, folder 1, PFPF, BYU.

97. Golden Woolf, Terminal Report, 1961, folder 1, PFPF, BYU.

98. Malno Reichert, End of Tour Report, 1961, folder 1, PFPF, BYU.

99. Malno Reichert, Completion of Tour Report, 1959, folder 1, PFPF, BYU.

100. Royce Flandro, Terminal Report, June 1961, folder 1, PFPF, BYU.

101. See terminal reports of Dean Farnsworth, Malno Reichert, and John Ord, folder 1, PFPF, BYU.

102. John Ord, Terminal Report, June 1961, folder 1, PFPF, BYU.

103. Woolf, Terminal Report, PFPF, BYU.

104. David Geddes, End of Tour Report, July 1961, folder 1, PFPF, BYU.

105. Morris Shirts to family, no date. I am grateful to Jessie Embry for sharing her transcription of this letter with me.

106. Woolf, Terminal Report, PFPF, BYU; Reichert, Completion of Tour Report, 1959, PFPF, BYU.

107. Reichert, Completion of Tour Report, 1959, and End of Tour Report, 1961, PFPF, BYU.

108. Shirts to family, December 27, 1957. I am grateful to Jessie Embry for sharing her transcription of this letter with me.

109. Morrill, End of Tour Report, folder 1, PFPF, BYU.

110. Reichert, End of Tour Report, 1961, PFPF, BYU.

111. "Education in Iran with Special Reference to Teacher Education," PFPF, BYU. Emphasis in original.

112. Reichert, End of Tour Report, 1961, PFPF, BYU.

113. Warne, "Report of Contributions," PFPF, BYU.

114. Amuzegar, *Technical Assistance*, 13.

115. Morrill, "Appendix A" to End of Tour Report, PFPF, BYU.

116. Morrill, End of Tour Report, folder 1, PFPF, BYU.

117. John Allen Fitz, "Observations on Education in Ostan 2," July 27, 1960, box 124, entry 617, AID, Archives II.

118. Arasteh, *Education and Social Awakening*, 58–60, 114.

119. Nirumand, *Iran*, 153; Ayman, *Educational Innovation in Iran*, 3.

120. Reichert, End of Tour Report, 1961, PFPF, BYU.

121. Menashri, *Education and the Making of Modern Iran*, 180.

122. Berryessa interview, November 3, 1998, UUIOHP, BYU.

CHAPTER 6: LEGACIES

1. Milligan interview, June 23, 1998, UUIOHP, BYU.

2. Lt. Col. Alexis M. Gagarine, "Observations on the Situation in Iran," undated, folder Iran General 3/21/61–3/31/61, box 115B, PPNSF, JFKL.

3. Keddie, *Modern Iran*, 117.

4. Tarun Bose, "The Point Four Programme: A Critical Study," *International Studies: Quarterly Journal of the Indian School of International Studies* 7 (July 1965): 85.

5. Figures quoted in Gasiorowski, *US Foreign Policy and the Shah*, 102–3, 105.

6. Embry, "Utah Universities in Iran," 176.

7. Warne, *Mission for Peace*, 68–69.

8. Amuzegar, *Technical Assistance*, 127.

9. Amuzegar, *Technical Assistance*, 102, 132.

10. Kazemian, *Impact of US Technical Aid*, 76–79; Jessie Embry, "Point Four, Utah State University Technicians, and Rural Development in Iran, 1950–1964," *Rural History* 14, no. 1 (2003): 110.

11. Amuzegar, *Technical Assistance*, 238–40.

12. Nemchenok, "That So Fair a Thing Should Be So Frail," 273.

13. Hendershot, *Politics, Polemics, and Pedagogs*, 84.

14. A. Reed Morrill, "Appendix A" to Completion of Tour Report, 1961, folder 1, PFPF, BYU.

15. Roskelley, "Some Notes on Institution Building," Richard Welling Roskelley Papers, USU.

16. Clifford, *Counsel to the President*, 252.

17. Adams and Garraty, *Is the World Our Campus*, 149 (first quotation); Fred Cook, "The Billion Dollar Mystery," *The Nation*, April 12, 1965, 381 (second quotation).

18. Quoted in Amuzegar, *Technical Assistance*, 135.

19. Gagarine, "Observations on the Situation in Iran," PPNSF, JFKL.

20. Cook, "Billion-Dollar Mystery," 382–83.

21. Morris Shirts to family, December 16, 1958. I thank Jessie Embry for providing me with a partial transcript of this letter.

22. Arasteh, *Education and Social Awakening*, 89 (first quotation), 126 (second quotation).

23. Mehrzad Boroujerdi, *Iranian Intellectuals and the West: The Tormented Triumph of Nativism* (Syracuse, NY: Syracuse University Press, 1996), 53. See also Ali Mirespass, *Intellectual Discourse and the Politics of Modernity: Negotiating Modernity in Iran* (Cambridge: Cambridge University Press, 2009), 99–101.

24. Ahmad, *School Principal*, 84–86.

25. Anderson interview, March 1, 1999, UUIOHP, BYU.

26. Morris Shirts to family, May 27, 1958. I thank Jessie Embry for providing me with a partial transcript of this letter. For similar sentiments, see Bunnell interview, June 17, 1999; Farnsworth interview, November 6, 1998, both in UUIOHP, BYU.

27. Max Berryessa, interviewed by Jessie Embry, November 3, 1998, UUIOHP, BYU.

28. Anderson interview, March 1, 1999, UUIOHP, BYU.

29. Farnsworth interview, November 6, 1998, UUIOHP, BYU.

30. Brown interview, November 10, 1998; Kupfer interview, June 21, 1998, both in UUIOHP, BYU.

31. Berryessa interview, November 3, 1998, UUIOHP, BYU.

32. Bunnell interview, June 17, 1999, UUIOHP, BYU.

33. Farnsworth interview, November 6, 1998, UUIOHP, BYU.

34. Kupfer interview, June 21, 1999, UUIOHP, BYU.

35. Amuzegar, *Technical Assistance*, 134, 136.

36. Nirumand, *Iran*, 175.

37. Macekura, "The Point Four Program," 152–53.

38. Yergin, *The Prize*, 271, 477–78.

39. Figures quoted in Latham, *Right Kind of Revolution*, 144–45.

40. NSC 5504, "Statement of Policy by the National Security Council on US Policy toward Iran," January 15, 1955, *FRUS* 1955–57, vol. 12, 690–92.

41. Warne, *Mission for Peace*, 151–69, 270.

42. Latham, *Right Kind of Revolution*, 44–53. See also Gilman, *Mandarins of the Future*; Michael Latham, *Modernization as Ideology: American Social Science and "Nation Building" in the Kennedy Era* (Chapel Hill: University of North Carolina Press, 2000).

43. Max Millikan and Walt Rostow, *A Proposal: Key to an Effective Foreign Policy* (New York: Harper Brothers, 1957).

44. Ekbladh, *Great American Mission*, especially chapters 5 and 6.

45. John F. Kennedy, "Special Message to the Congress on Foreign Aid," March 22, 1961, *Public Papers of the President*, 1961 (Washington, DC: GPO, 1962), 203–12.

46. Gasiorowski, *US Foreign Policy and the Shah*, 105.

47. Matthew K. Shannon, "American-Iranian Alliances: International Education, Modernization, and Human Rights during the Pahlavi Era," *Diplomatic History* 39 (September 2015): 678.

48. Amuzegar, *Technical Assistance*, 103.

49. Ekbladh, *Great American Mission*, 230–33; Milani, *Eminent Persians*, 738–41; Steven M. Neuse, *David E. Lilienthal: The Journey of an American Liberal* (Knoxville: University of Tennessee Press, 1996), 267–75.

50. George Baldwin, *Planning and Development in Iran* (Baltimore: Johns Hopkins University Press, 1964), 26–34; Kamran Mofid, *Development Planning in Iran: From Monarchy to Islamic Republic* (Wisbech, UK: Middle East and North African Studies Press, 1987), 34–41.

51. Katouzian, *Political Economy of Modern Iran*, 206.

52. Mofid, *Development Planning in Iran*, 47; Shannon, "American-Iranian Alliances," 664 (quotation).

53. Amuzegar, *Technical Assistance*, 105.

54. Action Program—Iran, Second Draft, June 28, 1963, folder Iran 1963 (1 of 2), box 424, PPNSF, JFKL.

55. John Bowling, "The Current Internal Political Situation in Iran," February 11, 1961, folder Iran General 3/21/61–3/31/61, box 115B; Memorandum for McGeorge Bundy, January 21, 1963, folder Iran General 1/63, box 116A; US Embassy in Iran to State, #1520, June 15, 1961, folder Iran General, 6/61, box 115B, all in PPNSF, JFKL.

56. Two concise overviews of the White Revolution are Gholam Reza Afkhami, *The Life and Times of the Shah* (Berkeley: University of California Press, 2009), 208–37; Saikal, *Rise and Fall of the Shah*, 71–96. For the shah's assessment, see Mohammad Reza Pahlavi, *The White Revolution* (Tehran: Kayhan, 1967); Mohammad Reza Pahlavi, *Answer to History* (New York: Stein and Day, 1980), chapter 9. Results of the 1963 referendum are quoted in Abbas Milani, *The Shah* (New York: Palgrave Macmillan, 2011), 294.

57. Mofid, *Development Planning in Iran*, 51.

58. Ansari, "Myth of the White Revolution," 1–24; James Goode, *The United States and Iran: In the Shadow of Musaddiq* (New York: Palgrave Macmillan, 1997), 176–77. The quotation is on Ansari, 2.

59. Farman Farmaian, *Daughter of Persia*, 262.

60. Quoted in Osamah F. Khalil, *America's Dream Palace: Middle East Expertise and the Rise of the National Security State* (Cambridge, MA: Harvard University Press, 2016), 203.

61. Kenneth Pollack, *Persian Puzzle: The Conflict between Iran and America* (New York: Random House, 2005), 95.

62. Van Epps interview, June 2, 1999, UUIOHP, BYU.

63. Royce Flandro, interviewed by Jessie Embry, March 19, 1999, UUIOHP, BYU.

64. Brown interview, November 10, 1999, UUIOHP, BYU.

65. Berryessa interview, November 3, 1998, UUIOHP, BYU.

66. Hubbard interview, February 28, 1999, UUIOHP, BYU.

67. Van Epps interview, June 2, 1999, UUIOHP, BYU.

68. Clarence Ashton, interviewed by Jessie Embry, June 4, 1999, UUIOHP, BYU.

69. First quotation: Neuse, *David E. Lilienthal*, 275; second quotation: David E. Lilienthal, *The Journals of David Lilienthal*, vol. 5 (New York: Harper and Row, 1971), 174.

70. Baldwin, *Planning and Development in Iran*, 95; Hooglund, *Land Reform and Revolution in Iran*, chapters 5 and 6; Mofid; *Development Planning in Iran*, 51–53; Najmabadi, *Land Reform and Social Change*, 264–68.

71. Halliday, *Iran*, 112–25.

72. McLachlan, *Neglected Garden*, 132–36, 166–70; Moghadam, *From Land Reform to Revolution*, 6, 94–97. The quoted phrase is in McLachlan, *Neglected Garden*, 133.

73. Katouzian, *Political Economy of Modern Iran*, 304; Mofid, *Development Planning in Iran*, 51, 53.

74. Charles Issawi, "The Iranian Economy 1925–1975: Fifty Years of Economic Development," in *Iran under the Pahlavis*, ed. George Lenczowski (Stanford, CA: Hoover Institution Press, 1978), 139–40.

75. Ekbladh, *Great American Mission*, 231–33; Christopher T. Fisher, "'Moral Purpose Is the Important Thing': David Lilienthal, Iran, and the Meaning of Development in the US, 1956–1963," *International History Review* 33 (September 2011): 445.

76. Nirumand, *Iran*, 153.

77. Ayman, *Educational Innovation in Iran*, 3.

78. Menashri, *Education and the Making of Modern Iran*, 213.

79. Reza Arasteh estimates that more than 10,000 Iranian students were studying abroad in 1958–59 in "The Education of Iranian Leaders in Europe and America," *International Review of Education* 8 (1962): 447–48.

80. George Baldwin, "The Iranian 'Brain Drain'", in *Iran Faces the Seventies*, ed. Ehsan Yar-Shater (New York: Praeger, 1972), 260–83; Afshin Matin-Asgari, *Iranian Student Opposition to the Shah* (Costa Mesa, CA: Mazda, 2002), 42–44, 50–55; Menashri, *Education and the Making of Modern Iran*, 186–209; Matthew K. Shannon, "'Contacts with the Opposition': American Foreign Relations, the Iranian Student Movement, and the Global Sixties," *The Sixties* 4 (2011): 4–5.

81. Farman Farmaian, *Daughter of Persia*, 263.

82. Ahmad quoted in Hamid Dabashi, *Theology of Discontent: The Ideological Foundations of the Islamic Revolution in Iran* (New York: New York University Press, 1993), 59.

83. Behrangi quoted in Boroujerdi, *Iranian Intellectuals and the West*, 74.

84. Jalal Al-e Ahmad, *Plagued by the West*, trans. Paul Sprachman (Delmar, NY: Caravan, 1982), 61, 89–90.

85. Marvin Zonis, "Educational Ambivalence in Iran," *Iranian Studies* 1 (Autumn 1968): 134.

86. Khomeini quoted in Menashri, *Education and the Making of Modern Iran*, 309–10. For a discussion of how American advisers from the University of Pennsylvania shaped Pahlavi University in Shiraz between 1962 and 1967, see Garlitz, "US University Advisors," 204–7.

87. Boroujerdi, *Iranian Intellectuals and the West*, 33.

88. Ahmad, *Plagued by the West*, 93.

89. Arasteh, *Education and Social Awakening*, 126.

90. Bill, *The Eagle and the Lion*, 158–61.

91. Ruhollah Khomeini, *Islam and Revolution: Writings and Declarations of Imam Khomeini (1941–1980)*, trans. Hamid Algar (Berkeley: Mizan, 1981), 182.

92. Roskelley, "Three Years in Iran," Richard Welling Roskelley Papers, USU.

93. Truman, "Inaugural Address," *Public Papers of the Presidents*, 112–15; Truman, *Years of Trial*, 232.

94. Stewart, "Iran: Pathway of the Middle East," 792.

95. Latham, *Right Kind of Revolution*, 4.

96. For more on Mossadegh's leadership, see Abrahamian, *Iran between Two Revolutions*, 250–80; Afkhami, *The Life and Times of the Shah*, 137–54; Azimi, *Iran*, 257–338; Gheissari and Nasr, *Democracy in Iran*, 51–54; Homa Katouzian, "Mosaddeq's Government in Iranian History: Arbitrary Rule, Democracy, and the 1953 Coup," in *Mohammad Mosaddeq and the 1953 Coup in Iran*, ed. Gasiorowski and Byrne, 1–26; Milani, *The Shah*, 157–70.

97. NSC 5504, "Statement of Policy by the National Security Council on US Policy toward Iran," January 15, 1955, *FRUS 1955–57*, vol. 12, 690–92.

98. "Multilateral Declaration Respecting the Baghdad Pact, Including Express United States Cooperation with Pact Nations," July 28, 1958; "Agreement of Defense Cooperation between the Government of the United States of America and the Imperial Government of Iran," March 5, 1959, both in *The United States and Iran*, ed. Alexander and Nanes, 305–7.

99. Ben Offiler, *US Foreign Policy and the Modernization of Iran: Kennedy, Johnson, Nixon, and the Shah* (New York: Palgrave Macmillan, 2015), 24.

100. Gasiorowski, *US Foreign Policy and the Shah*, 115–16; Jeremy Kuzmarov, *Modernizing Repression: Police Training and Nation-Building in the American Century* (Amherst: University of Massachusetts Press, 2012), 195.

101. Micol Seigel, "Objects of Police History," *Journal of American History* 102 (June 2015): 153, 156.

102. Quoted in Memorandum for the President, March 7, 1963, folder Iran General, 3/63, box 116A, PPNSF, JFKL. See also Kuzmarov, *Modernizing Repression*, 195–96.

103. Gasiorowski, *US Foreign Policy and the Shah*, 117.

104. Robert Graham, *Iran: The Illusion of Power* (New York: St. Martin's, 1978), 143.

105. Gasiorowski, *US Foreign Policy and the Shah*, 152.

106. Graham, *Iran: The Illusion of Power*, 143.

107. Barry Rubin, *Paved with Good Intentions: The American Experience and Iran* (New York: Oxford University Press, 1980), 177–78.

108. John F. Kennedy, *The Strategy of Peace* (New York: Harper and Brothers, 1960). The quotation is on pages 107–8.

109. Robert Komer to McGeorge Bundy, November 5, 1962, folder Iran 1961–62 White House Memoranda, box 424, PPNSF, JFKL. See also Ansari, *Confronting Iran*, 46–47; Bill, *The Eagle and the Lion*, 137; Cottam, *Iran and the United States*, 126; Saikal, *Rise and Fall of the Shah*, 75.

110. Kennedy quoted in William O. Douglas, *The Court Years, 1939–1975* (New York: Vintage Books, 1981), 303. Attorney General Robert Kennedy, the president's brother, developed a strong antipathy for the shah and called him an "S.O.B." See Telcon Attorney General Robert F. Kennedy and George Ball, January 29, 1962, folder Iran 1961–63, box 5, George W. Ball Personal Papers, JFKL. For a good overview, see James Goode, "Reforming Iran during the Kennedy Years," *Diplomatic History* 15 (1991): 13–29.

111. April R. Summitt, "For a White Revolution: John F. Kennedy and the Shah of Iran," *Middle East Journal* 58 (Autumn 2004): 562–63.

112. David R. Collier, "To Prevent a Revolution: John F. Kennedy and the Promotion of Democracy in Iran," *Diplomacy and Statecraft* 24 (2013): 461–62. The quotation is from Offiler, *US Foreign Policy and the Modernization of Iran*, 39.

113. "Position Paper on Iran," undated, folder Iran General 1/61–2/62, box 115B, PPNSF, JFKL.

114. University of Tehran Chancellor Dr. A. Forhad quoted in Nirumand, *Iran*, 156–57.

115. Afkhami, *Life and Times of the Shah*, 233–35; Keddie, *Modern Iran*, 146–48; Milani, *The Shah*, 296–99.

116. Memorandum for Mr. Komer, December 20, 1961, folder Iran General 12/11/61–12/31/61, box 116A, PPNSF, JFKL.

117. Memorandum for the Record, December 15, 1962, folder Iran 1961–62 White House Memoranda, box 424, PPNSF, JFKL. See also John Bowling, "Political Characteristics of the Iranian Urban Middle-Class and Implications Thereof for United States Policy," March 20, 1961, in *The United States and Iran*, ed. Alexander and Nanes, 325; Milani, *The Shah*, 299–300.

118. T. Cuyler Young to Walt Rostow, April 19, 1961, folder Iran General 4/61, box 115B, PPNSF, JFKL.

119. Goode, *The United States and Iran*, 171. See also Edward Wailes to Secretary of State, May 10, 1961, folder Iran General 5/1/61–5/14/61, box 115B; Memorandum for McGeorge Bundy, August 11, 1961, Subject: Task Force Meeting on Iran, folder Iran General 8/1/61–8/14/61, box 116A; Memorandum for the Attorney General, October 20, 1962, folder Iran 1961–62 White House Memoranda, box 424, all in PPNSF, JFKL.

120. Bowling quoted in Offiler, *US Foreign Policy and the Modernization of Iran*, 36–37.

121. Julius Holmes to Armin Meyer, August 27, 1961, folder Iran General 8/15/61–9/9/61, box 116A, PPNSF, JFKL.

122. Robert Komer, Memorandum for the President, August 4, 1961; Robert Komer to McGeorge Bundy, November 5, 1962, both in folder Iran 1961–62 White House Memoranda, box 424, PPNSF, JFKL.

123. Telegram from the Department of State to the Embassy of Iran, July 16, 1963, *FRUS 1961–63*, vol. 17, document 297, accessed November 5, 2015, https://history.state.gov/historicaldocuments/frus1961-63v18/d297.

124. Rohan Alvandi, *Nixon, Kissinger, and the Shah: The United States and Iran in the Cold War* (New York: Oxford University Press, 2014), 23.

125. Bill, *The Eagle and the Lion*, 154–56; Gasiorowski, *US Foreign Policy and the Shah*, 99; Shannon, "American-Iranian Alliances," 676.

126. Claudia Castiglioni, "No Longer a Client, Not Yet a Partner: The US-Iranian Alliance in the Johnson Years," *Cold War History* 15 (2015): 491–509; Andrew Johns, "The Johnson Administration, the Shah of Iran, and the Changing Patterns of US-Iranian Relations, 1965–1967: 'Tired of Being Treated Like a Schoolboy,'" *Journal of Cold War Studies* 9 (Spring 2007): 65; Offiler, *US Foreign Policy and the Modernization of Iran*, 6–8.

127. Alvandi, *Nixon, Kissinger, and the Shah*, 25–26; Offiler, *US Foreign Policy and the Modernization of Iran*, 71–72.

128. Ali Ansari, *Confronting Iran: The Failure of American Foreign Policy and the Next Great Conflict in the Middle East* (New York: Basic Books, 2006), 75–76; Bill, *The Eagle and the Lion*, 226–33; Shannon, "American-Iranian Alliances," 680–86.

129. "Toasts of the President and the Shah at Dinner Honoring the Shah," and "White House Statement Issued Following the First Meeting between the President and the Shah," both November 15, 1977, *Public Papers of the Presidents*, Jimmy Carter, 1977, Book 2, 2028–29.

130. "Toasts of the President and the Shah at a State Dinner," December 31, 1977, *Public Papers of the Presidents*, Jimmy Carter, 1977, Book 2, 2220–22.

131. Shannon, "American-Iranian Alliances," 680–81.

132. Bill, *The Eagle and the Lion*, 186. See also Gary Sick, *All Fall Down: America's Tragic Encounter with Iran* (New York: Penguin Books, 1986), 26.

133. Shannon, "American-Iranian Alliances," 680.

134. Shah quoted in Bill, *The Eagle and the Lion*, 186.

135. Ashton interview, June 4, 1999, UUIOHP, BYU.

136. Van Epps interview, June 2, 1999, UUIOHP, BYU.

137. Hall interview, March 19, 1999, UUIOHP, BYU.

138. Ashton interview, June 4, 1999, UUIOHP, BYU.

139. Van Epps interview, June 2, 1999, UUIOHP, BYU.

140. Hall interview, March 19, 1999, UUIOHP, BYU.

141. Anderson interview, March 1, 1999, UUIOHP, BYU.

142. Anderson interview, March 1, 1999, UUIOHP, BYU.

143. The quotation is in Hall interview, March 19, 1999, UUIOHP, BYU. See also, Flandro interview, March 19, 1999, UUIOHP, BYU.

144. Nemchenok, "That So Fair a Thing," 265.

145. Roskelley, "Three Years in Iran," Richard Welling Roskelley Papers, USU.

146. Anderson interview, March 1, 1999, UUIOHP, BYU.

147. Hall interview, March 19, 1999, UUIOHP, BYU.

148. Hubbard interview, February 28, 1999, UUIOHP, BYU.

149. Shirts interview, June 21, 1999, UUIOHP, BYU.

150. Institute for International Rural and Community Development, folder 1, box 27, Richard Welling Roskelley Papers, USU. On Roskelley's work in East Asia, see Rosa M. Leyva, "Recent Progress and Development in Latin American Programs," March 28, 1966, folder 6, box 27, Richard Welling Roskelley Papers, USU.

151. "CID Project Experience," folder 2, box 3, Bruce Anderson Papers, USU; Parson, "International Students and Programs," 20.

152. National Association of State Universities and Land-Grant Colleges, *Serving the World: The People and Ideas of America's State and Land-Grant Universities* (Washington, DC: National Association of State Universities and Land-Grant Colleges, 1987), 550.

153. Berryessa interview, November 3, 1998, UUIOHP, BYU; Berryessa, "Our Life Together," 71, MSS SC 2954, BYU.

154. Leah Hart, interviewed by Jessie Embry, June 18, 1999, UUIOHP, BYU.

155. Griffin interview, March 23, 1999, UUIOHP, BYU; Bruce Anderson, *The Consortium for International Development: A History of the First 20 Years* (Tucson, AZ: Consortium for International Development, 1990), J13–J14.

156. Wood interview, March 1, 1999, UUIOHP, BYU.

157. Anderson, *Consortium for International Development*; "CID Project Experience," Bruce Anderson Papers, USU; Institute for International Rural and Community

Development, Richard Welling Roskelley Papers, USU; Parson, "International Students and Programs," 20; E. Boyd Wennergen and Maria Lourdes del Rosario Juan, "The Economic Importance of International Assistance Activities at Utah State University," Study Series no. 81–1, Economic Research Center, Department of Economics, Utah State University, 1981, 2–3, folder 7, box 27, Richard Welling Roskelley Papers, USU.

158. Gardner quoted in Minette Marcroft, "Mid-east Trip Nets Exchange Benefits," *Daily Utah Chronicle* [Salt Lake City] 84, no. 48, 1 (undated).

159. Quoted in Eugene Bliss to John Dixon, April 12, 1975; see also Frank Moody to Abdul Samiy, December 26, 1974, both in folder 8, box 26, VPHSR, Utah.

160. Cox quoted in "Utahns Anxious to Continue Working with Iranians," *Utah Statesman* [Logan], January 10, 1979, 3.

161. "The Iran Center for Agricultural Management: A Proposal for Implementation by the Consortium for International Development," folder 14, box 6, Bruce Anderson Papers, USU; Houra Yavari to Bruce Anderson, August 12, 1979. The Yavari letter is among materials that were still unprocessed as of June 2015. I am grateful to Bob Parson, USU university archivist, for allowing me to read those materials.

162. "Statement of Claim by the Consortium for International Development against Islamic Republic of Iran in the Iran–United States Claims Tribunal at the Peace Palace, The Hague, Netherlands," December 31, 1981, box 277c, Bruce Anderson Papers, USU. This document is among materials that were still unprocessed as of June 2015. I am grateful to Bob Parson, USU university archivist, for allowing me to read those materials.

163. Khosrow Mostofi, interviewed by Everett Cooley, September 17, 1985, Everett L. Cooley Oral History Project, Marriott Library, University of Utah, Salt Lake City.

164. Farnsworth interview, November 6, 1998, UUIOHP, BYU.

165. Mostofi interview, Everett L. Cooley Oral History Project, Marriott Library, University of Utah, Salt Lake City; University of Utah News Release, December 10, 1974, folder 8, box 26, VPHSR, Utah.

166. Haws, *Iran and Utah State University*, 113–15. The quotation is on page 115. See also Parson, "International Student and Programs," 7–8, University History Collection, USU.

167. Haws, *Iran and Utah State University*, 117–20.

168. Haws, *Iran and Utah State University*, 22.

169. Parson, "International Students and Programs," 21–25, University History Collection, USU.

170. Salehi quoted in Karen Lambert, "Utah State Alma Mater for Hundreds of Iranians," HJnews.com, June 14, 2008, accessed July 19, 2016, http://news.hjnews.

com/news/utah-state-alma-mater-of-hundreds-of-iranians/article_2fbeee8c-0291
546b-23c3-0026d306a604.html.

171. Alan Paxman, letter to the editor, *Utah Statesman* [Logan], November 26,
1979, 5. The hostage crisis began as a demand that the US government return the
deposed shah to Iran to face charges of human rights abuses. President Carter had
admitted him to the United States to receive treatment for advanced cancer.

172. C. Lynn Chidestar, letter to the editor, *Utah Statesman* [Logan], November 26,
1979, 4.

173. Matthew K. Shannon, "Losing Hearts and Minds: American-Iranian Relations
and International Education during the Cold War" (PhD dissertation, Temple University, Philadelphia, PA, 2013), 318–19.

174. Will Teague, "Hostages of the Crisis: Iranian Students in Arkansas," *Arkansas
Historical Quarterly*, forthcoming.

175. "Immigration Agents Import a Disaster," *Utah Statesman* [Logan], November
28, 1979, 4.

176. "Your Papers, Please," *Utah Statesman* [Logan], November 28, 1979, 4.

177. Timothy Ford, letter to the editor, *Utah Statesman* [Logan], November 28,
1979, 4.

178. Tim Conrad, letter to the editor, *Utah Statesman* [Logan], December 3, 1979, 5.

AFTERWORD

1. "Iran," University History Collection, USU.

2. Grubbs, *Secular Missionaries*, chapter 6; Immerwahr, *Thinking Small*, 166–67,
180.

3. A good overview of the scholarly literature is Daniel Immerwahr, "Modernization and Development in US Foreign Relations," *Passport* 43 (September 2012): 22–25.

4. Barack Obama, Inaugural Address, January 21, 2009, accessed June 25, 2016,
https://www.whitehouse.gov/blog/2009/01/21/president-barack-obamas-inaug
ural-address.

BIBLIOGRAPHY

ARCHIVAL COLLECTIONS

Brigham Young University. L. Tom Perry Special Collections. Provo, UT.
   Alva John Clarke Personal Histories.
   Alva John Clarke Point Four Program Files.
   LDS Family Life Oral History Project.
   A. Reed Morrill Collection.
   Our Life Together: A Personal History of the Max and Janet Berryessa Family.
   Dean Peterson Collection.
   Utah Universities in Iran Oral History Project.
   Rudger Harper Walker Oral History Interview.
   Ernest L. Wilkinson Papers.
Church History Library. Salt Lake City, UT.
   Franklin Harris Diaries, 1908–54.
Dwight D. Eisenhower Library. Abilene, KS.
   Milton S. Eisenhower Papers.

DOI: 10.7330/9781607327547.c008

John F. Kennedy Library. Boston, MA.
    George W. Ball Personal Papers.
    David E. Bell Personal Papers.
    Presidential Papers. National Security File.
    Presidential Papers. White House Central Subject Files.
Michigan State University. University Archives and Historical Collections. East Lansing, MI.
    John A. Hannah Papers.
    International Studies and Programs Records, 1943–84.
National Archives and Records Administration. College Park, MD.
    Record Group 286: Records of the United States Agency for International Development.
    Record Group 469: Records of the United States Foreign Assistance Agencies, 1948–61.
Harry S. Truman Library. Independence, MO.
    Dean G. Acheson Papers.
    Stanley Andrews Papers.
    Henry G. Bennett Papers.
    Benjamin H. Hardy Papers.
    John H. Ohly Papers.
University of Utah. Archives/Records Management. Salt Lake City, UT.
    Everett L. Cooley Oral History Project.
    Iranian Rural Improvement Program Records, Iran Project Files 1951–56.
    Vice President for Health Sciences Records, 1945–90.
Utah State University. Special Collections and Archives. Logan, UT.
    Bruce Anderson Papers.
    Daryl Chase Photograph Collection.
    Eldon J. Gardner Photograph Collection.
    International Programs (Global Engagement), Office Files, 1950–2011.
    Louis Madsen Papers.
    Richard Welling Roskelley Papers.
    Richard Welling Roskelley Photograph Collection.
    University History Materials.
    University Participation in Iran.
    University Participation, International Cooperation Administration.
    Luther M. Winsor Papers.

NEWSPAPERS

Daily Universe [Provo, UT]

Daily Utah Chronicle [Salt Lake City]

Department of State Bulletin [Washington, DC]

Deseret News [Salt Lake City]

Herald Journal [Logan, UT]

New York Times

Salt Lake Tribune

Utah Statesman [Logan]

BOOKS AND ARTICLES

Abdul-Jabar, Faleh, and Hosham Dawod, eds. *Tribes and Power: Nationalism and Ethnicity in the Middle East*. London: Saqi, 2003.

Abrahamian, Ervand. "Communism and Communalism in Iran: The *Tudah* and the *Firqah-I Dimukrat*." *Middle East Studies* 1 (1970): 291–316.

Abrahamian, Ervand. *The Coup: 1953, the CIA, and the Roots of Modern US-Iranian Relations*. New York: New Press, 2013.

Abrahamian, Ervand. *Iran between Two Revolutions*. Princeton, NJ: Princeton University Press, 1982.

Acheson, Dean. *Present at the Creation: My Years in the State Department*. New York: W. W. Norton, 1969.

Adams, Jane, ed. *Fighting for the Farm: Rural America Transformed*. Philadelphia: University of Pennsylvania Press, 2003.

Adams, Walter, and John A. Garraty. *Is the World Our Campus?* East Lansing: Michigan State University Press, 1960.

Afary, Janet. *The Iranian Constitutional Revolution, 1906–1911: Grassroots Democracy, Social Democracy, and the Origins of Feminism*. New York: Columbia University Press, 1996.

Afkhami, Gholam Reza. *The Life and Times of the Shah*. Berkeley: University of California Press, 2009.

Afzal, Manuchehr. "The Cultural Setting of the Problems of Teacher Training in Iran." PhD dissertation, Columbia University, New York, NY, 1956.

Ahmad, Jalal Al-e. *Plagued by the West*. Trans. Paul Sprachman. Delmar, NY: Caravan, 1982.

Ahmad, Jalal Al-e. *The School Principal*. Trans. John K. Newton. Minneapolis: Bibliotheca Islamica, 1974.

Alexander, Yonah, and Allan Nanes, eds. *The United States and Iran: A Documentary History*. Frederick, MD: University Publications of America, 1980.

Allen, Harold. "The Rural Factor." *Muslim World* 44 (1954): 171–80.

Allen, Harold. *Rural Reconstruction in Action: Experience in the Near and Middle East.* Ithaca, NY: Cornell University Press, 1953.

Alvandi, Rohan. *Nixon, Kissinger, and the Shah: The United States and Iran in the Cold War.* New York: Oxford University Press, 2014.

Amin, Camron Michael, Benjamin C. Fortna, and Elizabeth B. Frierson, eds. *The Modern Middle East: A Sourcebook for History.* New York: Oxford University Press, 2009.

Amuzegar, Jahangir. *Iran: An Economic Profile.* Washington, DC: Middle East Institute, 1977.

Amuzegar, Jahangir. *Technical Assistance in Theory and Practice: The Case of Iran.* New York: Praeger, 1967.

Anderson, Bruce. *The Consortium for International Development: A History of the First 20 Years.* Tucson, AZ: Consortium for International Development, 1990.

Ansari, Ali. *Confronting Iran: The Failure of American Policy and the Next Great Conflict in the Middle East.* New York: Basic Books, 2006.

Ansari, Ali. "The Myth of the White Revolution: Mohammad Reza Shah, 'Modernization,' and the Consolidation of Power." *Middle Eastern Studies* 37 (July 2001): 1–24.

Anshel, Kurt, Russell Brannon, and Eldon Smith, eds. *Agricultural Cooperatives and Markets in Developing Countries.* New York: Praeger, 1969.

Arasteh, Reza. *Education and Social Awakening in Iran, 1950–1960.* Leiden: E. J. Brill, 1962.

Arasteh, Reza. "The Education of Iranian Leaders in Europe and America." *International Review of Education* 8 (1962): 444–50.

Atabaki, Touraj, ed. *Iran and the First World War: Battleground of the Great Powers.* New York: I. B. Tauris, 2006.

Avery, Peter. *Modern Iran.* Bristol: Praeger, 1965.

Ayman, Iraj. *Educational Innovation in Iran.* Paris: United Nations Educational, Scientific, and Cultural Organization Press, 1974.

Azimi, Fakhreddin. *Iran: The Crisis of Democracy from the Exile of Reza Shah to the Fall of Musaddiq.* New York: I. B. Tauris, 2009.

Badeau, John, and Georgiana Stevens, eds. *Bread from Stones: Fifty Years of Technical Assistance.* Englewood Cliffs, NJ: Prentice-Hall, 1966.

Baldwin, George. *Planning and Development in Iran.* Baltimore: Johns Hopkins University Press, 1964.

Barton, James L. *The Story of Near East Relief (1915–1930): An Interpretation.* New York: Macmillan, 1930.

Bass, Paul William. *Point Four: Touching the Dream: A Bold, New US Foreign Policy.* Stillwater, OK: New Forums, 2009.

Bayandor, Darioush. *Iran and the CIA: The Fall of Mosaddeq Revisited.* Houndmills, UK: Palgrave Macmillan, 2010.

Beck, Lois. *Nomads in Postrevolutionary Iran: The Qashqa'i in an Era of Change.* London: Routledge, 2015.

Beck, Louis. *The Qashqa'i of Iran.* New Haven, CT: Yale University Press, 1986.

Behrooz, Maziar. *Rebels with a Cause: The Failure of the Left in Iran.* London: I. B. Tauris, 2000.

Bill, James. *The Eagle and the Lion: The Tragedy of American-Iranian Relations.* New Haven, CT: Yale University Press, 1988.

Bill, James, and William Roger Louis, eds. *Musaddiq, Iranian Nationalism, and Oil.* Austin: University of Texas Press, 1988.

Bingham, Jonathan. *Shirt Sleeve Diplomacy: Point Four in Action.* New York: John Day, 1954.

Bonine, Michael E., and Nikki Keddie, eds. *Modern Iran: The Dialectics of Continuity and Change.* Albany: State University of New York Press, 1981.

Boroujerdi, Mehrzad. *Iranian Intellectuals and the West: The Tormented Triumph of Nativism.* Syracuse, NY: Syracuse University Press, 1996.

Bose, Tarun. "The Point Four Programme: A Critical Study." *International Studies: Quarterly Journal of the Indian School of International Studies* 7 (July 1965): 66–97.

Brigham Young University. *Franklin Stewart Harris: Educator, Administrator, Father, Friend: Vignettes of His Life.* Provo, UT: Brigham Young University Press, 1965.

Brigham Young University Contract Team. *Evaluation and Recommendation for Daneshsaraye Ali.* Tehran, 1961.

Brigham Young University Contract Team. *Technical Aid: An Investment in People: The Point Four Program in Iran.* Provo, UT: Brigham Young University, 1960.

Brown, Edward. *The Persian Revolution of 1905–1909.* London: Frank Cass, 1966 [1910].

Brunner, Henry S. *Land Grant Colleges and Universities, 1862–1962.* Washington, DC: Government Printing Office, 1962.

Building Institutions to Serve Agriculture: A Summary Report of the C.I.C.-A.I.D. Rural Development Research Project. West Lafayette, IN: Purdue University, 1968.

Butterfield, Samuel. *US Development Aid—an Historic First: Achievements and Failures of the Twentieth Century.* Westport, CT: Praeger, 2004.

Butts, Robert Freeman. *American Education in International Development.* New York: Harper and Row, 1963.

Castiglioni, Claudia. "No Longer a Client, Not Yet a Partner: The US-Iranian Alliance in the Johnson Years." *Cold War History* 15 (2015): 491–509

Castle, Eugene. *Billions, Blunders, and Baloney: The Fantastic Story of How Uncle Sam Is Squandering Your Money Overseas.* New York: Devin-Adair, 1955.

Castle, Eugene. *The Great Giveaway: The Realities of Foreign Aid.* New York: Live Line, 1957.

A Century of Missionary Work in Persia, 1834–1934. Beirut: American Press for the Presbyterian Church in the USA, Iran Mission, 1936.

Chaqueri, Cosroe. "Did the Soviets Play a Role in Founding the Tudeh Party in Iran?" *Cahiers du Monde Russe* 40, no. 3 (July–September 1999): 497–528.

Chaqueri, Cosroe, ed. *The Left in Iran, 1905–1940*. Pontypool, UK: Merlin, 2010.

Clifford, Clark. *Counsel to the President: A Memoir*. New York: Random House, 1991.

Collier, David R. "To Prevent a Revolution: John F. Kennedy and the Promotion of Democracy in Iran." *Diplomacy and Statecraft* 24 (2013): 456–75.

Cook, Fred. "The Billion Dollar Mystery." *The Nation*, April 12, 1965, 380–97.

Cottam, Richard. *Iran and the United States: A Cold War Case Study*. Pittsburgh: University of Pittsburg Press, 1988.

Cronin, Stephanie. *Tribal Politics in Iran: Rural Conflict and the New State, 1921–1941*. London: Routledge, 2007.

Cullather, Nick. *The Hungry World: America's Cold War Battle against Poverty in Asia*. Cambridge, MA: Harvard University Press, 2010.

Cullather, Nick. "Miracles of Modernization: The Green Revolution and the Apotheosis of Technology." *Diplomatic History* 28 (April 2004): 227–54.

Curti, Merle, and Kendall Birr. *Prelude to Point Four: American Technical Missions Overseas, 1838–1938*. Madison: University of Wisconsin Press, 1954.

Dabashi, Hamid. *Theology of Discontent: The Ideological Foundations of the Islamic Revolution in Iran*. New York: New York University Press, 1993.

Daneshvar, Simin. *Savushun*. Trans. M. R. Ghanoonparvar. Washington, DC: Mage, 2001.

Daniel, Robert. *American Philanthropy in the Near East, 1820–1960*. Athens: Ohio University Press, 1970.

Daniels, Walter M., ed. *The Point Four Program*. New York: H. W. Wilson, 1951.

Daryaee, Touraj, ed. *The Oxford Handbook of Iranian History*. New York: Oxford University Press, 2012.

De Bellaigue, Christopher. *Patriot of Persia: Muhammad Mossadegh and the Tragic Anglo-American Coup*. New York: Harper Perennial, 2012.

Department of State. *The Point Four Program*. Publication 3347. December 1949. Accessed April 1, 2017. https://babel.hathitrust.org/cgi/pt?id=umn.31951p010925273;view=1up;seq=2.

Donovan, Robert J. *Conflict and Crisis: The Presidency of Harry S Truman, 1945–1948*. New York: W. W. Norton, 1977.

Douglas, William O. *The Court Years, 1939–1975*. New York: Vintage Books, 1981.

Dueck, Colin. *Hard Line: The Republican Party and US Foreign Policy since World War II*. Princeton, NJ: Princeton University Press, 2010.

"Education." *Encyclopedia Iranica*. Accessed June 28, 2016. http://www.iranicaonline.org/articles/education-index.

Education and World Affairs. *The University Looks Abroad: Approaches to World Affairs at Six American Universities*. New York: Walker, 1965.

Ehsani-Nia, Sara. "'Go Forth and Do Good': US-Iranian Relations during the Cold War through the Lens of Public Diplomacy." *Penn History Review* 19 (Fall 2011): 1–41.

Ekbladh, David. *The Great American Mission: Modernization and the Construction of an American World Order*. Princeton, NJ: Princeton University Press, 2011.

Elm, Mostafa. *Oil, Power, and Principle: Iran's Oil Nationalization and Its Aftermath.* Syracuse, NY: Syracuse University Press, 1994.

Embry, Jessie. "The Church Follows the Flag: US Foreign Aid, Utah Universities, the LDS Church, and Iran, 1950–1964." *Journal of Mormon History* 32 (Fall 2006); 141–79.

Embry, Jessie. "The LDS Church and Iran: The Dilemmas of an American Church." *John Whitmer Historical Quarterly* 21 (2001): 51–68.

Embry, Jessie. "Point Four, Utah State University Technicians, and Rural Development in Iran, 1950–1964." *Rural History* 14, no. 1 (2003): 99–113.

Embry, Jessie. "Utah Universities in Iran, 1950–1964." *Journal of the Utah Academy of Sciences, Arts, and Letters* (2002): 164–79.

Ernst, John. *Forging a Fateful Alliance: Michigan State University and the Vietnam War.* East Lansing: Michigan State University Press, 1998.

Esfandiary, Malek Mansour. "The Agricultural Phase of the Technical Assistance Program of the United States in Iran, with Special Reference to the Role of Utah State University." Master's thesis, Utah State University, Logan, 1958.

Executive Sessions of the Senate Foreign Relations Committee. Volume 2, *Eighty-first Congress, 1949–50.* Washington, DC: Government Printing Office, 1976.

Farman Farmaian, Sattareh. *Daughter of Persia: A Woman's Journey from Her Father's Harem though the Islamic Revolution.* New York: Anchor Books, 1993.

Fattahipour, Ahmad. "Educational Diffusion and Modernization of an Ancient Civilization: Iran." PhD dissertation, University of Chicago, 1964.

Fink, Carole. *Cold War: An International History.* Boulder: Westview, 2014.

Fisher, Christopher T. "'Moral Purpose Is the Important Thing': David Lilienthal, Iran, and the Meaning of Development in the US, 1956–1963." *International History Review* 33 (September 2011): 431–51.

Foreign Relations of the United States. Annual volumes. Washington, DC: Government Printing Office, 1964–2017.

Frame, Margaret A. *Passage to Persia: Writings of an American Doctor during Her Life in Iran, 1929–1957.* Stamford, UK: Summertime, 2014.

Funk, J. Arthur. "The Missionary Problem in Persia." *Muslim World* 10 (1920): 138–43.

Gaddis, John Lewis. *The Cold War: A New History.* New York: Penguin, 2005.

Gagon, Glen. "A Study of the Development and Implementation of a System of Elementary Education for the Ghasghi and Basseri Nomadic Tribes of Fars Ostan, Iran." Master's thesis, Brigham Young University, Provo, UT, 1956.

Galbraith, John Kenneth. "Making 'Point 4' Work: Some Unresolved Problems in Aiding Backward Areas." *Commentary* (September 1950). Accessed June 2, 1016. https://www.commentarymagazine.com/issues/1950-september/.

Galbraith, John Kenneth. "A Positive Approach to Economic Aid." *Foreign Affairs* 39 (April 1961): 444–57.

Garlitz, Richard. "Academic Ambassadors in the Middle East: The University Contract Program in Turkey and Iran, 1950–1970." PhD dissertation, Ohio University, Athens, 2008.

Garlitz, Richard, and Lisa Jarvinen, eds. *Teaching America to the World and the World to America: Education and Foreign Relations since 1870.* New York: Palgrave Macmillan, 2012.

Gasiorowski, Mark. *US Foreign Policy and the Shah: Building a Client State in Iran.* Ithaca, NY: Cornell University Press, 1991.

Gasiorowski, Mark, and Malcolm Byrne, eds. *Mohammad Mosaddeq and the 1953 Coup in Iran.* Syracuse, NY: Syracuse University Press, 2003.

Gavin, Francis J., and Mark Atwood Lawrence, eds. *Beyond the Cold War: Lyndon Johnson and the New Global Challenges of the 1960s.* New York: Oxford University Press, 2014.

Geselbracht, Raymond, ed. *Foreign Aid and the Legacy of Harry S. Truman.* Kirksville, MO: Truman State University Press, 2015.

Gheissari, Ali, and Vali Nasr. *Democracy in Iran: History and the Quest for Liberty.* New York: Oxford University Press, 2006.

Gilman, Nils. *Mandarins of the Future: Modernization Theory in Cold War America.* Baltimore: Johns Hopkins University Press, 2003.

Glick, Philip. *The Administration of Technical Assistance: Growth in the Americas.* Chicago: University of Chicago Press, 1957.

Goode, James. "A Good Start: The First American Mission to Iran, 1883–1885." *Muslim World* 74 (April 1984): 110–18.

Goode, James. "Reforming Iran during the Kennedy Years." *Diplomatic History* 15 (1991): 13–29.

Goode, James. *The United States and Iran: In the Shadow of Musaddiq.* New York: Palgrave Macmillan, 1997.

Goulden, Joseph. *The Best Years: 1945–1950.* New York: Atheneum, 1976.

Government of Iran, Ministry of Agriculture. *Agricultural Extension in Iran.* Tehran, 1959.

Government of Iran, Ministry of Education, Bureau of Statistics. *Educational Statistics in Iran.* Tehran, 1965.

Government of Iran, Ministry of Education. *Tribal Education in Iran.* Tehran: Kayhan, 1965.

Graham, Robert. *Iran: The Illusion of Power.* New York: St. Martin's, 1978.

Graves, William. "Iran: Desert Miracle." *National Geographic Magazine,* January 1975, 2–47.

Grosvenor, Gilbert N., ed. *Nomads of the World.* Washington, DC: National Geographic Society, 1971.

Grubbs, Larry. *Secular Missionaries: Americans and African Development in the 1960s.* Amherst: University of Massachusetts Press, 2009.

Hadary, Gideon. "The Agricultural Reform Problem in Iran." *Middle East Journal* 5 (Spring 1951): 181–96.

Hadjiyanis, Demos. "Point Four in Iran." Master's thesis, Ohio University, Athens, 1954.

Halliday, Fred. *Iran: Dictatorship and Development.* Harmondsworth, UK: Penguin, 1979.

Hamby, Alonzo. *Man of the People: A Life of Harry S. Truman.* New York: Oxford University Press, 1995.

Hardin, William H. "John Kee and the Point Four Compromise." *West Virginia History* 41 (Fall 1979): 40–58.

Harris, Franklin S. "The Beginnings of Point Four Work in Iran." *Middle East Journal* 7 (1953): 222–28.

Hart, Justin. *Empire of Ideas: The Origins of Public Diplomacy and the Transformation of US Foreign Policy.* New York: Oxford University Press, 2013.

Haws, Gwen, ed. *Iran and Utah State University: Half a Century of Friendship and a Decade of Contracts.* Logan: Utah State University, 1963.

Hayden, Lyle. "Living Standards in Rural Iran." *Middle East Journal* 3 (Spring 1949): 140–50.

Hazlitt, Henry. "Foreign Investment vs. Foreign Aid." *Freeman,* October 1, 1970. Reproduced by the Foundation for Economic Education. Accessed December 21, 2016. https://fee.org/articles/foreign-investment-vs-foreign-aid/.

Hazlitt, Henry. *Illusions of Point Four.* Irving-on-Hudson, NY: Foundation for Economic Education, 1950.

Heiss, Mary Ann. *Empire and Nationhood: The United States, Great Britain, and Iranian Oil, 1950–1954.* New York: Columbia University Press, 1997.

Hendershot, Clarence. *Politics, Polemics, and Pedagogs: A Study of United States Technical Assistance in Education to Iran, Including Negotiations, Political Considerations in Iran and the United States, Programming, Methods, Problems, Results, and Evaluations.* New York: Vantage, 1975.

Hendershot, Clarence. *White Tents in the Mountains: A Report on the Tribal Schools of Fars Province.* Tehran: United States Agency for International Development, 1965.

Higgins, Benjamin. "The Evaluation of Technical Assistance." *International Journal* 25 (March 1970): 34–55.

History of the Office of the Coordinator of Inter-American Affairs. Washington, DC: Government Printing Office, 1947.

Hoffman, Elizabeth Cobbs. *All You Need Is Love: The Peace Corps and the Spirit of the 1960s.* Cambridge, MA: Harvard University Press, 1998.

Hogan, Michael. *A Cross of Iron: Harry S. Truman and the Origins of the National Security State, 1945–1954.* New York: Cambridge University Press, 1998.

Hogan, Michael. *The Marshall Plan: America, Britain, and the Reconstruction of Western Europe, 1947–1952.* New York: Cambridge University Press, 1987.

Hooglund, Eric. *Land Reform and Revolution in Iran, 1960–1980.* Austin: University of Texas Press, 1982.

Humphrey, Richard A., ed. *Universities . . . and Development Assistance Abroad.* Washington, DC: American Council on Education, 1967.

Immerwahr, Daniel. "Modernization and Development in US Foreign Relations." *Passport* 43 (September 2012): 22–24.

Immerwahr, Daniel. *Thinking Small: The United States and the Lure of Community Development*. Cambridge, MA: Harvard University Press, 2015.

International Cooperation Administration. *Technical Cooperation through American Universities*. Washington, DC: International Cooperation Administration, no date.

"Iran: Reds Taking Over." *Newsweek*, August 10, 1953, 36–38.

Jacobs, Norman. *The Sociology of Development: Iran as an Asian Case Study*. New York: Praeger, 1966.

Jenson, Janet. *The Many Lives of Franklin S. Harris*. Provo, UT: Brigham Young University Press, 2002.

Johns, Andrew. "The Johnson Administration, the Shah of Iran, and the Changing Patterns of US-Iranian Relations, 1965–1967: 'Tired of Being Treated Like a Schoolboy.'" *Journal of Cold War Studies* 9 (Spring 2007): 64–94.

Jones, Geoffrey. "The Imperial Bank of Iran and Iranian Economic Development, 1890–1952." *Business and Economic History* 16 (1987): 69–80.

Jones, Randolph. "Otto Passman and Foreign Aid: The Early Years." *Louisiana History* 26 (Winter 1985): 53–62.

Jordan, Samuel. "Constructive Revolutions in Iran." *Muslim World* 24 (1934): 347–53.

Kamalipour, Yahya, ed. *The US Media and the Middle East: Image and Perception*. Westport, CT: Praeger, 1997.

Kardan, Ali Mohammad. *L'Organisation Scolaire en Iran*. Geneva: Imprimerie Reggiam et Jacond, 1957.

Karnow, Stanley. *In Our Image: America's Empire in the Philippines*. New York: Random House, 1989.

Katouzian, Homa. *The Political Economy of Modern Iran: Despotism and Pseudo-Modernism, 1926–1979*. New York: New York University Press, 1981.

Kazemian, Gholam Hossein. *Impact of US Technical Aid on the Rural Development of Iran*. New York: Theo Gaus's Sons, 1968.

Kazemzadeh, Firuz. *Russia and Britain in Persia, 1864–1914: A Study of Imperialism*. New Haven, CT: Yale University Press, 1968.

Keddie, Nikki. *Modern Iran: Roots and Results of Revolution*. New Haven, CT: Yale University Press, 2003.

Keddie, Nikki, and Rudi Matthee, eds. *Iran and the Surrounding World: Interactions in Culture and Cultural Politics*. Seattle: University of Washington Press, 2002.

Kennedy, John F. *The Strategy of Peace*. New York: Harper and Brothers, 1960.

Kerwin, Harry W. "An Analysis and Evaluation of the Program of Technical Assistance to Education Conducted in Iran by the Government of the United States from 1952 to 1962." PhD dissertation, American University, Washington, DC, 1964.

Khalil, Osamah F. *America's Dream Palace: Middle East Expertise and the Rise of the National Security State*. Cambridge, MA: Harvard University Press, 2016.

Khomeini, Ruhollah. *Islam and Revolution: Writings and Declarations of Imam Khomeini (1941–1980)*. Trans. Hamid Algar. Berkeley: Mizan, 1981.

Kinzer, Stephen. *All the Shah's Men: An American Coup and the Roots of Middle East Terror.* Hoboken, NJ: John Wiley and Sons, 2008.

Kuniholm, Bruce. *The Origins of the Cold War in the Near East: Great Power Conflict and Diplomacy in Iran, Turkey, and Greece.* Princeton, NJ: Princeton University Press, 1980.

Kuzmarov, Jeremy. *Modernizing Repression: Police Training and Nation-Building in the American Century.* Amherst: University of Massachusetts Press, 2012.

LaFeber, Walter. *Inevitable Revolutions: The United States in Central America.* 2nd ed. New York: W. W. Norton, 1993.

Lambton, Ann. *The Persian Land Reform: 1962–1969.* Oxford: Clarendon, 1969.

Latham, Michael. *Modernization as Ideology: American Social Science and "Nation Building" in the Kennedy Era.* Chapel Hill: University of North Carolina Press, 2000.

Latham, Michael. *The Right Kind of Revolution: Modernization, Development, and US Foreign Policy from the Cold War to the Present.* Ithaca, NY: Cornell University Press, 2011.

Lear-Nickum, Ian Cole. "Mossadegh in America: A Turning Point, October 9, 1951– November 18, 1951." Master's thesis, North Carolina State University, Raleigh, 2013.

Lederer, William J., and Eugene Burdick. *The Ugly American.* New York: W. W. Norton, 1958.

Lemelin, Bernard. "An Internationalist Republican in a Time of Waning Bipartisanship: Congressman Christian A. Herter of Massachusetts and the Point Four Program, 1949–1950." *New England Journal of History* 58 (Fall 2001): 61–90.

Lenczowski, George. *Russia and the West in Iran, 1918–1948: A Study in Big Power Rivalry.* Westport, CT: Greenwood, 1968.

Lenczowski, George, ed. *Iran under the Pahlavis.* Stanford, CA: Hoover Institution Press, 1978.

Leuchtenburg, William. *In the Shadow of FDR: From Truman to Ronald Reagan.* Revised ed. Ithaca, NY: Cornell University Press, 1985.

Lilienthal, David E. *The Journals of David E. Lilienthal.* Volumes 4 and 5. New York: Harper and Row, 1969, 1971.

Louis, William Roger. *The British Empire in the Middle East, 1945–1951.* Oxford: Oxford University Press, 1984.

Lytle, Mark Hamilton. *The Origins of the Iranian-American Alliance, 1941–1953.* New York: Holmes and Meier, 1987.

Macekura, Stephen. "The Point Four Program and US International Development Policy." *Political Science Quarterly* 128 (March 2013): 127–60.

"Man of the Year: Challenge of the East." *Time,* January 7, 1952, 18–21.

Manela, Erez, Amy Sayward, David Ekbladh, Meredith Oyen, and Nick Cullather. "A Roundtable Discussion of Nick Cullather's *The Hungry World: America's Cold War Battle against Hunger in Asia.*" *Passport* 42 (January 2012): 6–16.

Matin-Asgari, Afshin. *Iranian Student Opposition to the Shah*. Costa Mesa, CA: Mazda, 2002.

McAdams, Margaret. "Billions, Blunders, and Baloney." *Hanover Historical Review* 10 (Spring 2009): 46–47.

McAlister, Melani. *Epic Encounters: Culture, Media, and US Interests in the Middle East, 1945–2000*. Berkeley: University of California Press, 2001.

McCullough, David. *Truman*. New York: Touchstone, 1992.

McLachlan, Keith. *The Neglected Garden: The Politics and Ecology of Agriculture in Iran*. London: I. B. Tauris, 1988.

McMahon, Robert J. *Dean Acheson and the Creation of an American World Order*. Washington, DC: Potomac Books, 2009.

McVety, Amanda. *Enlightened Aid: US Development as Foreign Policy in Ethiopia*. New York: Oxford University Press, 2012.

McVety, Amanda. "Pursuing Progress: Point Four in Ethiopia." *Diplomatic History* 32 (2008): 371–404.

Menashri, David. *Education and the Making of Modern Iran*. Ithaca, NY: Cornell University Press, 1992.

Merrill, Dennis, ed. *Documentary History of the Truman Presidency*. Vol. 27: *The Point Four Program: Reaching Out to Help the Less Developed Countries*. Bethesda, MD: University Publications of America, 1995.

Milani, Abbas. *Eminent Persians: The Men and Women Who Made Modern Iran, 1941–1979*. Syracuse, NY: Syracuse University Press, 2008.

Milani, Abbas. *The Shah*. New York: Palgrave Macmillan, 2011.

Miller, Merle. *Plain Speaking: An Oral Biography of Harry S. Truman*. New York: G. P. Putnam's Sons, 1973.

Millikan, Max, and Walt Rostow. *A Proposal: Key to an Effective Foreign Policy*. New York: Harper Brothers, 1957.

Mirespass, Ali. *Intellectual Discourse and the Politics of Modernity: Negotiating Modernity in Iran*. Cambridge: Cambridge University Press, 2009.

Mofid, Kamran. *Development Planning in Iran: From Monarchy to Islamic Republic*. Wisbech, UK: Middle East and North African Studies Press, 1987.

Moghadam, Fatemeh E. *From Land Reform to Revolution: The Political Economy of Agricultural Development in Iran 1962–1979*. New York: I. B. Tauris, 1996.

Monroe, Paul, R. R. Reeder, and James I. Vance. *Reconstruction in the Near East*. New York: Near East Foundation, 1924.

Musaddiq, Mohammad. *Musaddiq's Memoirs*. Trans. Homa Katouzian. London: National Movement of Iran, 1988.

Najmabadi, Afsaneh. *Land Reform and Social Change in Iran*. Salt Lake City: University of Utah Press, 1987.

National Association of State Universities and Land-Grant Colleges. *Serving the World: The People and Ideas of America's State and Land-Grant Universities*. Washington, DC: National Association of State Universities and Land-Grant Colleges, 1987.

National Security Archive. "CIA Confirms Role in 1953 Iran Coup." Accessed June 6, 2016. http://nsarchive.gwu.edu/NSAEBB/NSAEBB435/.

Nemchenok, Victor. "'That So Fair a Thing Should Be So Frail': The Ford Foundation and the Failure of Rural Development in Iran, 1953–1964." *Middle East Journal* 63 (Spring 2009): 261–84.

Neuse, Steven M. *David E. Lilienthal: The Journey of an American Liberal.* Knoxville: University of Tennessee Press, 1996.

Niehoff, Richard O. *John A. Hannah: Versatile Administrator and Distinguished Public Servant.* Lanham, MD: University Press of America, 1989.

Nirumand, Bahman. *Iran: The New Imperialism in Action.* Trans. Leonard Mins. New York: Modern Reader Paperbacks, 1969.

Oberling, Pierre. *The Qashqa'i Nomads of Fars.* Paris: Mouton, 1974.

Offiler, Ben. *US Foreign Policy and the Modernization of Iran: Kennedy, Johnson, Nixon, and the Shah.* New York: Palgrave Macmillan, 2015.

Offner, Arnold. *Another Such Victory: President Truman and the Cold War.* Stanford, CA: Stanford University Press, 2002.

Örnek, Cangül, and Çağdaş Üngör, eds. *Turkey in the Cold War: Ideology and Culture.* Houndmills, UK: Palgrave Macmillan, 2013.

Pach, Chester. *Arming the Free World: The Origins of the Military Assistance Program, 1945–1950.* Chapel Hill: University of North Carolina Press, 1991.

Packenham, Robert. *Liberal America and the Third World: Political Development Ideas in Foreign Aid and Social Science.* Princeton, NJ: Princeton University Press, 1973.

Pahlavi, Mohammad Reza. *Answer to History.* New York: Stein and Day, 1980.

Pahlavi, Mohammad Reza. *Mission for My Country.* New York: McGraw-Hill, 1961.

Pahlavi, Mohammad Reza. *The White Revolution.* Tehran: Kayhan, 1967.

Painter, David S. *Oil and the American Century: The Political Economy of US Foreign Oil Policy, 1941–1954.* Baltimore: Johns Hopkins University Press, 1986.

Paterson, Thomas G. "Foreign Aid under Wraps: The Point Four Program." *Wisconsin Magazine of History* 56 (Winter 1972–73): 119–26.

Paterson, Thomas G. *Meeting the Communist Threat: Truman to Reagan.* New York: Oxford University Press, 1988.

Peterson, Christian. *Globalizing Human Rights: Private Citizens, the Soviet Union, and the West.* New York: Routledge, 2012.

Pollack, Kenneth. *Persian Puzzle: The Conflict between Iran and America.* New York: Random House, 2005.

Popp, Roland. "An Application of Modernization Theory during the Cold War? The Case of Pahlavi Iran." *International History Review* 30 (March 2008): 76–98.

Public Papers of the Presidents. Volumes for Harry S. Truman, Dwight D. Eisenhower, John F. Kennedy, and Jimmy Carter. Washington, DC: Government Printing Office, 1964–81.

Rahnema, Ali. *Behind the 1953 Coup in Iran: Thugs, Turncoats, Soldiers, and Spooks.* Cambridge: Cambridge University Press, 2015.

Ramazani, Rouhollah. *The Foreign Policy of Iran, 1500–1941.* Charlottesville: University of Virginia Press, 1966.

Ramazani, Rouhollah. *Iran's Foreign Policy, 1941–1973: A Study of Foreign Policy in Modernizing Nations.* Charlottesville: University of Virginia Press, 1975.

Rasmussen, Wayne D. *Taking the University to the People: Seventy-Five Years of Cooperative Extension.* Ames: Iowa State University Press, 1989.

Renda, Mary. *Taking Haiti: Military Occupation and the Culture of US Imperialism, 1915–1940.* Chapel Hill: University of North Carolina Press, 2001.

Richardson, John M., Jr. *Partners in Development: An Analysis of AID-University Relations, 1950–1966.* East Lansing: Michigan State University Press, 1969.

Ringer, Monica. *Education, Religion, and the Discourse of Cultural Reform in Qajar Iran.* Costa Mesa, CA: Mazda, 2001.

Roosevelt, Kermit. *Countercoup.* New York: McGraw-Hill, 1979.

Rosenberg, Emily. *Spreading the American Dream: American Economic and Cultural Expansion, 1890–1945.* New York: Hill and Wang, 1982.

Rostow, Walt. *The Stages of Economic Growth: A Non-Communist Manifesto.* New York: Cambridge University Press, 1960.

Rubin, Barry. *Paved with Good Intentions: The American Experience and Iran.* New York: Oxford University Press, 1980.

Ruttan, Vernon. *United States Development Assistance Policy: The Domestic Politics of Foreign Economic Aid.* Baltimore: Johns Hopkins University Press, 1996.

Sadiq, Issa. *Modern Persia and Her Educational System.* New York: Columbia University Press, 1931.

Saghaye-Biria, Hakimeh. "United States Propaganda in Iran: 1951–1953." Master's thesis, Louisiana State University, Baton Rouge, 2009.

Saikal, Amin. *The Rise and Fall of the Shah.* Princeton, NJ: Princeton University Press, 1980.

Salih, Ali Pasha. *The Cultural Ties between Iran and the United States.* Tehran: Her Majesty's National Committee for the American Revolution Bicentennial, 1976.

Scott, James C. *Seeing Like a State: How Certain Schemes to Improve the Human Condition Have Failed.* New Haven, CT: Yale University Press, 1998.

Seigel, Micol. "Objects of Police History." *Journal of American History* 102 (June 2015): 152–61.

Shahbazi, Mohammad. "The Qashqa'i Nomads of Iran (Part I): Formal Education." *Nomadic Peoples* 5 (2001): 37–63.

Shahbazi, Mohammad. "The Qashqa'i Nomads of Iran (Part II): State-Supported Literacy and Ethnic Identity." *Nomadic Peoples* 6 (2002): 95–123.

Shahshahani, Soheila, "Tribal Schools of Iran: Sedentarization through Education." Commission on Nomadic Peoples. *Nomadic Peoples* 36–37 (1995): 145–56.

Shannon, Matthew K. "American-Iranian Alliances: International Education, Modernization, and Human Rights during the Pahlavi Era." *Diplomatic History* 39 (September 2015): 661–88.

Shannon, Matthew K. "'Contacts with the Opposition': American Foreign Relations, the Iranian Student Movement, and the Global Sixties." *The Sixties* 4 (2011): 1–29.

Shannon, Matthew K. "Losing Hearts and Minds: American-Iranian Relations and International Education during the Cold War." PhD dissertation, Temple University, Philadelphia, PA, 2013.

Shannon, Matthew K. *Losing Hearts and Minds: American-Iranian Relations and International Education during the Cold War.* Ithaca, NY: Cornell University Press, 2017.

Shenin, Sergey Y. *America's Helping Hand: Paving the Way for Globalization, Eisenhower's Foreign Aid Policy and Politics.* New York: Nova Science, 2005.

Shuster, Morgan W. *The Strangling of Persia: A Record of European Diplomacy and Oriental Intrigue.* New York: Century, 1912.

Sick, Gary. *All Fall Down: America's Tragic Encounter with Iran.* New York: Penguin, 1986.

Smuckler, Ralph. *A University Turns to the World.* East Lansing: Michigan State University Press, 2003.

Statler, Kathryn C., and Andrew Johns, eds. *The Eisenhower Administration, the Third World, and the Globalization of the Cold War.* Lanham, MD: Rowman and Littlefield, 2006.

Stewart, George. "Iran: Pathway of the Middle East." *Improvement Era*, October 1950, 790–92.

Summitt, April R. "For a White Revolution: John F. Kennedy and the Shah of Iran." *Middle East Journal* 58 (Autumn 2004): 562–63.

Szyliowicz, Joseph S. *Education and Modernization in the Middle East.* Ithaca, NY: Cornell University Press, 1973.

Technical Cooperation with Iran: A Case Study of Opportunities and Policy Implications for the United States. Washington, DC: Agency for International Development, 1972.

Thomas, David A. *Michigan State College: John Hannah and the Creation of a World University, 1926–1929.* East Lansing: Michigan State University Press, 2008.

Truman, Harry S. *Years of Trial and Hope.* Garden City, NY: Doubleday, 1956.

United States Operations Mission/Iran. "A Ten Year Summary of the United States and Iran—a Joint Effort in Public Health, 1951–1960." Accessed June 27, 2016. http://pdf.usaid.gov/pdf_docs/PNABI618.pdf.

University Projects Abroad: Papers Presented at the Conference on University Contracts Abroad. Washington, DC: American Council on Education, 1956.

Warne, William. *Mission for Peace: Point Four in Iran.* Bethesda, MD: IBEX, 1999.

Weidner, Edward W. *The World Role of Universities.* New York: McGraw-Hill, 1962.

Wood, Robert E. *From Marshall Plan to Debt Crisis: Foreign Aid and Development Choices in the World Economy.* Berkeley: University of California Press, 1968.

Woytinsky, Wladimir S., and Emma S. Woytinsky. *World Population and Production: Trends and Outlook.* New York: Twentieth Century Fund, 1953.

Yar-Shater, Ehsan, ed. *Iran Faces the Seventies.* New York: Praeger, 1972.

Yergin, Daniel. *The Prize: The Epic Quest for Oil, Money, and Power.* New York: Simon and Schuster, 1991.

Young, T. Cuyler. "The Race between Russia and Reform in Iran." *Foreign Affairs* 28 (January 1950): 278–89.

Zabih, Sepehr. *The Communist Movement in Iran.* Berkeley: University of California Press, 1966.

Zabih, Sepehr. *The Mossadegh Era: Roots of the Iranian Revolution.* Chicago: Lake View, 1982.

Zirinski, Michael. "Harbingers of Change: Presbyterian Women in Iran, 1883–1949." *American Presbyterians* 70 (Fall 1992): 173–86.

Zonis, Marvin. "Educational Ambivalence in Iran." *Iranian Studies* 1 (Autumn 1968): 133–52.

ABOUT THE AUTHOR

RICHARD GARLITZ is associate professor of history at the University of Tennessee at Martin, where he teaches courses on the history of United States foreign relations and the Middle East. He is coeditor of *Teaching America to the World and the World to America: Education and Foreign Relations since 1870.*

INDEX